BAD FOOD BRITAIN

Joanna Blythman is Britain's leading investigative food journalist and an influential commentator on the British food chain. She has won five Glenfiddich Awards for her writing, including a Glenfiddich Special Award for her first book, *The Food We Eat*, and the Glenfiddich Food Book of the Year Award in 2005 for *Shopped*, as well as a Caroline Walker Media Award for 'Improving the Nation's Health by Means of Good Food', and a Guild of Food Writers Award for *The Food We Eat*. In 2004 she won the prestigious Derek Cooper Award, one of BBC Radio 4's Food and Farming Awards. She has also written two other groundbreaking books, *How to Avoid GM Food* and *The Food Our Children Eat*. She writes and broadcasts frequently on food issues.

Also by Joanna Blythman:

Shopped
The Food We Eat
The Food Our Children Eat
How to Avoid GM Food

BAD FOOD BRITAIN

JOANNA BLYTHMAN

FOURTH ESTATE • London

First published in Great Britain in 2006 by
Fourth Estate
An imprint of HarperCollins*Publishers*
77–85 Fulham Palace Road
London W6 8JB
www.4thestate.co.uk

A catalogue record for this book is
available from the British Library

ISBN-13 978-0-00-721994-0
ISBN-10 0-00-721994-6

Typeset in PostScript Minion with Railroad Gothic Display by
Rowland Phototypesetting Ltd, Bury St Edmunds, Suffolk

Printed in Great Britain by Clays Ltd, St Ives plc

For Derek Cooper

CONTENTS

ACKNOWLEDGEMENTS

This book started out as a germ of an idea and might never have proceeded any further but for the tremendous enthusiasm of my then agent, John Saddler, now of the Saddler Literary Agency. As always, I would never put pen to paper were it not for the encouragement and confidence that I get from my editor at 4th Estate, Louise Haines. Her calmness, intelligence, quiet determination and sense of humour make it a privilege to work with her. I have also benefited from warmth and optimism about the project of the wider team at 4th Estate. I doubt that I would ever have managed to complete this book without the constant support, and sometimes practical assistance, of my fellow food writer and dear friend, Lynda Brown. Camilla Hornby at Curtis Brown inherited the book late in the day, but took it on with much enthusiasm.

Hundreds of research sources were plundered for this book, all recorded in the References. Many colleagues, friends, and even total strangers took the time to pass on nuggets of information, anecdotes and helpful insights, especially Alex Buchan, Janey Buchan, Nicholas Cooper, Anita Cormac, David Craig, Chris Duncan, Bob Granleese, Nick Howell, John Irving, Bob Kennard, Eva Merz, Charlotte Mitchell, Ebongué Mouanjo, Claudia

Nicholson, Dr Richard North, Judith O'Hagan, Frances Sloane and Claudia Zeiske.

My sister Margo, my mother Marion, and my daughter Amy supplied me with an ongoing diet of support and ideas long-distance. At home, my daughter Zoe and husband Nick put up with a moody, distracted writer and helped me untangle ideas. My best love and thanks to them all.

INTRODUCTION

One afternoon in early 2006, my phone rang. It was a fellow journalist looking for quotes for an article he was writing about the significance of Britain's doyenne of food writers, Elizabeth David. 'Was it thanks to her that we have become a nation of foodies?' he wanted to know. The next morning, the *Today* programme on Radio 4 was repeating a story about how sales of olive oil in Britain were now outstripping those of all other cooking oils put together, a phenomenon attributed to Britain's increasing sophistication in food taste – yet another manifestation of the nation's much-vaunted food revolution.

Nation of foodies! Food revolution! Who are we kidding? British eating habits are getting worse, not better. In reality, Britain is second only in notoriety to the United States in the bad food stakes. Of course, this flies in the face of the perceived wisdom that we are in a 'You've Never Had It So Good' phase of British gastronomy, in the throes of a dynamic food renaissance. After all, isn't London's restaurant scene the envy of the rest of the planet? What about all the farmers' markets, regional food festivals, and new artisan food products that are popping up left, right and centre, the length and breadth of the land? And how about our regiment of chef celebrities? Isn't cool Food Britannia a runaway success? At last, after all those decades of cringing on the world food stage, surely we can now strut our stuff with conviction, and show off our new-found gastronomic credentials.

This is how Britain likes to see itself nowadays, as a fully functioning, participatory food culture. In truth, this vision is a chimera, an unconvincing construction built and talked up by the media, the chattering classes, the hospitality, tourism and food industries, and TV chefs on the make. It is a delusion that selectively ignores the gaping discrepancies that don't fit the story:

- Our growing incompetence in the domestic kitchen and the endangered status of home cooking – surely one of the most telling indicators of a nation's culinary health.
- Our inability to feed our children on a diet of life-sustaining, healthy food, either at home or at school.
- The stifling of an independent local grocery sector or small food commerce under the hulking boot of supermarket monoculture.
- Our addiction to industrial techno-foods.
- Our growing resistance to devoting any time to food shopping or preparation.
- Our unwillingness to take the time to eat a meal.
- Our bulging waistlines.
- Our city centres studded with chain eateries and 'gastropubs' where everything on the menu comes straight out of a lorry into the freezer, and from there to the microwave or deep-fat fryer.

- Our near dependence on foreign cuisines because of the weakness of our own native one.

And that's just for starters!

This book explores all the contemporary manifestations of Britain's unhappy relationship with food; the embedded ideas, patterns and practices that keep us locked in a Bad Food mindset and which feed the nation's profound gastronomic illiteracy. Not the least of our current troubles is our inability to admit that something is wrong. Like an alcoholic who can't accept that he or she has a drink problem, Britain is in denial that it has a Bad Food problem. Yet such an acceptance is a necessary preliminary to identifying creative solutions that might enable us to appreciate the pleasure we might derive from better food, and in the process transform the quality of our life.

Bad Food Britain is not a history book, although the roots of Britain's current difficulties with food would richly reward such an approach. Perhaps the weak food culture in Britain is due to early industrialization, and a consequent rapid growth of an urbanized population divorced from the countryside and food production? Religion may play its part in the form of a Protestant work ethic which spawned a breed that would rather build an empire or factory than waste hours preparing and eating food; a peculiarly Anglo-Saxon form of Puritanism which holds that it is immoral to enjoy or cherish food too much, parsimony and abstinence being the higher goals. Other factors might include our grey northern climate, the legacy of post-war rationing, our close identification with the United States and 'time is money' American capitalism. Or might it be a matter of simple xenophobia, complicated by a fine overlay of class; the notion that food is something fancy that only foreigners, or those who ape them, enjoy? Whatever the historical explanation, the fact remains that food never has been a British priority and shows no signs of becoming one in the near future.

One of the most amusing but telling insights I happened on in the course of writing this book was the following letter, published in *The Times* during the wave of concern that flowed through Britain in the wake of the transmission of *Jamie's School Dinners*:

Sir,
A letter from my daughter's primary school in Essex reads:

Change to the School Menu
In response to recent publicity, 'Turkey Twizzlers' have been taken off the school menu and replaced by 'Chicken Teddies'.

What is it about the British and food? We just don't get it, do we? Well, it's time that we did.

BAD FOOD BRITAIN IN NUMBERS

1   One in every four British households no longer has a table that everyone can eat around

57   The percentage of British men who have little interest in food

38   The percentage of British women who have little interest in food

1   One out of every three Britons say they do not eat vegetables because they require too much effort to prepare

50   The percentage of Britons who really enjoy eating

2003   The year by which Britain ate more ready meals than the rest of Europe put together

40   The percentage of patients entering and leaving British hospitals in 2004 with malnutrition. The equivalent figure in British nursing homes is 60 per cent

29   The number of unique British products with protected status in the EU in 2005. Italy had 149, France had 143, Portugal 93, Spain 91, Greece 84

40   The percentage of food bought in Britain, but never eaten

35   The average amount in pence spent on food ingredients for a primary school meal in 2003.

This is half what is spent on lunch for residents in HM Prisons and a quarter of the sum allocated to feeding an army dog

48 The percentage of Britons who say they are fed up being told what to eat

20 The percentage of British viewers who say that TV food programmes encourage them to cook

4 Only four out of ten Britons enjoy eating meals with their children

69 The percentage of Britons who are still confused about which foods are healthy

1 One out of every two meals eaten in Britain is now eaten alone

63 The percentage of the food eaten by Britons in 2004 that was home-produced, down from 75 per cent in 1994

1 Only one in five Britons will go out of their way to buy British food if it means paying more for it

50 The percentage of all British shoppers who say that they do not care where their food comes from

2020 The year by which at least a third of all British adults, one fifth of British boys and one third of British girls will be obese, if current trends continue

51 Britain eats more than half of all the crisps and savoury snacks eaten in Europe

BRITAIN'S TOP 10 BAD FOOD BELIEFS

* Eating is about refuelling, not pleasure. A part of life's routine, just like going to the lavatory.
* Home cooking takes too long. Successful Britons buy ready-made food instead.
* Food is not important. Pretty much everything else in life matters more.
* A dining table is a redundant item of furniture.
* The single most important thing to know about food is what it costs.
* There is no point in giving children good food. They won't appreciate it.
* There is no such thing as bad foods, only bad diets.
* British supermarkets stock such great food, there is no need to shop elsewhere.
* You can live on a diet of processed food and still stay healthy and slim.
* A microwave is the only piece of kitchen equipment you really need.

1

FANTASY FOOD

Britain lives in a fantasy food world, a virtual food state. Our shelves are laden with cookbooks. Books about eating or cooking are never out of the bestsellers lists. In 2005, cookbooks – already one of the book trade's richest earners – reached new money-spinning heights. Sales of food and drink books grew by 22 per cent, while fiction grew by only 5 per cent. Our television schedules are studded with programmes about food: *Ready, Steady, Cook, Full on Food, You Are What You Eat*, Jamie's this, Gordon's that, Nigella's this, that or the other . . . there is no avoiding them. Newspapers and magazines spew out a diet of recipes, discussions of ingredients, restaurant and cookery book reviews. The number of column inches and amount of air time given to food in Britain dwarfs that in every other comparable country. According to *Vogue* magazine: 'How we cook, what we cook with, where we last ate, what our children are eating . . . is an obsession that has stretched its sticky, lickable hands across society.'

The pages of weekend supplements are populated by beautiful people plucked from a nation of lip-licking gastronomes, a nation that grows food, cooks food and rejoices in the eating of it. They live in lofts and stylish townhouses, or – depending on the newspaper's readership profile – in covetable country houses and hollyhocked cottages. Wherever they are located, these people are ultra-literate in food and gastronomy. They take a great interest in foodie arcana, soaking up articles on items such as shade-grown peppercorns and salted, sun-dried Sardinian tuna roe, like children devouring the latest Harry Potter book. They weigh up the pros and cons of Lacanche ranges versus Agas. It matters to them that their crème brulée is correctly caramelized, so they give each other blow torches as Christmas presents. They are endlessly fascinated with the contents of famous people's refrigerators. Their own capacious American-style, double-door fridges are filled with organic goat's milk yogurt, juice squeezed from English heritage apples and Toulouse sausages made from rare breed, acorn-fed porkers. They savour obscure cocktails dreamed up by someone purporting to be the world's most innovative mixologist. Their shelves are stacked with at least six different estate-bottled extra virgin olive oils. Their drawers are filled with expensive Japanese knives as recommended by Bad Boy chef, Anthony Bourdain. These people constantly give dinner parties or, more fashionable these days, informal, relaxed 'suppers' for foodie friends. They are tuned into every little nuance of food provenance, seeking out products of impeccable pedigree as they navigate their way around farmers' markets, specialist food shops and mail order companies supplying everything from samphire to smoked eel. When you see the picture of them sitting around their craft-made dinner table, hewn from a vast trunk of fallen oak or elm by a local architect who downshifted to the country, they are surrounded either by adorable, food-appreciating offspring weaned on puréed allotment parsnips, or by stimulating food enthusiast guests. Attentive readers of *Heat* or *Hello!* magazines may even be able to spot the odd celebrity peeping out from their assembled ranks.

And you know what? They don't exist. Correction – they account for a vanishingly small percentage of the British population. Anyone from abroad who skims through these supplements or switches on UK television could be forgiven for gaining the impression that Britain is a country that celebrates matters alimentary, one that devotes huge swathes of its waking time to living and breathing food. In fact this is merely a construction of how the British like to see themselves, as a switched-on, fully-participatory food culture. Our diligently prepared diet of 'what to eat, where to buy it' foodie lifestyle is engineered and highly accomplished, but the edifice is all the more audacious because of the scale of the lie it sells. Welcome to the peculiarly British world of food pornography, where watching other people cooking food or talking about cooking food has become a substitute for doing it yourself. Chef Simon Hopkinson put his finger on it when he wrote:

> 'Something seems to be ever so slightly rotten in the state of the British kitchen just now. I sometimes feel that we have all but lost the grasp of how to cook nicely at all. We watch endless cookery programmes, but prefer, finally, to spend lots of money on supermarket ready-meals while idly turning the pages of spotlessly clean cookery books until the microwave pings.'

The more media space food and cooking occupies in Britain, the less it reflects any grass roots practical activity. We have become a nation of food voyeurs. The broadcaster Jeremy Paxman provided an explanation for this apparent contradiction when asked if he was interested at all in food. 'Well, I would be if I had more time, but it's one of those things that's gone to the wall as life has got busier,' he explained. 'I might read a recipe and think "That sounds absolutely delicious", or "That seems an interesting idea". So I tear out the page but never make the recipe.' Mr Paxman speaks for the nation in this respect. It has a theoretical interest in cooking and earnestly means to get around to doing it at some point. But when time is at a premium and there is too much to do, then cooking, being an optional extra as opposed to a core British activity, is the first thing that must go. And yet the British continue to turn out one glossy cookbook after another. As the *Evening Standard*'s Literary Editor, David Sexton, observed, their marketability is more to do with the generous dollop of lifestyle with which they are garnished, than the recipes. 'Such incessant activity is only achieved, of course, by emphasizing everything but the food ... We are sold instead the personality of the cook, the romance of the foreign journey, the superior lifestyle that somehow the food is supposed to supply. Recipes become almost irrelevant. Now the cookbook is not a manual at all but rather an aberrant species of literary composition, one of the most baroque products of the age.'

Britain has now built a lovingly-assembled, reassuring image of itself as a country that has undergone a second coming on the food front, but unfortunately this is not predicated on any day to day reality. Quite the opposite. We have become detached from reality by persuading ourselves that the frequency of practical cooking is no longer the most telling indicator of a country's culinary health. Just as agony aunts will advise that in their experience, infrequent sex is often a sign of a relationship in terminal decline, Britain's reluctance to cook suggests that all is not well in its relationship with food. But the British are in denial. Rather than face this unpalatable truth and do something about it, we have preferred to buy into the myth that a diet of well-chosen 'tried and tested' processed meals and savvy eating out is a viable substitute for hands-on cooking.

The last time significant sections of the British population actually showed any signs of seriously improving their cooking skills, and hence the quality of the food they ate, was in the heyday of Delia Smith. Delia caught the BBC's eye at the end of the 1960s with cookery columns in the *Daily Mirror*, the *Evening Standard* and the *Radio Times*. Her television career began in 1973 with the BBC series *Family Fare*, a title which now would be dismissed out of hand by commissioning editors because of its in-built assumption that viewers might be interested in cooking family meals.

Family Fare proved so popular, however, that after running for two years, it was followed in 1975 by the megaseries *Delia's Cookery Course*. The aim of this major series, which was broadcast repeatedly over more than a decade, was systematically to take viewers through the basics of cooking and teach fundamental techniques to home cooks. The goal was unashamedly educational – Delia's series came under the auspices of the BBC's education programming – and what she taught on screen was backed up by affordable paperback manuals filled with easy-to-follow, well-tested recipes which, if instructions were followed, would guarantee sound results. It became the model for other influential series in the same education slot: Madhur Jaffrey's *Indian Cookery* in 1982 and Ken Hom's *Chinese Cookery* in 1984. These presenters all shared the same neutrally pleasant but essentially functional approach: We are here to teach a practical skill. You are watching because you want to learn so that you can try it out.

Delia's style of presentation was that of an ever so slightly glamorous domestic science teacher: encouraging, straightforward, business-like and not at all show-offy. She assumed the traditional female cookery demonstrator's pose, face on to the camera, standing behind a worktop covered with basic kitchen equipment and a small sea of glass bowls, and she took viewers through a few recipes with thoroughness and detail, flagging up possible variations on the theme. She communicated her knowledge of cookery in a factual way, taking nothing for granted, stopping regularly to explain or introduce a new ingredient or the usage of a less common item of kitchen equipment. Her attitude was not a patronizing 'Poor you, haven't you heard of balsamic vinegar? Oh do keep up!' but an unthreatening 'Here's an interesting Italian vinegar that I like and I think you might like too'. Delia came over more like an approachable member of the local Women's Institute than a scion of some elite society of food connoisseurs. She did not fit the mould of the distinguished, upper-class, English cookery writers, such as the wonderfully acerbic memsahib Elizabeth David, or the erudite, well-travelled Jane Grigson. They had performed a stalwart service by helping to drag British food out of its post-war austerity, but they influenced a select audience of people rather like themselves. Whether or not she consciously set out to do so, Delia Smith became a food democrat whose mission was to broaden the food knowledge and cooking capability of the great mass of ordinary Britons. As such she developed a strongly female following who found her recipes realistic and do-able.

Out there in Middle Britain, the Delia effect was tangible. In the 1980s and early 1990s, it was always a great relief when visiting family, friends and acquaintances with a less than impressive record on the cooking front to hear the phrase 'I didn't know what to make so I just made a dish from Delia Smith'. That usually ominous introduction from the nervous, unconfident cook 'I've never made this before . . . I hope it's all right' was instantly less perturbing when followed up with '. . . It's a Delia recipe'.

By the late 1990s, the Delia brand increasingly became seen as old-fashioned, a bit plodding, in need of lightening up, and out of touch because of its patronage of the unglamorous, primarily female realm of home cooking. Delia had been upstaged by a new generation of TV cooks who fitted in with broadcasters' notions that food now belonged not in an education, but light entertainment slot. Keith Floyd was the vanguard for this new genre of TV food entertainment. His recipes were rough and inexact, unlike Delia's meticulously weighed centilitres and grams. An ageing, rakish bon viveur with a diverting line in banter, he appealed to male viewers, to the kind of man who likes to show off his cooking skills at high-profile events but doesn't like to muck in with everyday domestic cooking. The efficacy of Keith Floyd's recipes was considered by broadcasters to be secondary to his entertainment value. They liked him because he rescued cookery from what they considered to be a female ghetto.

He got out of the studio and cooked up impromptu feasts on boats, in fields, on beaches. He supplied excitement and added value. He did something more than just cook.

Keith Floyd provided a prototype for a new breed of TV cook or 'celebrity chef'. It was no longer good enough merely to teach people to cook. Celebrity chefs had to offer the viewing public something different, because – and here's the irony – they now had to appeal to people with little or no interest in food, people who quite possibly had no intention to cook. Consequently, Jennifer Paterson and Clarissa Dickson-Wright were not allowed to be just two patrician, middle-aged women with a formidable knowledge of food, but had to be portrayed as PG Wodehouse stereotypes, Two Fat Ladies travelling around, Biggles-style, with a motorbike and side car. The gimmicks abounded. Jamie Oliver had to keep up a constant stream of chippy barrow-boy prattle and slide down banisters to boost ratings figures amongst younger viewers. Nigella Lawson had to look eternally gorgeous and seductive and spout a script heavily overlaid with sexual nuance. These added-value cookery shows demonstrated, yet again, Britain's traditional lack of conviction that food in its own right merits intelligent interest. The underlying thinking was that cooking is a chore which, in its unadorned form, could not be expected to appeal to British people. It had to be spiced up with a series of innovations if ratings were not to flag. Food and cooking needed something else to sell it: sex, travel, eccentricity, adventure, farce, incessant swearing – anything.

The success of these new-wave food programmes created a mass delusion, the idea that British people were already so sophisticated in their appreciation of good food, and accomplished in the cooking of it, that they had no more elementary lessons to learn. In 1998, Delia Smith had launched a new series, *Delia's How To Cook*, a back-to-basics cooking primer aimed at reintroducing Britons living on processed food to the pleasures of cooking. This was blatantly at odds with the assertion that Britain was in the throes of a good food revolution and provoked an outburst from chef Gary Rhodes who attacked *How To Cook* as 'offensive'. 'I don't need to be shown what boiling water looks like and I tend to think that the rest of the population don't need to be shown it now,' he said. 'It is insulting to their intelligence.' Soon after, chef Antony Worrall Thompson jumped on the anti-Delia bandwagon dubbing her 'the Volvo of cooking' because he considered that she was reliable but dull.

Delia Smith retaliated, voicing her aversion to celebrity chefs and the whole 'food as light entertainment' approach, laying into BBC2's prime-time popular food show in particular. 'I will never, ever know, as long as I live, how the BBC or the general public can tolerate *Food and Drink*,' she said. *Food and Drink* was the progenitor of a new strand of live audience programmes in the game show mould. It was made to be undemanding and unintimidating, so presenters who actually knew anything about their subject had to pretend that they were just punters. Those who knew no more than the average citizen were awarded the status of idiot savants and charged with talking garrulously and hyperactively, so reinforcing the British suspicion that anyone who goes on about food is either mad, irrevocably pretentious or downright ridiculous. It was geared to viewers with the attention span of a flea.

Then, in 2003, after selling ten million books, Delia Smith announced her retirement from cookery. She said that she was 'reciped out', but fired one last salvo at the massed ranks of celebrity chefs before she went. 'What's happened to the amateur cook in the country house? Or that lady down the pub who only the locals knew about and cooked up a storm?' she asked. Delia's retirement marked the consignment of any serious attempt to teach Britain practical cooking skills to the dustbin.

The balance of culinary power in Britain has now swung away from the domestic zone, where its keepers were women who passed on their accumulated knowledge with their egos held well in check, to the male zone, where its new luminaries are a bunch of flashy performance artists. The success of these performers is not measured by whether the woman along the road successfully cooked one of their dishes, but by their ratings and book sales.

The focus of food fashion has become more rarefied, arcane and preoccupied with the endless pursuit of novelty; in fact, it is entirely detached from most Britons' domestic cooking experience. A lot of media attention has been given to Heston Blumenthal, chef of the Fat

Duck at Bray and his particular style of cooking – 'molecular gastronomy'. Mr Blumenthal's gastronomy is complex, and is best contemplated only by the most seriously skilled chefs, yet his recipes turn up with regularity in programmes and magazines aimed at ordinary people, most of whom seem impressed. Writing in the *Evening Standard*, Yasmin Alibhai-Brown declared herself to be perplexed by the whole Blumenthal phenomenon: 'I watched him on TV last week making mashed potatoes – twelve steps, one and a half hours, eight different pots and utensils and an end result that looked like thick soup. Is he taking the mickey?'

Food as a spectator sport has now become a huge industry in Britain. In countries that are feted for their cuisine, such as Italy and France, food has a much lower profile in the media. Weekend newspapers carry a restaurant review, perhaps a profile of a chef, a diary of local food and wine festivals, and the odd recipe. News-stands sell a number of cheap, practical magazines filled with seasonal recipes for everyday cooking. Commonly these recipes are not authored, since the object of the exercise is to show what the dishes look like and explain how to make them, not sell the lifestyle of food celebrities. When chefs appear on French and Italian television, viewers do not get a through-the-keyhole snoop into their lives to see their children, homes or long-suffering partners. They simply stand up, demonstrate a recipe and leave it at that. If you talk about 'celebrity chefs', Europeans look blank and are not sure what you mean.

The justification advanced for the Great British Media Food Circus with its clowns, acrobats and survival artists is that it has helped Britain catch up with established food cultures and rekindled the flame of British gastronomy. Jamie is turning on young people to cooking by making it seem trendy and youthful. Gordon is drumming up recruits for the catering profession by reducing B-list celebrities to tears in front of the camera. Paul and Brian are supplying stressed-out housewives with barnstorming 15-minute menus using hideously incompatible and unfamiliar ingredients that will invigorate their lacklustre cooking. The only problem with this noisy and ever more attention-seeking circus is that it has had the opposite effect. As the food writer Tamasin Day-Lewis has commented: 'What strikes me is the number of perfectly competent cooks who say they have become frightened of cooking. They feel that what they once cooked with confidence is no longer fashionable. Restaurant and television food has added to their insecurity.' A case in point is comedienne Arabella Weir, who confesses: 'All that plethora of cookery shows really does is make me feel insecure. They don't make me think, "Oh what a great thing to do with scallops and chives." I just think, "Oh God! I'm just a fat oaf who lives in a horrible kitchen!"'

As far as the media is concerned, food and cooking in Britain should be viewed similarly to advertising. Its job is to sell us an aspirational lifestyle in which food occupies its time-honoured place in British society as a way of defining class, status and refinement. But, like parading a line of skinny supermodels before a local Weightwatchers group, its effect is not empowering but paralysing. The people who are apparently showing us how to cook are asking too much of us. They offer a menu of incessant choice, seasoned with a perpetual stream of possibility. But they are not like us, they do not represent us, and we can never be like them. They live in a world glossy with food fashion, rich with knowledge and busy with perpetual novelty. We watch them, talk about them, and let ourselves be entertained by their antics as a form of diversion and escapism, but we know that all this has little or nothing to do with real life.

2

HOW OTHERS SEE US

Just days before the 2005 G8 Summit meeting at Gleneagles in Scotland, French President Jacques Chirac put his diplomatic foot in it. At a high-level meeting in Russia to celebrate the 750th anniversary of the founding of Kaliningrad, and in earshot of reporters from the French daily newspaper, *Libération*, President Chirac entertained the Russian President Vladimir Putin and German Chancellor Gerhard Schroeder by mocking British food. 'We can't trust people who have such bad food,' he was quoted as saying, compounding the insult with, 'the only thing they [the British] have ever done for European agriculture is mad cow.' President Putin and Chancellor Schroeder seemed to appreciate his humour, laughing and joining in with the banter.

Britain, on the other hand, was not at all amused. Rather than brushing it off as might a country confident about its food culture and cuisine, the UK rose to the bait – big time. 'Don't talk crepe, Jacques!' bellowed the

Sun. 'How would Mr Chirac feel if others descended to this level of argument and called him a snob and a has-been who pongs of garlic?' asked the *Daily Telegraph*. Egon Ronay, publisher of the eponymous restaurant guide, accused the French President of being ill-informed. 'A man full of bile is not fit to pronounce on food. There's no other country in the world whose food has improved so greatly and more quickly in the last 15–20 years than this country,' he said. In the *Evening Standard*, Fay Maschler, doyenne of British restaurant critics, denounced President Chirac's 'ignorant, witless remarks', retaliating with a tirade against French food:

> 'The simple little restaurant run by maman and papa straight off the pages of Elizabeth David's *French Provincial Cooking*, where a carefully composed meal made from local produce was sold for a song, exists no more. Or at least it needs a Sherlock Holmes detective to find. Menus in various departments of France are repetitive and monotonous ... Restauration in its homeland (France) has become a depressed and cynical exercise ... Even getting a good cup of coffee and a noble loaf of bread is nowadays easier in London than in Paris.'

The rivalry between the French and the British is historic. France and Britain have been best of enemies for centuries. Cross-Channel insults are nothing new, and the French President's remarks were bound to provoke a certain amount of retaliatory flag-waving and chauvinism. Back in 1999, a light-hearted article published in the *New York Times* in which the critic William Grimes said that Cornwall 'probably offers more bad food per square mile than anywhere else in the civilized world' and likened the Cornish pasty to a doorstop, actually provoked one pasty maker into burning an American flag in protest.

But the strength and stridency of the reaction to President Chirac's comments demonstrated that he had wounded our national pride in a fundamental way. But why such vulnerability? The French President had exposed our long-standing Achilles heel. However much commentators try to promote a rehabilitated image of British food with inspiring tales of booming farmers' markets, new-wave artisan producers and innovative restaurants, the unpalatable fact is that other nationalities either just don't buy it or, at best, they judge any improvement to be minimal. For instance, in 2001 the *New Yorker* magazine talked of 'the baby steps the British are taking away from their tradition of gruesomely bad cooking'.

The United States enjoys being rude about Britain's food. Thinking Americans feel embarrassed about their own fast-food diet which is universally hailed as unhealthy and obesogenic. Britain gives them a country to which they can feel superior, one with worse food than their own. Even high-profile ambassadors for Britain's revitalized food culture such as Jamie Oliver can't escape the sneers and curled lips. Mr Oliver complains that when he travels abroad, he frequently ends up listening to people bad-mouthing British food. 'You go on Jay Leno [a US talk show] for the third time and he's still making cracks about shitty English food.' The British take it particularly badly when Americans criticize our food. It feels like a best friend swapping sides and ganging up with the enemy – that's France, Italy and any other country that outshines us on the gastronomic front.

Britain becomes tetchy very easily when negative comparisons are made with countries that have thriving food cultures, using attack as a form of self-defence. This sideswipe at Italian food, from the *Daily Telegraph*'s restaurant critic, Jan Moir, is a classic example. She took exception to chef Antonio Carluccio pointing out that Italian labourers eat truffles – an illustration of how good food in Italy is regarded as a democratic entitlement, enjoyed by all social classes.

> 'Really, stuff like this does get tiresome. We all know about the excellence and seasonality of Italian food, but every time I go to Italy, the supermarkets there are full of the same old rubbish that they sell here, but we're always led to believe that every grotty little shepherd is dining like a king on heavenly risottos and garlic-infused baby lambs, while ignorant John Bull has to make do with boiled hoof and carrots because he knows no better.'

In contrast to such defensiveness, our king in waiting, His Royal Highness, Charles, Prince of Wales, has accepted that Britain does have a serious problem with what it eats:

> 'Over the last two generations we have managed to create a nation of fast food junkies to whom food, often processed by industrialised farming systems, is nothing but fuel. The result is a growing obesity and health problem and a disconnection in the minds of too many people between the food on their plate and where and how it is produced.'

Whether or not we choose to face up to it, Britain has always had a particular credibility problem in convincing the rest of the world of its culinary credentials, and that perception has not substantially shifted. Viewed from outside its borders, Britain is a strange and aberrant country, a cultural exception in Europe, and second only to the US in its capacity to shock outsiders with its eating habits. As one Chinese writer, looking forward to his first trip to London, told the *Guardian*: 'I've tasted an English breakfast but otherwise I've heard the food is awful.'

So common are the negative perceptions of British food abroad that bodies charged with attracting visitors to the UK are well-rehearsed in fielding them. The British Council in Japan, for instance, has a website aimed at students who are considering studying in Britain. The site has a Frequently Asked Questions section: Question number 3 (following questions about the cost of study and the weather) deals with what is clearly one of the biggest disincentives to people contemplating visiting, studying or working in the UK:

> *Q:* 'I've heard that British food is boring. Will I be able to find the sort of food that I like?'

> *A:* 'Britain used to have a bad reputation as far as food is concerned. This has changed dramatically. Britain is a land of lovers of good food. As well as traditional British food which is currently seeing a revival after years of neglect, Indian, French, Greek, Chinese, Italian, Malaysian, Turkish, Mexican and many other ethnic restaurants can be widely found. Japanese food has become popular in Britain during the last few years. There are even kaiten-zushi bars in London!'

While more optimistic potential students might feel reassured, the more cynical might interpret the sub-text as follows: 'Take it on trust from us that the ghastly things you have heard about British food no longer apply, but just in case you don't believe us, let us reassure you that there are lots of other cuisines to go for. And if you don't fancy those, there's always sushi – in London at least.'

Foreign students contemplating taking a course at the University of Oxford are likewise pre-warned as to what to expect:

'British food does not have a good reputation overseas. However, there is in fact a very wide variety available, both traditional British food and international cuisine, especially in bigger cities. There are many fresh ingredients which are delicious when cooked well. However, many busy people don't pay much attention to preparing food well and prefer instant meals.'

Of course, it is only natural for foreign nationals to be attached to their own cuisine, to cling on to what they know and even be somewhat suspicious of the food they might encounter when they travel abroad. But the fact remains that British food continues to be notorious worldwide. When *Malaysia Tatler* magazine sent a reviewer to sample the British food at the Ivy restaurant in Kuala Lumpur (no relation to the eponymous London establishment) in 2005, she enjoyed chicken with Stilton and leek, but queried whether it could really be a British dish, as she was 'surprised that something as tasty could come from there [Britain]'. As *Malaysia Tatler* pointed out: 'The British have given many things to the world – television, the steam train, even the internet ... But nowhere, on any listing of the island's achievements will you find the phrase "culinary finesse".'

In 2003, the results of a survey of Polish attitudes towards British food were almost universally negative – 108 out of 111 responses. A great many critical comments were recorded, including: 'tasteless', 'unhealthy', 'lot of fat', 'not many vegetables', 'cheap', 'industrial', 'no specific cuisine', 'no traditional food', 'not nutritious' and 'no good bread'. Indeed, there was repeated amazement at the state of British bread. 'They [the British] don't eat normal bread, only tosty' [white sliced bread],' one respondent expanded. The existence of vinegar-flavoured crisps raised eyebrows too. Many people commented on the proliferation of fast food and the lack of home cooking in the UK. The problem, concluded one respondent, was that 'the British don't really know what good food tastes like'. Another opined that 'if British people can survive their cooking they can survive anything'.

Speak to people of diverse foreign origins who live or work in the UK, and it will quickly become evident that food is one of their biggest obsessions. Wherever they come from, they pick out habits and customs that strike them as incomprehensible and strange, even though they are considered unremarkable by many natives. Most preface their opinions diplomatically with the things they really like about Britain – more personal freedom to live your life as you want being the compliment that crops up most frequently. But when it comes to food, the floodgates open. One German student told me:

> 'When I moved to London from Berlin, my first experience of British food was on the boat from Dunkirk to Ramsgate. We wanted to eat something and waiting in the queue I saw them serving lasagne with chips and peas. I just felt so shocked by that, I left the queue and didn't eat anything, thinking that I really couldn't cope

with this kind of food. The idea of eating chips with lasagne!'

That hoary old stereotype – chips with everything – still crops up regularly in outsiders' images of British food. The traditional fish supper, in particular, described by Egon Ronay as Britain's 'most distinctive contribution to world cuisine', finds few admirers; on the contrary, most people from abroad are bemused by Britain's fondness for what they see as an unappetizingly greasy meal, served without knives and forks and eaten from dirty newspaper. Others cannot get over Britain's addiction to food consumed on the hoof. 'When I first arrived I was surprised to see how people walk about eating in the street and quite astonished to see school children walking around at lunchtime eating a packet of crisps and some sweets,' a French Cameroonian engineer told me. 'The French have a completely different attitude. Either you go home for lunch or stay and eat in the canteen.' People from other countries are gobsmacked by the food that British children eat. A Dutch mother told me:

'Until I came to Britain, my children had never been exposed to sweets at all. My kids didn't even think about them. They liked fruit but it was impossible to keep that up because always when they entered the nursery or playgroup in Britain there were people giving them sweets; not just biscuits – things like sticky sweets and fizzy drinks. In kindergarten in Holland, the kids got fruit and yogurt, but no sweets. It would be unheard of in Holland if the kids brought in crisps and sweets from home. They would not be allowed, a bit like bringing cigarettes into school. Here the kids open a lunch pack and there is at least one packet of crisps, one Mars bar or similar, and then they have these really weird takes on real food like cheese strings or something where they make the food into a funny, dinosaur shape. In order to persuade a child to eat a piece of cheese in Britain they have to make it into a shape!'

A Danish artist told me that when she arrived in the UK, she could not get over the contents of British shopping trolleys:

'When standing in line I noticed what people had in their shopping baskets, all that sugar and fat in there, and I would be really amazed to see even old people stocking up with junk. Three years later I stand at the checkout here and still can't get over all those trolleys filled with big amounts of pies, ready-made food, and lots of crisps – but without any vegetables. A Danish trolley, irrespective of social class, would look much different. In a word, "greener". We eat a lot more green food and our dishes look nicer as a result because we eat more salads, more stewed vegetables, more vegetables on the side as a garnish.'

An Italian teacher recounted her first encounter with prospective in-laws, picking out what she saw as the entirely alien habit of staggered eating, the unceremonious speed of eating, and the lack of effort that goes into food in the UK.

'I went to my [British] husband's family for Christmas. It was a huge cultural shock, the saddest Christmas in my life. If somebody had come to my house in Emilia Romagna at any time, not even a festive period, my mum would make an extra effort – a special pasta, a special secondo [meat or fish course], more of everything, a real welcome. But I don't think his mum is cooking at all. She doesn't care about that. When it was lunchtime she said "Everything is in the fridge, everybody can help themselves" and off she went. At about 12 o'clock, his dad would go to fridge and make himself a sandwich, at 12.30 his sister served herself and so on. The day after was the same. At the actual Christmas dinner, after half an hour, all the food had already disappeared from the table. I have had to adapt to it, but for me, it was definitely shocking.'

People from abroad are regularly baffled by what they see as a lack of family meals and communal eating. One Austrian arts administrator explained:

'Now that I live in Britain I still cook every night. We eat together every night and that is a most important time for us. But I see from other British families that this is considered really strange. In the UK, eating together is almost something you do on a Sunday if you are a "good" family. It's really important to me that we sit properly, half an hour or so – not like in France where they take one and a half hours – and not a fancy meal necessarily, just something that's properly cooked. We would not sit at the TV and eat either. I notice people do that here. You don't come across much of what I would call proper, normal eating in the UK.'

For an executive summary of the outsider's verdict on British food and eating habits, click onto the web pages of 'Grenouilles au Royaume Uni' ('Frogs in the UK'), a reportage by French people living in Britain, and look under the ironic heading 'The Delights of British Cuisine':

'The British no longer consider a meal as a family ritual. That's a growing trend in France too but it's more noticeable here. English families cook less in general and rely more on food delivered to their homes. Members of the same family tend to eat on their own when they feel hungry. Hence the profusion of junk food, fast food, takeaway and so on. Direct consequence: 39 per cent of Britons are overweight, 19 per cent are obese.'

Although most Britons view it as entirely normal, Terry Durack, restaurant critic for the *Independent on Sunday*, has voiced the ongoing incomprehension with which British eating habits are viewed internationally:

'As an Australian, I often find myself blinking in disbelief at the average Briton's relationship with food, at how unimportant it is to so many people. But then, I grew up in a country where good food was available to all at a good price. Here [in Britain], eating well is an economic issue, a class issue, and an education issue. Good food is available – at a price. And nobody is going to pay the price if good food is simply not a priority in their lives.'

Whether we like to admit it, Britain is seen abroad as a country that has well and truly lost the gastronomic plot, a food recidivist, demonstrating precious little capacity for improvement.

3

BRIT FOOD

Any country with a healthy food culture has a distinct body of ingredients and dishes that that can be recognized widely as constituting a national cuisine, but in Britain even the native population has some difficulty agreeing on such a definition. Expatriate Britons, on the other hand, seem entirely clear. Scan the catalogues of companies that purvey distinctive British foods to Britons in the diaspora, such as Best of British – a chain of stores throughout France – and you will be left in no doubt about what they crave. Their mission statement reads:

'It is good, from time to time, to be able to have some of those traditional British foods we so enjoyed in the UK; a good fry-up with bacon, pork sausages and beans, steak and kidney pies, battered cod with mushy peas, proper curry, syrup sponge with real custard, trifle, etc. You will find them all at Best of British.'

To French people who happen on Best of British, the stock must appear bizarre. For the most part, the goods on offer represent a drab, sad testament to Britain's addiction to over-processed, industrial food: Plumrose pork luncheon meat, Jackson's white sliced bread, Tunnock's marshmallow snowballs, Cadbury's Curly Wurlys, Bisto gravy granules, Walker's prawn cocktail crisps, Angel Delight, Spam, Pot Noodles, Heinz tinned coleslaw, spaghetti hoops and salad cream, Princes Hot Dogs, Campbell's condensed mushroom soup, Hula Hoops, Fray Bentos tinned steak and kidney, frozen sausage rolls and Birds Dream Topping are just a few of the treats in store. For some Britons based abroad, these are delights to seek out and savour.

Wherever they go in the world, Britons like to uphold their food traditions and remain loyal to an unedifying portfolio of industrial products whose main selling point is that they make cooking more or less redundant. An internet search for 'British food' will find a bevy of other companies – Brit Essentials, UK Goods, The British Shoppe, British Delights, Brit Superstore, British Corner Shop, amongst others – with a flourishing trade in much-loved, quintessential British foods. Branston pickle, Daddy's Sauce, Bovril, Twiglets, Ribena, Bird's custard powder, Oxo cubes, instant coffee, Heinz tomato soup, Ambrosia creamed rice, Coleman's Cook-In sauces, tinned meat paste, Paxo sage and onion stuffing, fruit-free fruit-flavour jellies, Burton's Wagon Wheels, 'fun-size' confectionery, and Yorkshire pudding mix are all typical offerings.

Far from being food best left back in Blighty, these products are very much in demand, as one company that sends them to customers' doorsteps all around the world explains: 'As ex-expats ourselves, we fully understand your frustrations in obtaining a taste of Britain in your new country. It seemed like Christmas when we did find a shop selling British products.' Frequently, these much-missed British foods are on show at social events run by Britons living abroad. Bemused local guests might be invited to British 'curry suppers' or parties where a common offering is the nominally Mexican chilli con carne, made in the British style using mince and served with rice, to be eaten from a bowl while standing up – followed by mini Mars bars.

Back in the UK, those intent on promoting the idea that Britain has lately undergone a food revolution and developed a food culture that can hold its head up, not only in Europe but in the world at large, would hasten to point out that many of these products are reminiscent of the stock list of a 1960s convenience store, and not at all representative of the way most British people now like to eat. If this is the case, then what exactly is 'British food' nowadays?

In reality, this is a bit of a puzzle, both to the British and to other nationalities. Up until the 1970s, we had something that amounted to a national cuisine, a repertoire of commonly eaten dishes which most citizens would agree were British; toad-in-the-hole, roast meat with roast potatoes, Lancashire hotpot, boiled beef and carrots, mince and potatoes, bangers and mash, tripe with onions, boiled ham with parsley sauce, broths and hearty soups, shepherd's pie, oxtail stew, cauliflower cheese, potted shrimp, steak pie, kippers, raised pies, steak and kidney pudding, jellied eel and any number of stick-to-the-ribs puddings. Depending on who you listen to, this cuisine was either a) monotonous and almost invariably badly cooked or b) straightforward, appetizing and wholesome. Either way, at least it was based on native raw ingredients – give or take a few billion packets of gravy powder.

Even then, a certain confusion reigned. In countries with consolidated eating traditions, 'national' is the sum of the 'local' parts. In Britain, on the other hand, what was once 'local' – Cumberland sausage, York ham, Melton Mowbray pie – becomes a 'national' dish, which may be a reflection of the absence of regional food pride, or perhaps a sign of desperation about the thinness of Britain's food culture.

In 1998, the food writer Sybil Kapoor made a valiant attempt to map out a newer, more relevant definition for British food in her evocative book *Simply British*. She abandoned any attempt at classification based on a body of popular dishes or culinary techniques, in favour of a collection of intrinsically British ingredients. 'In my opinion,' she wrote, 'there is only one thing that unifies and defines British cooking and that is its ingredients.' But while the book was an appetizing and much-needed reminder to the British that good cooking starts with fresh, indigenous materials, any territorial claim to ingredients is bound to be subject to counter-claim. For all we may try to assert the gastronomic equivalent of intellectual property rights over ingredients such as lamb, beetroot, lavender and greens, neither the Greeks, the Russians, the French nor the Chinese, respectively, will accept it.

In 2004, the author and chef William Black set out on a tour around Britain to seek out the country's traditional specialities for his book *The Land That Thyme Forgot*. He wanted to taste 'enigmatic, mysterious dishes' like Hindle Wakes (boiled fowl stuffed with prunes served with a rich lemony butter sauce and herbs), Clanger (a suet crust pastry with meat in one end and jam in the other) and Salamangundie (a sort of salad made with eggs, anchovies, onion, chicken and grapes). At the beginning of his journey, Mr Blake was 'absolutely convinced that somewhere there was a vibrant regionalism just waiting to blossom', but he never did get to taste most of the dishes he wanted to because they had simply dropped off Britain's culinary map. In the spirit of an archaeologist hastily excavating a site before the developers move in, he catalogued a list of British specialities or GODs (Great Obscure Dishes), appealing to readers to adopt a dish as a contribution towards nursing British food back to culinary health. Into this sanatorium he put regional specialities that one might have expected to be in a more healthy state, such as Yorkshire Fat Rascals (a fruit scone/ rock cake hybrid), Syllabub (wine sweetened with whipped cream) and Liverpool Scouse (meat and potato stew). His conclusions made gloomy reading:

> 'As I travelled around the country I did get a sense of a revival in regional food but it seemed a very one-sided, haphazard affair indeed, Yes, farmers' markets are springing up all over the place, and these arenas at least allow us to talk to producers and begin to amass a degree of awareness about food, nutrition and seasonality, but at a price. Much of the produce seems so insanely expensive to most of us when compared to the mass-produced pap we are accustomed to buying in the local supermarket that we often find it hard to get it into perspective. In other words, any good food movement is perceived as elitist . . . Is it too late for us ever to revive this disappearing gastronomy? Quite possibly. But we can nag. And rootle around and search for this golden grail, a renascent food culture that has to be more than just the ability to buy carrots with mud on them, and the odd farmhouse cheese.'

Slowly but surely, over the last 20 years, as our food shopping tastes have been shaped and increasingly dominated by supermarkets, Britain has abandoned its native gastronomy and become the culinary magpie of the world, raiding other countries' gastronomic heritages and stockpiling their offerings for its nest. Although we live in a globalized age where true diversity is ever more elusive, most countries, both rich and poor, can still point to dishes that are more or less uniquely their own and perceived by outsiders as such. Germans eat sauerkraut; Vietnamese enjoy pho; Czechs are loyal to goulash and dumplings; Sri Lankans won't go long without eating a stringhopper. The British? Well, that will be lasagne, moussaka, chicken kiev, pizza, fajitas, baltis, Thai red curry, hummus – basically, anything other than British.

The British actively project this magpie persona abroad. Every two years, different countries proudly showcase their cutting-edge food wares at the Anuga trade show in Germany. In 2005, smiling staff at the 'Best of British' section were pictured by *The Grocer* magazine standing proudly in front of displays, not of Lincolnshire chine or Bakewell tarts, but of pot noodles and crisps with 'authentic British flavours'. What the word 'authentic' meant in relation to laboratory flavourings was not made explicit, but it was evidently thought to be a selling point that these crisps offered six months' shelf-life, and labelling in eleven foreign languages. Britain's weakness for junk food is now so longstanding, that our taste for it can almost count as traditional. In the same article, *The Grocer* noted that while other countries focused on traditional products normally associated with them – pasta and olive oil from Italy, cheese from Holland, and so on – 'the 63-strong Food From Britain section was a real cornucopia of world cuisine with Indian and Oriental brands putting on a strong show'. This is what Britain's food industry does best these days: snack-bar sushi, instant noodles, frozen pizza, gloopy stir-fry sauce, long-life Peking duck wraps . . . We are now the international specialists in making inferior industrial copies of other countries' favourite foods.

No one jumped to contradict the Foreign Secretary Robin Cook in 2001 when he hailed chicken tikka masala as the most popular British dish. Chicken tikka masala is a British 'Indian' dish, unrecognized in India, invented by a Bangladeshi cook. Mr Cook hailed it as 'a perfect illustration of the way Britain absorbs and adapts external influences' on the grounds that the masala sauce was devised to 'satisfy the desire of British people for gravy'. But this dish is really a symbol of the weakness of the indigenous cuisine in Britain, and is a demonstration of the British tendency to fill this vacuum by importing and traducing misunderstood foreign dishes.

At a more nostalgic, emotional level, the British do still want to cling on to a more coherent, traditionally British food identity. However, an attempt to unite our culinary past with our eclectic culinary present is not without difficulties – witness the marketing pitch for chef James Martin's 2005 book, *Easy British Food*:

'Typically when asked about British food, thoughts turn immediately to a plate of good old fish and chips followed by the less inspiring meat and two veg. This is just not the case anymore – Britain is jam-packed with a diverse and delicious variety of food . . . James has packed the book full of classic dishes you thought only your mother had the secret to from homemade

Cumberland sausages to Welsh rarebit, from jam roly poly to raspberry Pavlova, *Easy British Food* does not disappoint.'

That is the British bit of the sell, but everyone from the editor to the sales manager knows that a volume of straight, traditional British cooking is not commercial enough or sufficiently seductive to market to Britons sceptical about their own culinary heritage, so it needs a hint of foreign promise added:

'Inherited British favourites from overseas have not been overlooked – Margarita pizza, lamb curry, salmon risotto and crème brulée are all now firm favourites in the heart of the British nation, all of these and more are made easy in this delicious collection . . .'

This voices the almost pathetic British need to make foreign dishes our own in order to compensate for what we consider to be the inadequacies of our own native cooking tradition. This is our new food identity, dipping into cuisines from all over the world and trying to unite them in a new composite product that can plausibly be regarded as British. While Queen Elizabeth II may still represent a more conservative British palate – she is said not to like garlic or long pasta – market research has shown that Britain is the country in Europe most fond of foreign tastes. Seven out of ten Britons say that they 'like foreign food' compared to 29 per cent of Spaniards.

One survey of European eating habits remarked on how Germans were 'conservative consumers' favouring traditional German food. The same applied to Spaniards whose eating habits remain 'still very much based on a Mediterranean-type diet'. While Britain likes to commend itself, quite legitimately, on its openness to foreign culinary ideas and influences, there is no escaping the fact that this taste is powered by lack of belief in our indigenous gastronomy.

The British lack of culinary confidence was demonstrated rather spectacularly (twice) during US President George Bush's 2003 visit to the UK. At Buckingham Palace, the Queen served him a meal – billed as 'Le Menu' – consisting of potage Germiny, délice de flétan aux herbes, suprême de poulet fermier au basilica, and bombe glacée Copelia, which was French both in language and concept. Dining at Downing Street with Tony Blair, eating a menu created by Nigella Lawson, the American President was treated to roast pumpkin, radicchio and Welsh feta salad, braised ham with honey and mustard glaze, creamed potatoes and seasonal vegetables, followed by double-baked apple pie with cheddar crust and vanilla ice cream. The *Guardian*'s Matthew Fort, for one, was unimpressed:

'You might have thought that the occasion of the state visit of an American president would herald a little tub-thumping of our own, for the culinary fireworks which we have been so busy claiming for ourselves . . .

It sounds quite tasty and homely ... but I can't help feeling that Queen Nigella may have gone a bit far in the hand of friendship direction in an effort to make Citizen Bush feel at home. Pumpkin has a greater following in America than it does here ... and what is more American than apple pie, with or without the cheddar crust? ... Come to that, when has radicchio been a British vegetable of choice? And why feta cheese, Welsh or not? What's wrong with Caerphilly?'

When ambassadors for Britain are so half-hearted about serving British food, it is no surprise that ordinary people feel the same way. By 2004, only 63 per cent of the food eaten in Britain was home-produced, down from 75 per cent in 1994. We seem to be eating less native produce, not more. This situation is in part a reflection of the preference of British supermarkets for global sourcing which leads to diminishing amounts of British food on British shelves. In 2005, a survey by Friends of the Earth found that two-thirds of the apples sold in the height of the UK apple season came from overseas. Some of the apple varieties being offered had travelled more than 12,000 miles. The reliance of supermarkets on cheap imported foods means that Britons who do want to buy British food find it difficult to do so.

For decades, British consumers have been exhorted by numerous food industry marketing bodies such as the Meat and Livestock Commission and the National Farmers Union to support British farmers, but this has fallen mainly on deaf ears. In countries with a thriving food culture, consumers feel connected to those who produce food, not least because many of them have a producer in their extended family or circle of friends. In Britain, on the other hand, few consumers have any connection with farming or primary food production, largely because it has now become so intensive, industrial and factory-based, that fewer and fewer people are engaged in it. The vast majority of Britons are divorced from the countryside and know little or nothing about what it can produce. Indeed, the urban masses tend to see farmers in an unsympathetic light as potential chisellers and fiddlers of European Union subsidies, people who are not to be trusted. Consequently, they do not get a sympathetic hearing.

In recent years, a slight but significant resurgence of interest in smaller-scale, less industrialized food amongst opinion formers has opened up a more positive dialogue between producers and consumers. In 2002, the chief executive of the Countryside Alliance, Richard Burge, launched an initiative called British Food Fortnight and took the opportunity to appeal to consumers, using the term 'producers' rather than 'farmers', and emphasizing pleasure rather than patriotic duty: 'The time has come to stand up for British food and its producers! We have to remind consumers of the great pleasure which comes from eating locally-grown, high-quality foods, and just how important it is to the British countryside at this time that we eat its produce.'

Now an annual event each October, British Food Fortnight aims to make everyone in the UK more aware of the diversity and quality of home-grown, locally-sourced British produce. Consumers are urged to seek out seasonal produce, cook a British meal for friends and explore British regional cooking. This may be a surprisingly tall order: according to a survey carried out by the Institute of Grocery Distribution just before British Food Fortnight 2005, only one in five Britons will go out of their way to buy British food if it means paying more for it, while over half of all shoppers polled said that they didn't care where their food came from. The Institute pointed out that while 87 per cent of respondents considered farming to be an important part of British heritage, the challenge was to translate this patriotism into purchasing British food because Britons did not generally 'see the connection with food production and the countryside'.

By 2005, British Food Fortnight was still being run as a cottage industry. Despite pressure on the government from both Houses of Parliament, the media at large and the farming press, the government's contribution was actually reduced in 2005 from some £46,000 to £45,000. The event went ahead on a paltry budget of £108,000, cobbled together from sponsorship from the Nationwide building society, retailers Booths and Budgens, and other supportive organizations. 'The sad reality,' commented organizer Alexia Robinson, 'is that there is no overall body representing British food producers and, therefore, there is no consensus, no unified marketing and no easy mechanism for raising funding on behalf of the industry as a whole ... Asking the public to buy British food because they feel sorry for farmers will not cut it.'

As always in Britain, any attempt to have small food businesses – or anything that smacks of the artisan – taken seriously turns out to be a lonely battle. The relevant government departments in successive government administrations have put their efforts into pleasing the captains of the processed food industry, and have continued to dismiss small-scale food producers as marginal – and therefore irrelevant – to the country's food effort. There is a persistent strand in British regulatory thinking that views the existence of anything akin to peasant farming as retrograde because it might be taken as an indicator of economic backwardness.

More recently, small food projects have begun to attract a little support from government and local authority departments charged with regeneration and tourism. Some city centre management teams are beginning to wake up to the fact that independent shops and farmers' markets can increase the number of people who use the town centre by making them more interesting and lively places to visit. In British cities dominated by supermarket monoculture, a thriving business has sprung up in 'Continental markets' – imported, highly stereotyped, usually French-themed markets – because they appear to inject some gastronomic life. Tourism authorities have latched on to the idea of culinary tourism and have begun to promote small food operations, such as farm shops, that help create a new, more favourable image of Britain in the visitor's mind. But, again, this new-found enthusiasm does not stem from a belief in good food for good food's own sake, but derives from the realization that it can bring other social and economic benefits.

Indeed, small-scale British food is in danger of turning into a heritage industry. Stately homes, garden centres, museum and farm shops are filling their shelves with edible souvenirs made to an antique recipe – real or imagined – loading their shelves with jars of jams, jellies, chutneys, sweets and endless cakes and biscuits, masquerading as something you might pick up at a Women's Institute market. Most such enterprises are run by well-intentioned people who are naive enough to believe that by buying local and British, this is automatically some guarantee of quality. In fact, there is a danger that purchasing home-produced food is being transformed into a quaint, nostalgic Sunday afternoon leisure activity instead of a viable everyday alternative to the tedium and uniformity of the supermarket. The local food shops that actually improve shopping choice are the small minority that take risks with really fresh meat, fish, and seasonal fruit and vegetables; these are places where you can buy the raw ingredients for a meal, not just a jar of redcurrant and rose petal jelly for your elderly auntie.

Medium-sized food companies, struggling to make ends meet because of the crippling low returns they receive from their supermarket masters, are keen as English mustard to come up with new 'British' products that cash in on the vogue for British food. Large industrial creameries are inventing more profitable 'speciality' cheeses, basically the same old push-button cheese, tarted up in gimmicky forms with stripes and swirls of colour. Take your pick from white Stilton with a raspberry and strawberry ripple, added 'orange crumble', apricots or cranberries, or rubbery cheddar with pizza, 'Mexican', or even tandoori flavour.

At the same time, the 'Big Food' interests that are inimical to the development of any genuine grass roots British food culture based on diversity in retailing and food production are also getting in on the 'Fly the Flag for British Food' act as a self-promotional tool. In the autumn of 2005, a government quango, the Sustainable Farming and Food Implementation Group, organized a conference to discuss what might be done to reconnect British consumers with British food. The event was chaired by Tesco's director of corporate affairs. Many farmers blame this retailer for the downturn in their fortunes because it demands such low prices from its suppliers that it makes food production unsustainable for all but the very largest farmers and growers. The Tenant Farmers' Association refused to attend the event because of Tesco's involvement. 'Tesco is simply not interested in allowing farmers to communicate with consumers,' said the Association's chief executive, George Dunn.

Shortly after this event, the supermarket chain Sainsbury's ran a 'Taste of Britain' competition in conjunction with the *Daily Telegraph* to find the best suppliers of British food and drink. This provided another platform for exaggerated claims about the UK's food revival. 'British food and drink has gone through somewhat of a renaissance in recent years, after decades of ridicule from our European contemporaries,' read Sainsbury's advertorial, 'so much so that we can now compete with the best of them within the gastronomic world.' It also gave Sainsbury's a chance to associate itself with Britain's struggling small producers. All British supermarket chains now seize every opportunity to be seen hand in hand with these 'food heroes' because they occupy the moral high ground in the eyes of British consumers – even if few of us actively support them with our purchases. At the same time as this competition was running, farmers across the UK – led by the campaign group Farmers For Action – were either throwing out or giving away their produce in protest against the unfair trading practices that had led to hundreds of farms going out of business while supermarket profits soared.

On paper, it is possible to mount a reasonably convincing argument that in the last few years, we have moved towards a clearer, saner definition of what British food should mean; a vision of a new, modern British food culture. The buzz words are now 'local' and 'small-scale'; farmers' markets go from strength to strength; more towns have a specialist food shop selling some hand-made, regional food; organic box schemes have waiting lists; increasing numbers of artisans are scraping a living by dealing direct with the public using mail order. But these are little green shoots in an otherwise bleak and homogenous British food landscape where globalized industrial food and supermarket monoculture is the order of the day.

A tiny, dedicated band of Britons actively seeks out and encourages high-quality, independent, locally-produced food. Such people are probably even more committed to their cause than food-loving citizens in other countries who tend to take the availability of good food for granted. A slightly bigger fringe in Britain sees such food as an interesting and desirable minor accessory to the main business of shopping in supermarkets and living on a mass-produced, industrial diet. As the food writer Tamasin Day-Lewis put it:

'We're in a very different place in this country, food-wise, from where we were 20 years ago. And it's mostly disadvantageous. Industrialization of food production, the supermarkets persuading us that it's OK to eat things that have been imported thousands of miles with no regard to seasonality . . . we're totally losing our heritage. There's a dwindling band of people growing rare apple breeds or planting traditional tomatoes, but they're regarded as rather eccentric.'

Our attitude to food in Britain has certainly moved on, but it has not improved.

4

RENAISSANCE RESTAURANTS

A loose coalition of interest groups in Britain likes to suggest that British cuisine has been so thoroughly over-hauled and improved that it can now be considered as one of the most dynamic and exciting in the world. This is a rainbow alliance, composed of Fly the Flag patriots, perpetual optimists who believe that our tendency to self-deprecation is more worrying than our cooking, Little Englanders who resent the mere suggestion that Johnny Foreigner might eat better than we do, and food processors, restaurateurs, hoteliers and assorted tourism experts who have spent too much time reading their own marketing propaganda. People attempting to mount a convincing case for Britain's supposedly rehabilitated food culture have become adept at drawing a veil over the cooking (or lack of it) that goes on in the domestic sphere. They prefer not to focus on the nation's growing daily dependence on push-button industrial food and quickly skip to what appears to be firmer ground –

Britain's Great Restaurant Renaissance. Where Britain once had to cringe when its food was under discussion, nowadays its restaurants have allowed it to assume a cocky swagger.

At some point in the 1990s, London began to be hailed – in Britain at least – as 'the restaurant capital of the world', a grandiose claim attributed to design guru and restaurateur, Sir Terence Conran. It is a theme to which many people, some with vested interests, others without, have since warmed. The small, London-based *Restaurant* magazine picked up the ball and ran with it in 2002 when it took it upon itself to run a competition to judge nothing less ambitious than 'The World's 50 Best Restaurants'. Now held on an annual basis, it habitually locates British restaurants at the forefront of global gastronomy, thereby generating fulsome media coverage. In 2005, the Fat Duck, run by the much-lauded chef Heston Blumenthal, scooped both the 'Best in the World' and 'Best in Europe' awards. British restaurants in general were awarded 14 of the 50 illustrious slots, with 11 of these in the capital. England had four restaurants in the top ten, France just one and Italy none. According to its editor the awards represented a combination of 'commonsense' and the considered, informed opinions of 'our contacts in the industry', some 500 judges in all – chefs, food journalists, people from cook schools and academies and top companies. Their precise identity and nationality, however, remains confidential to *Restaurant* magazine.

Not everyone was convinced by this top 50. Irish chef

Richard Corrigan dared to suggest that Britain did not deserve to be judged any better than France, Italy or Spain. 'There is a slight bias in the list,' he said. 'You have to take it with a very big pinch of salt.' Yet this vision of Britain as being in the vanguard of world restaurant culture has become firmly embedded. It feeds our almost pathological need to shake off our Bad Food Britain image and display some good food credentials on a world stage while simultaneously rubbing our rivals' noses in it. 'The world has had enough of red-checked tablecloths and fat cheerful men called Carlo ladling gloops of choleric ragout atop plates of overcooked pasta,' wrote Rod Liddle in the *Sunday Times*. 'It has wearied very quickly too of the rough'n'ready Piedmont and Tuscan peasant cuisines that kept our increasingly capricious palates briefly engaged in the 1990s. And meanwhile, classic French cooking with its epic hauteur has become about as fashionable as Marshal Pétain or Johnny Halliday, which is why the French are desperately trying to reinvent their whole cuisine.'

Britain is now convinced that London is firmly ensconced as the planet's restaurant capital. 'The city fizzes with gastronomic challenge and enthusiastic, knowledgeable customers,' wrote the *London Evening Standard*'s highly respected restaurant critic, Fay Maschler. Indeed, London does have some exceptionally fine restaurants with serious, accomplished chefs who would attract recognition anywhere, but any suggestion that they constitute the glittering pinnacle of a solid, broad-based restaurant culture, rather than beacons of hope in a predominantly bleak British food landscape, amounts to wishful thinking.

Tellingly, it is hard to think of any restaurant of note in the UK that willingly brands itself as 'British' pure and simple, because of the negative connotations that adjective has when attached to the noun 'cookery'. In the words of the *Harden's London Restaurants* guide: 'As the capital of a country which, for at least two centuries, has had no particular reputation for gastronomy, London's attractions are rarely indigenous. By and large, only tourists look for "English" restaurants.' Traditionally, Britain has a pub culture, rather than a restaurant culture, which is why, according to *Harden's*, there are 'very few traditional restaurants of note and even fewer which can be recommended'.

The nearest you might get to most people's idea of traditional British food would be Rules in London's Covent Garden, a venerable establishment commended by the *Tatler* restaurant guide in 2005 as the place 'to impress visiting American friends' with its 'age-old but not old-fashioned dishes in an atmosphere of Edwardian exuberance'. Diners at Rules can savour dishes such as dressed crab, smoked venison with juniper, roast Lincolnshire rabbit with bacon and black pudding, leeks Mornay, steak, kidney and oyster pudding, and roast beef with Yorkshire pudding. Rules, remarked *Field* magazine, 'fills a vital role in educating an increasingly ignorant public who have lost touch with what their countryside can provide'.

Otherwise, apart from brewery-owned chains of provincial hotels which serve up something approximating to the traditional Sunday lunch 'roast dinner', most serious and ambitious chefs prefer to describe their cookery as 'modern British'. The 'modern' delineates what they serve from the negative connotations attached to 'British' and leaves ample room for manoeuvre when it comes to using foreign cooking techniques and ingredients. Fergus Henderson, chef-owner of St John restaurant in London, who serves dishes that might reasonably be construed as British, such as nettle soup, ox heart and chips, and marrow bones with parsley salad, avoids any 'British' tag. 'I prefer to see myself as a modernist who happens to be cooking good, indigenous food,' he has said. Gary Rhodes, the chef widely credited with promoting the joys of traditional British food, called his television series and book *New British Classics* – surely a contradiction in terms – but the 'new' in the title distances it from unreconstructed 'British' cookery.

Just how British are the most highly-rated 'modern British' restaurants? Many could just as easily be categorized as French. Naturally, they use the finest British ingredients, but their cooking techniques and kitchen organization pay homage to Escoffier. Chef Tom Aikens was reportedly 'quite miffed' when the *Independent on Sunday*'s food writer, Sybil Kapoor, said that she considered his Michelin-starred food British. He himself saw his food as 'more French than anything'. In the top British kitchens, a Franco-British patois is frequently the order of the day with diligent 'sous' and 'commis' chefs barking out 'Oui, chef!' countless times in one service. Their menus are dotted with French words such as 'nage', 'jus', 'velouté', 'tranche' and 'confit' for which British chefs can find no suitable simple English translation.

The *Good Food Guide 2006* awarded its top rating to four restaurants – Gordon Ramsay, the Fat Duck, Le Manoir aux Quat' Saisons and Winteringham Fields – all of which are essentially French in approach. But it also acclaimed the emergence of 'Food Britannia', which it characterized as more chefs using local and seasonal produce and boasting about it. The guide commended restaurants such as the Three Fishes, at Mitton in Lancashire, for serving dishes such as heather-reared Bowland lamb, and Lancashire hotpot with pickled red cabbage, and the Buttery in Glasgow for its Isle of Mull mussels with Finnan haddock and bacon. This encouraging trend was instantly seized on by *The Times* as more evidence of Britain's new, reformed food culture. 'No longer will the maitre d' at Maxi be able to curl his lip in quite such supercilious disdain at the mention of British cuisine . . . *The Good Food Guide* has made it official: British food, like British art, music and sport, is now at Europe's cutting edge.' A more circumspect conclusion, against the larger backdrop of Britain's restaurant and catering industry, would be that native food is still a rarefied minority experience amongst British catering establishments. A quick head count of British restaurant menus will reveal thousands of establishments that continue to serve 'roasted Mediterranean vegetables' made using Dutch hydroponic vegetables as a winter staple, or seared, imported Sri Lankan tuna as the fish of the day, in preference to the local foods on their doorstep.

Britain's accommodating, some might say globalized, attitude to food is reflected in the capital's restaurant scene which is rich in flavours and techniques that are not indigenous. London is one the world's most diverse and cosmopolitan cities with an array of eating-out possibilities – everything from Peruvian, Ethiopian and Indonesian through to Korean, Ghanaian and Afghani – that reflects its lively, multicultural personality. 'Where London does score – and score magnificently – is the range and quality it offers of other national styles of cooking. Always an entrepot, London is now a culinary melting pot too: in terms of scale and variety, its only obvious competitor is New York,' says *Harden's London Restaurants*. Outside the metropolis, Indian, Chinese and Thai restaurants throw a much-needed lifeline to the cause of restauration on every small shopping parade and obscure outpost throughout the British Isles, where otherwise there would be little else in the air apart from the distinctively British odour of deep-fat frying.

Just how good or representative of their parent cuisines many British 'ethnic' restaurants are is a moot point, but we love to talk them up anyway. 'I would argue that in London you will find better Thai, Indian, Chinese, Italian and French cooking than you would in the indigenous countries,' proclaimed Rod Liddle. This is a ludicrous proposition but it exemplifies the new-found British ability to pontificate confidently on matters gastronomic from a basis of colonial-style ignorance. It is true that many Indian restaurants have now ditched their flock wallpaper 1960s curry-house image and adopted classier names that evoke tourist board images of India. Some are excellent, but many more continue to serve little more than pre-cooked cubes of meat in a 'variety' of chameleon sauces derived from a small number of bought-in, factory-made spice pastes, served with chemically-coloured rice. Many of these meals are cooked by the children of first generation immigrants who consider themselves British first and foremost. Their appreciation of mother-country cooking is often limited. In the biggest British cities, where there is a local population of Chinese extraction, one can find restaurants serving quite authentic Chinese food. Commonly, these restaurants operate two distinct menus. One is written in English and offers Westernized 'Chinese' staples designed to please the British market. The hallmarks here are super-real flavours based on megadoses of salt, sugar and vinegar, and lots of deep-frying. Another, written in Chinese, offers an authentic, healthy repertoire of traditional Chinese dishes considered to be too real and too daunting for the British: everything from fish-head soup through braised chicken feet to rice congee. British diners are rarely able to eat from a true Chinese menu unless they are fortunate enough to speak a Chinese dialect fluently or are in the same party as a Chinese friend. Generally, the Chinese community likes to keep real Chinese food to itself. Staff will positively steer non-Chinese customers away from more authentic dishes because they worry that they will not go down well. Timothy Mo's novel, *Sour Sweet*, which follows two first generation Chinese immigrants, Chen and Lily, who set up a takeaway restaurant in Greater London, gave an insight into the thinking behind it.

'The food they sold, certainly wholesome, nutritious, colourful, even tasty in its way, had been researched by Chen. It bore no resemblance at all to Chinese cuisine. They served from a stereotyped menu, similar to countless other establishments in the UK. The food was, if nothing else, thought Lily, provenly successful: English tastebuds must be as degraded as their care of their parents; it could, of course, be part of a scheme of cosmic repercussion. "Sweet and sour pork" was their staple, naturally: batter musket balls encasing a tiny core of meat, laced with a scarlet sauce that had an interesting effect on the urine of the consumer the next day. Chen knew because he tried some and almost fainted with shock the morning after, fearing some frightful internal haemorrhaging ... "Spare ribs" (whatever they were) also seemed popular. So were spring rolls, basically a Northerner's snack, which Lily parsimoniously filled mostly with beansprouts. All to be packed in the rectangular silver boxes, food coffins, to be removed and consumed statutorily off-premises. The only authentic dish they served was rice, the boiled kind; the fried rice they sold with peas and ham bore no resemblance to the chowfaan Lily cooked for themselves . . .'

Although Britain's willingness to embrace world cuisine – albeit in bogus forms – is admirable, the huge success of non-British restaurants in the UK reflects the relative weakness of our indigenous cuisine. The natives of Bremen, Bruges, Bratislava, Bologna, Barcelona and Bordeaux feel less need to eat foreign food and remain largely immune to its charms quite simply because they are more content with their own home-grown offering. For them, a restaurant specializing in a foreign cuisine represents a potentially interesting novel addition to native cuisine, but it is not a substitute for it.

Because there is nothing much to defend in the way of a British restaurant tradition, our new-found claim to gastronomic distinction lies in our eclecticism, our willingness to break rules and invent new traditions. We have no baby to throw out with the bath water. We start with a clean sheet of ideas and a healthy openness to ingredients and culinary approaches from all over the world. But the pitfalls are obvious – a mongrel mish-mash of misunderstood foreign cuisine, cooked by amateur chefs and served to naive and inexperienced diners. As Jonathan Meades, the most authoritative of all recent British restaurant critics, pointed out, this is not a recipe for success, but a culinary Tower of Babel:

'Instead of repairing or reinventing its own cooking, it has crazes: French, Thai, Swedish, Cantonese . . . There is no kitchen in the world that is safe from the depredations of the British cook exhibiting both a denial of confidence in national identity and the dumb conviction that the grass is always greener.'

Britain's globetrotting culinary tastes reach their nadir in the country's secondary cities, where restaurants strive to show sophistication by their bold synthesis of diverse ingredients and cooking styles. Here is a typical menu from a 'modern British' brasserie in one of Britain's largest cities:

STARTERS

Thai fishcakes with sweet chilli sauce
French onion soup and toasted cheese
Blackened Cajun chicken Caesar salad
Chicken liver parfait, toast and spiced fig chutney
Seared scallops, sunblush tomato, potato and rocket salad
Moules marinières
King prawn tempura and ponzu sauce
Roast field mushroom bruschetta, pesto and parmesan
Seared squid with rocket, chilli and lime
Crispy duck, beansprouts and watercress with soy and sesame dressing
Tiger prawn salad with mango

MAIN COURSES

Shepherd's pie and peas
Calves liver and bacon, mash and onion gravy
Tuna burger with wasabi mayonnaise and chilli fries
Braised lamb shank with mint, garlic and root
   vegetable couscous
Five-spiced duck with sweet potatoes, pak choi and
   shitake mushrooms
Steak frites
Nasi Goreng with roast chicken supreme
Salmon fishcake with spinach, lemon and parsley
   sauce
Fish and chips with mushy peas
Seabass fillet with hot and sweet sour vegetable
   noodles
Smoked haddock, mash, poached egg and Mornay
   sauce
Risotto with sweetcorn, peas and mushrooms
Roasted shellfish spaghetti with lemon, garlic and
   parsley
Jumbo macaroni three cheeses, roast tomato and toast
Rigatoni, tomato, spicy sausage and mozzarella bake
Red onion and mulled cheddar tart
Coq au vin

DESSERTS

Tarte Tatin and vanilla ice cream
Sticky toffee pudding and custard
White chocolate chip brownie with chocolate sauce
Lemon cheesecake with strawberries
Warm chocolate brownie with vanilla ice cream
Pannacotta with spiced poached pear

If they were so minded, diners in this type of establishment could construct a meal with some territorial integrity – French onion soup, say, followed by steak frites and tarte Tatin. They might head East and feast on tiger prawn salad with mango and five-spiced duck. In an Italophile mood they could tuck into roast field mushroom bruschetta, rigatoni and pannacotta. But more than likely, most British diners will find themselves eating a combination like prawn tempura and ponzu sauce, followed by risotto, followed by chocolate brownie. In other words, it is a mongrel menu that cannibalizes world cuisine and spawns meals that do not gel into a coherent whole because they lack any sound unifying principle.

The existence of such menus might cause the trusting diner to suppose that the kitchen has mastered a repertoire of diverse skills and tastes, when, in reality, these are far beyond the reach of the average second division city bistro or brasserie. Nonetheless, many British people will turn up and pay for this type of package and go away pleased with what they are given because they lack the experience to know whether of its type it is any good or not. Once again, we are putting ourselves at a disadvantage by overlooking what is familiar and on our doorstep, instead dabbling with exotica we rarely understand. Italians have strong ideas about what constitutes a good risotto. Indians recognize a fine masala dosa when they see one. Japanese people know when their sashimi is truly fresh and refuse to settle for less. Back in Britain, any undertrained, ill-equipped outfit can trade on the advantage that if it serves foreign food, then few people – the chefs included – will be equipped to judge it. It is a case of the blind leading the blind. Bill Knott, editor of *Caterer and Hotelkeeper*, likened it to a game of Chinese whispers where the original message gets more and more distorted in the transmission.

'The average menu [in the UK], even in restaurants proudly describing themselves as "modern British", is written in a curious mixture of French, Italian, Spanish and just about any other language that doesn't involve hieroglyphs. Even worse, many of the foreign terms used are thoroughly inaccurate and deeply misleading. Millefeuille of aubergine, cappuccino of white beans, chicory tarte Tatin ... the game of gastronomic Chinese whispers, in which a modish, foreign-sounding dish goes through so many incarnations that it becomes completely meaningless, is all the rage.'

Study the restaurant reviews in national newspapers and you will notice that some 80–90 per cent consist of restaurants in central London. Indeed, restaurant critics frequently get it in the neck from readers for overlooking restaurants outside the metropolis. Claims that newspapers are London-centric in this respect do have some basis, but it overlooks the plight of the British restaurant reviewer. Although it is entertaining to read the occasional excoriating review, readers mainly look for recommendations from critics. The minute they travel beyond the M4, however, the critics have a problem because there are simply not enough establishments worth writing about, and those that are have already been reviewed ten times over. So the critic faces an invidious choice: step outside London and face the risk of having to write a negative review of the 'elitist London critic attacks popular local institution' variety – certain to incense the locals – or leave well alone and court criticism for lazily ignoring 'The Regions'.

The *Observer*'s restaurant reviewer, Jay Rayner, attracted a large mail bag, many letters using language 'ripe enough to make a navvy blush', amounting to 'string the bastard up', when he wrote a scathing review of a Desperate Dan-style pub lunch in the West Midlands wherein he lamented the absence of decent restaurants in the area. 'I sit down with guidebooks and scan furiously, hoping, with each new study, that somehow, something might have changed since the last time I looked. I scan the net. I beg for recommendations. But nothing.' In response to the heated post bag, Mr Rayner countered accusations of London-centrism by clarifying that he had in fact reviewed establishments from the Isle of Wight to Edinburgh and from the west of Devon to the eastern-most tip of Norfolk, and he remained recalcitrant.

> 'London really is the best place in Britain in which to eat out, and I refuse to pretend otherwise. There are so many more restaurants here. The food is better. The variety is better. The inventiveness is greater . . . I'm not claiming that it is always the best value . . . Nor am I claiming that there are no good restaurants outside London. Obviously there are. Certain cities – Man-chester, Leeds, Edinburgh – are serious contenders. But still nothing matches the capital's range. One virtue of a crowded city like London is that it forces everyone to raise their game.'

Such candour is refreshing. However much Britons living outside London attempt to deny it, there is a dearth of good eating places outside the capital. Londoners may well have a terrific choice of restaurants on their doorstep, but their good fortune is not shared by the would-be eating-out public elsewhere. It is no surprise that top British chef, Gordon Ramsay, chose to make a television series entitled *Ramsay's Kitchen Nightmares*: the only sur-prise is that no one thought up such a project sooner since there is no shortage of ailing restaurants in Britain to provide ample fodder. Nor is it a coincidence that the establishments featured were all outside central London in places where evidence of the much-vaunted British Food Revolution is often thin on the ground. Mr Ramsay's thumbnail sketch of one Essex Kitchen Nightmare might easily apply to thousands of other aspiring eateries throughout the UK:

> 'With over 40 dishes to choose from, Philippe's menu is global both in size and choice – everything from the traditional all-day English breakfast to Hoisin noodles and Mexican platters. And 70 per cent of the food is bought-in, ready-prepared then often reheated and not cooked to order – an expensive, false economy . . . The Ramsay take? Definitely more confusion than fusion.'

Ramsay's Kitchen Nightmares identified the key short-comings of too many British restaurants: inadequately trained chefs with ridiculously large, over-ambitious, globalized menus, relying on bought-in food that can be either deep-fried or microwaved. Anyone who takes a stroll past a parade of British catering establishments between 10.00 and 12.00 on a weekday morning can count on seeing fleets of 'food service' chilled vans delivering supplies. Short cuts for chefs are not unique to the UK – in every affluent country lesser restaurants do buy in labour-saving items such as pre-cut chips – but in Britain such companies can provide a total service for the caterer, to the extent that if you scan the public notices in local newspapers, it is now common to see catering licences that have been granted on a 'microwave-only' basis.

When he wrote his *Bad Food Guide* in 1967 – a book in which he lampooned low standards in British restaurants – Derek Cooper noted the growing trend towards a uniform blandness or 'untaste', a consequence of the creep of convenience food into restaurants, and he predicted more to come:

> 'The era of technical development that the catering industry in Britain is undergoing will inevitably mean more standardization, less and less food will be cooked in the kitchens of small restaurants, and more and more will be prepared in factories under conditions of the utmost hygiene, and deep-frozen for consumption hundreds of miles away and months later.'

His comments proved prescient. These days, British chefs don't need to cook at all. There is no need to do a catering course or serve your time as an apprentice in a reputable kitchen. No need to pay professional wages that will interest a serious young chef. All it takes is someone with half a brain who can be relied upon to turn up each shift and not run out of food; someone whose job it is to reheat, deep-fry, plate and assemble. Like lazy domestic cooks who pop out to Tesco or Marks & Spencer for a boxed ready meal, the chef only needs the catalogue and phone number for catering suppliers who will do all the work for him: delivering to the kitchen door every short cut from pre-balled tri-colour melon, hand-tied bundles of frozen haricots verts, olive oil mash, through to ready-poached egg and ready-to-use Hollandaise sauce. In 2005, complete dishes supplied by two such companies – Brakes and 3663 – included paella, Malaysian beef rendang, lamb with dumplings in cider sauce, asparagus and lemon risotto, braised lamb with flageolets, three-cheese pasta and broccoli bake, char-grilled vegetable and mozzarella timbale, pre-cooked omelettes, cod and pancetta fish-cakes, moules marinières, peperonata terrine, char-grilled chicken with mango salsa, Mediterranean vegetable bake, Moroccan lamb tagine, pork hock with fruit compote, Thai ginger fish brochettes and mushroom, brie, rocket and redcurrant filo bundle. They were doubtless consumed with reasonable enthusiasm by millions of diners who remained blissfully unaware that they were not fully prepared from scratch on the premises.

The one area where British restaurants really do push the boat out for their consumers is children's food. Britain is unique in Europe in that it likes to make a fuss of children by offering them an especially bad menu. A separate 'children's menu' is an alien concept in any other country except the US. Restaurateurs elsewhere take the attitude that children will eat the same sort of food as adults, the only concessions being that dishes may be offered in smaller portions, or produced more promptly to pre-empt outbursts from hungry toddlers. Foreign restaurateurs do not live in fear of hysterical children throwing tantrums in the dining room because they can count on the fact that the children have been socialized at home by family meals and can usually be relied upon to sit round a table and eat alongside others. Britain, on the other hand, believes that a dining room is a hostile and foreign environment for a child, a potential war zone. Before contemplating a restaurant visit with their children, the British seem to believe that children must be pacified with a distinct repertoire of 'child-friendly' foods (for which read 'junk') and bribed with free, non-food gifts. Otherwise, how else can they be expected to sit through an exclusively adult dining experience that is widely considered to be intolerable for a British child? Viewed from abroad, when it comes to food Britain's treatment of children amounts to neglect, a national embarrassment, even to the British. One Englishwoman told me:

'We often go to this seafood restaurant in Marbella. We like it because it is chilled and laid-back. You can sit on the balcony and eat fantastic prawns and squid while you look out at the sea. The people who eat there are very international: Dutch, Germans, Belgians, Swiss, Austrians, Canadians, Scandinavians. When they come in a family group, you notice how the kids just sit down and eat the same food as their parents, no nonsense. The British families stand out because the children won't eat this or that, and so their parents start asking the waiters for something different for them that's not on the menu. Why can't they just appreciate food like European children seem to?'

In 2003, the Parents Jury – a group that campaigns for better children's food – surveyed the food in British restaurants that commonly serve to children, based on responses from 1,400 parents. The judging panel concluded that, because the standard was so low, the idea of children's menus should be done away with altogether. The children's menu in one prominent chain was summarized by a judge as follows: 'No fresh food. Everything is out of the freezer and into the fryer or microwave. I bet they haven't got a chopping board in the kitchen.' The Parents Jury went on to highlight one typical children's menu with a prehistoric dinosaur theme. It consisted of heavily processed foods: 'Raptor hot dog', 'Jungle chicken', 'Jurassic sausages', 'Bronto burger', 'T-Rex pizzas' and 'Big Dino breakfast'. All these were served with chips and a refreshing ice lolly with 'fruit-flavour'. To make the package more attractive, it was available in a larger or super-size version for 50 pence extra. Good children who finished up this assembly were rewarded with a free lollipop. A subsequent survey of 141 children's meals served in cafés and restaurants in London found that every one failed to meet even the basic nutritional standards set down for school meals.

Almost 40 years ago, Derek Cooper summed up his conclusions about the state of Britain's eating-out scene. 'There is, alas, no optimism on the eating front. For the minority prepared to pay for the privilege there will always be a small number of good restaurants. The majority of us will continue to put up uncomplainingly, perhaps even with a sort of masochistic pleasure, with bad food.' Four decades on, his remarks still seem extraordinarily apt.

5

NO TIME TO COOK

Britain has become a nation that steadfastly believes it no longer has the time to cook, except for Christmas Day and the odd weekend when we dabble in the ancient art of cooking and try to work up some enthusiasm for the pleasures of the table. As little as 20 years ago, we used to look on cooking as part and parcel of daily life, then reports came from the United States of the emerging trend towards 'no-cook' eating. It was said to have started in Manhattan, where apartment kitchens were tiny and the possibilities for eating out were rich and varied. 'Grazing' became a new buzz word as consumers took to roaming fertile foodie pastures, eating what they felt like, when they felt like it. So the modern myth was born that it is possible to abandon cooking entirely but still continue to eat great food every day of the week.

The British had their doubts about no-cook eating. To start with, few neighbourhoods in the UK have a dazzling food emporium such as Zabar's or Dean & DeLuca on the street corner. Then there were those tales – possibly apocryphal – of Americans who stood over their toasters in the morning shouting 'Faster, faster!' at a slice of bread, just so they could jog off to work at six in the morning to work a ten-hour day. It all sounded a bit manic.

But at the beginning of the 21st century, Britain seems determined to follow in the footsteps of the US when it comes to eating habits. While it would be an exaggeration to say that home cooking in Britain is dead, it is most certainly in a chronic state. In 2001, the average British household cooked from scratch – that is, prepared a meal from mainly raw ingredients – just 3.36 times a week. By 2002, 45 per cent of Britons agreed with the statement 'I am so tired in the evening, I don't have the energy to do anything'. Many British people are now convinced that they don't have the time or energy to cook and they are acting upon that conviction. While in 1980, the average meal took one hour to prepare, now on average it takes 13 minutes. On current trends, it is predicted that by 2010, this will shrink to 8 minutes. Cooking is now widely seen in Britain as an optional activity, a reflection of how little importance the country gives to food. Why would one want to cook, so the thinking goes, when nearly everything else in life is potentially more interesting and rewarding? As the convenience food manufacturer Geest observed: 'People generally are trying to fit more pleasurable things [than cooking] into their lives.'

This attitude which sees food preparation and cooking as an oppressive burden draws us closer to the US – and further from Europe. Though most women are attracted by the idea of not having to cook every day of their life, the prospect of not cooking routinely and relying instead on ready-made food for sustenance is entirely alien to most Europeans – unless, that is, they are rich enough to afford a personal cook. For example, four out of every five Spanish adults believe that they do have the time to spend preparing and cooking food. The French writer Mireille Guiliano, author of *French Women Don't Get Fat*, notes that French women love to shop for food and prepare it. 'Prepare your own meals. Shun prepared foods, especially processed ones with artificial anything' is one of the guiding precepts that she identifies as keeping her countrywomen svelte. The French instantly recognize that when you give up cooking you abdicate responsibility for what you put in your mouth to an industry that is generally less trustworthy than yourself.

One survey of European food habits noted that Italians were even more committed to cooking than the French. 'They [Italians] pride themselves on how much they spend on food and time spent preparing food would appear to be no effort . . . Some seven in ten Italian women love to cook . . . Going shopping everyday is considered much more acceptable than having to consume food that is laden with preservatives and additives.' This attitude is also typical of Germans for whom health and proper nutrition are especially important considerations. Like Italy, seven out of every ten German women say that they love to cook. To most Europeans, it is obvious that any abandonment of home cooking not only leaves you at the mercy of the food industry's chemical henchmen, but also amounts to a surrender in control over what you eat, even a form of self-neglect. This is why they make space for it in their daily routine. One working German mother put it this way: 'I think I would find myself a loser if my work left me in such a state that I couldn't cook any more. I would feel that I was not coping, like not washing myself or brushing my teeth any longer.'

Meanwhile in Britain, the no-time-to-cook culture continues to grow, feeding off the deeply-rooted British idea that food is of trivial importance in the great span of things, and also picking up more modern justification along the way by wrapping itself in the language of feminism. All over the world, since time immemorial, women have taken responsibility for domestic cooking. As late as the 1950s, the preparation of food at home by women was not only expected, but encouraged – the presumption being that women did not work. In 1955, *Housekeeping Monthly* magazine was still advising its female readers to keep their husbands happy as follows:

'Have dinner ready. Plan ahead, even the night before to have a delicious meal ready, on time for his return. This is a way of letting him know that you have been thinking about him and are concerned about his needs. Most men are hungry when they come home and the prospect of a good meal (especially his favourite dish) is part of the warm welcome needed.'

71

By the late 1960s, with the emergence of the Women's Liberation Movement, the image of the contented housewife happily cooking at home while tending to children and polishing floors had come under attack. The domestic arena had become a political one, a key contested area in the battle between the sexes. Viewed together with 'housework', cooking was seen as deeply politically incorrect. Once again, the critique of cooking originated, not in Europe, but in the United States. 'Women have been brainwashed more than even we can imagine,' wrote Pat Mainardi of Redstockings, an influential New York women's liberation group. 'Men have no such conditioning. They recognize the essential fact of housework right from the very beginning. Which is that it stinks.' No distinction was drawn between cooking a meal or cleaning up a baby's vomit. Ms Mainardi's list of 'dirty chores' began with 'buying groceries, carting them home and putting them away, cooking meals and washing pans and pots'. Another feminist collective denounced cooking as something that not only exhausted a woman but which tended to 'shackle her time, keeping her from more stimulating endeavours'. The message was loud and clear: Cooking is demeaning and oppressive, so ditch it as soon as you can.

Food manufacturers are always keen to cash in on what the industry refers to as 'lifestyle trends'. By the end of the 1960s, a large number of short-cut convenience foods were already on the British shopping list. One of the first commentators to pick up on this trend was the broadcaster Derek Cooper. In *The Bad Food Guide*, his bold 1967 attack on British gastronomy, he drew a witty but troubling pen portrait of 'Mrs Average Housewife' (Mrs A.H.), portraying her as putty in the hands of the food industry and its advertisers:

'She is far too busy forcing grey out and forcing white in to her husband's shirts to spend more than a few minutes a day at the cooker. For her, everything must be EASY ... What she likes to do is to un-zip the foil envelope, place contents in pan of water and stir over a low flame for two minutes. Or she likes to empty a packet into a bowl, add an egg, whisk, and there you have it ready to pop in the oven. Or she likes to open tins full of rich fresh goodness (just add half a pint of milk) or little containers of chemicals that will, theoretically, make featherlight pancakes or heavenly buns or whatever it says on the packet ... For Mrs A.H., as portrayed in television commercials, the less time spent in the kitchen the better. Nobody has yet done a survey on what the children of Mrs A.H. have for supper, but I wouldn't mind betting that in 98 per cent of homes it's some kind of quick convenience food: baked beans, frozen hamburgers, spaghetti with tomato sauce, tinned soup, fish fingers, tinned meat loaf.'

Nowadays, Mrs Average Housewife has been supplanted in the eyes of the food industry by Mrs or Ms Average Working Woman, and just like Mrs Average Housewife before her, she represents a wonderful business opportunity. Here are four miracle British products that aim to make Ms Average Working Woman's life that bit easier:

Fast Feasters instant burger

Click! Tick! Ping! A pre-cooked, ready-assembled cheese burger in a bun that only needs to be microwaved, then have the accompanying sachet of tomato relish squirted over it. It is designed to appeal to the person who sincerely believes that life is too short to slice open a burger bun and grill a burger. The person who can't be bothered getting out of their chair to pick up one at McDonald's. Fast Feasters come with the number of seconds the product takes to reheat – 90 seconds in the case of an Xtra Large burger – printed prominently on the front of the packet, so start that stopwatch ticking. Cartoon-style diagrams illustrate the simplicity of the preparation process. You just 'Click' open the microwave, set the timer to 'Tick' and then wait for the 'Ping' that tells you it is ready. They are cheap as chips too. Just £1.49 for two six-ounce burgers in a Buy One Get One Free promotion!

Marks & Spencer's ready prepared coffee

Ready-brewed filter coffee sold chilled in litre cartons at the not inconsiderable price of £1.99. All you have to do is pour it into a mug and reheat in a microwave oven. Arguably preferable in taste terms to Britain's beloved staple, instant coffee, which now accounts for 90 per cent of the British coffee market, ready-brewed filter is designed to appeal to well-heeled Britons who are too indolent and lacking in discernment to take the time to make a proper cup of coffee, but who fancy something a little bit more up-market than granules. After all, stirring instant coffee granules into water from a boiling kettle, or emptying out grains from a cafetière, is such an exhausting business.

Bisto Gravy Granules for chicken dishes

We all know that Britons love their gravy, and there's nothing quite like Bisto to evoke the mood of a traditional British roast dinner. This product comes in a jolly orange tub with a mouth-watering golden roast chicken, flanked with green beans and roast potatoes on the front. The only thing is, it does not contain any chicken at all, being a mixture of potato starch, maltodextrin, hydrogenated oil, salt, wheatflour, flavourings, colours, flavour enhancers, sugar, emulsifiers, spice, herb and vegetable extracts. Still, it's no-fuss and quick. Just add the 'finer granules' with the 'smoother taste' to water and stir. Add more granules for a thicker gravy.

Warbies All In One Riddlers

Oppressive, isn't it, having to split open a roll and squirt cheese spread on it? Warburtons, known to kids and mums by its diminutive fun title 'Warbies', the company that brought a whole new take to the quintessentially English crumpet in the form of the orange and green-flecked Pizza Flavour Crumpet, has come up with Riddlers, a bap that comes with a delightful cheese spread, or ham-flavoured cheese spread, already in the middle. What a breakthrough for busy mums, fretting over their offspring's lunchboxes! With 25 ingredients, it is a triumph of British cutting-edge food technology. In the company's own words: 'A really clever, but bonkers, scientist has invented a machine just for us. It makes rolls with yummy cheese already in the middle.' The 'riddle' for children to solve is 'How does the cheese get in?' Suggestions to Warburtons on postcards please.

A 2002 report which looked at how amenable or otherwise various European countries were to increased 'penetration' of convenience foods, identified Britain as the country offering the richest pickings for food processors. Britain, it pointed out, was the country where traditional eating habits were the most eroded; this was a situation which it attributed to the changing role of women. 'Working women, particularly full-time workers, have less time and inclination for preparing family meals; additional incomes also make more money available for spending on convenience foods, such as ready meals, or on takeaways and meals out.'

You can almost hear the food industry licking its lips. Its legions of supermarket pundits, retail analysts and new-product developers have all taken up with gusto the idea of the no-cook consumer, quickly coining the term 'cash rich, time poor shopper', a stereotype that fits the industry's purpose rather well.

Contrary to urban myth, longer working hours do not seem to be the main factor behind Britain's perceived time shortage for cooking. Official data released in 2004 showed that the average length of the working week in Britain for all occupations, both full and part time, fell to 31.8 hours in July 2004 – the lowest on record. So it is not so much that Britons do not have the time to cook, than that they no longer see cooking as a good use of their time. Yet food processors and retailers continue to appeal to consumers who like to think they belong to this new 'cash rich, time poor' breed. They are an easy market for products with 'added value', products that generate more money from basic natural ingredients by altering them in a technological way and repackaging them imaginatively. But there is also a baser motive for this. People shopping in a hurry can generally be relied on to pick up almost anything without asking too many questions about it, providing it looks the part. Food processors and manufacturers have a financial interest in fostering the bogus idea that it is possible for the country to abandon routine cooking, yet still consider itself a nation of gastronomes by virtue of its adventurous processed food tastes. This is a proposition that countries with healthy food cultures would find preposterous.

Like the archetypal forgetful husband, who dashes out guiltily to luxurious shops to buy a hasty, badly-chosen and expensive present for his largely ignored wife, many working women in Britain now dash out to the supermarket, in search of products that look as though they approximate to an idea of likeable, edible food. Indeed, in the age of the 'cash rich, time poor' shopper, not having time to cook has become a sign of status. If you do still cook on a humdrum daily basis, you risk being seen as less of an achiever than those who don't – by implication, your time should be taken up with something more worthwhile and improving than cooking.

This attitude has proven disastrous for the nation's cooking skills. Gordon Ramsay was accused of sexism in 2005 when he declared that too many British women were surviving on a daily diet of expensive and unhealthy ready meals. 'You'd be amazed how little cooking the girls are doing. When they eat, they cheat – it's ready meals and pre-prepared meals all the way.' But his conclusion that most young British women 'can't cook to save their lives' had more than a ring of truth to it.

This peculiarly British no-time-to-cook ideology has become so deeply ingrained over the last 20 years that it is now enshrined in public policy. Dame Deirdre Hutton, boss of the Food Standards Agency, admitted in 2005 that Britain's ever-growing consumption of ready meals was having a grave effect on the nation's health. However, she ducked the opportunity to encourage people to cook more fresh food for themselves, plumping instead for the wholly inadequate option of coaxing the food industry into making its techno-food a little better. 'Processed food is here to stay. In that sense we need to make it as healthy as possible. It is up to us to work with what people are doing – it is no good trying to take people back to some largely mythical golden age,' she said.

In Britain, despite the weighty repercussions of a diet of processed food, it seems no politician or public servant is prepared to risk promoting home cooking as a public health strategy. Although the government is not afraid to promote breast feeding over formula milk substitutes – 'Breast Is Best' – it will not contemplate a parallel 'Home Cooked Is Best' campaign when it comes to solid food. This is because Britain has swung so far away from the idea that cooking is a basic, nourishing life skill, that to champion it locates you on the margins of political life and culture, like an eccentric flat-Earther or incurable romantic. You might as well advise women to abandon their washing machines and start doing their laundry on stones in the river.

The more you earn in Britain, the more aspiring and

ambitious you are, the more you are under pressure not to cook as this may lead you to put your success under stress. One senior manager in a large north-eastern company building homes for the middle to upper end of the housing market told me how they operated a 'buy back' scheme in which someone who buys a new-build house can trade it in for another new-build house a few years later. 'When we get the houses back we are surprised by how many people have never used the oven. We know this because the instruction manuals are still inside.' I heard of a complex of holiday homes, hand-somely refurbished with an eye to the foreign tourist market, that got into difficulties because the kitchens were equipped with a microwave in place of a traditional oven. 'The visitors all complained and asked: "Where's the oven?" The British letting agents were totally taken aback by this because they had calculated that no one would want to cook.'

Unlike Europe, where women clearly think they can cook and still be considered as rounded, successful people who are effective in other spheres of their life, British women who see home cooking as a priority for health, well-being and a life-enriching pleasure, risk being seen as being in the slow lane of modern life, not using their intellect to its fullest potential.

This point was made forcefully by columnist Decca Aitkenhead whose view is that cooking, like cleaning the toilet, is no more than a daily domestic grind. 'Nigella Lawson is a highly educated, intelligent woman who has been congratulated for producing a book and television show about cooking,' she wrote. 'Salman Rushdie was one of her dinner guests, and was fulsome in his praise. If you had this man round to your house for dinner, you might think it less an achievement than a shame if the topic of conversation was your cooking.' Likewise, the interviewer, Lynn Barber – in feminist mode – defended young British women against the criticism, levelled by male chefs, that they will not learn to cook, by once again portraying a 'no-cook' philosophy as social progress. 'Nobody these days wants to be a peasant and girls have better things to do than pluck chickens,' she wrote.

In Britain, unlike the rest of Europe, feminist sister-hood has proven spectacularly bad for the cause of good food, yet perversely, it does not appear to have liberated women from their obligation to feed others. An increas-ing number of men do take some responsibility for cook-ing as more women now work than before. The UK has the third highest rate of female employment in Europe with a record 70 per cent of women at work, but the stereotypical image of the woman at the kitchen sink still fits British contemporary life. Although less cooking is going on in British households, women still take the responsibility for seeing that everyone has something to eat. One survey found that in 61 per cent of British households, women do all or most of the cooking that takes place. They may not necessarily be cooking from scratch, but women still have to solve the daily puzzle of what everyone is going to eat, even though a 'no-cook' culture makes this a less time-consuming and demanding task.

As fewer people cook from scratch, the concept of everyone sharing the same meal has also waned. Today's working women, unlike their mothers and grandmothers before them, can no longer expect everyone to eat one meal because a 'no-cook' culture makes it possible for everyone to eat something different. If Mum doesn't actually cook the dinner, just buy it, then there is no need for everyone to eat the same thing. Consequently, the erstwhile 'cook' in the house is now expected to plan purchases to reflect everyone's likes and dislikes; 43 per cent of British mothers now make up to three different meals each night, presumably to cater for members of the household unwilling to eat the same thing. So it may be turkey nuggets, baked beans and potato shapes for one child, a pizza and oven chips for another, and a Tesco's 'Finest' ready meal for the adults. Instead of settling on one communal meal that everyone can eat – albeit in relays – women now have to produce a different meal for everybody.

This task is supposedly made easier by the availability of ready meals or flexible food items that can be put together allowing women to serve up easily-made dishes tailored to each individual's picky tastes. In reality, deciding what everyone is going to eat each night may be more stressful than simply cooking a single straightforward communal meal from scratch. This is a new pressure on women that their female forebears who followed a cyclical repertoire – roast on a Sunday, cottage pie on a Monday, fish on a Friday and so on – never had. Repetitive staple family meals no longer seem good enough, and seemingly sophisticated ready-prepared foods appear to be tempting solutions. Yet many women are now so overloaded with choice when it comes to convenience foods that they find it harder and harder to make decisions. And when they do settle on certain products, they can be left with a guilty feeling that they have not made the best selection, either because other household members say they don't like them, or because they worry that the dishes that do go down well are not that healthy or wholesome.

In theory, the availability of a huge range of convenience food should be a boon to the woman (or man) who wants to cook sometimes, but not always – a handy stand-by on occasions. In practice this has a corrosive effect because the less you cook, the less you are likely to feel able to cook. Regular cooking is largely a question of momentum and establishing a rhythm. People who cook regularly see it as fairly easy, and some actively enjoy the experience. Others view it as worth the effort for the end result and preferable to the alternatives. People who are out of the habit of cooking, on the other hand, come to see it as a big deal. After a few nights eating ready meals, the fridge is bare. There is no cold meat left over from the night before on which to base an evening salad, or a pilaf, or a packed lunch sandwich. There is no stock from a roasted chicken carcass to make the base for an easy vegetable soup which might feature in several meals and fill a lunchtime flask. There is no longer the option of eating up the remaining half of Sunday's apple crumble.

Convenience food shopping is geared to specific 'meal solutions', as the supermarkets like to call them, rather than the basic re-provisioning of a household with a versatile larder of fresh and dried ingredients. The more you buy convenience foods, the more real cooking seems like a bridge too far, perhaps something you do for a dinner party for friends at weekends, or for extended family at Christmas, but not something that is practically achievable on a daily basis. As dependency on convenience foods grows in Britain, cooking is perceived as an optional leisure interest like taking dressmaking classes or doing Pilates, rather than a life-enhancing everyday activity.

6

DISAPPEARING DINNER TABLES

In 1999, Oxo officially laid to rest the corpse of the British family meal. Ever since 1983, the stock cube company had based its TV advertising around images of a family, sitting down around a dinner table all eating roast beef and Yorkshire pudding, predictably anointed with Oxo gravy. But as the 20th century drew to a close, Oxo was forced to admit that this once iconic image of British family life was no longer appropriate for the new millennium. Consequently, it dropped the advert. The nation's food habits had changed radically and adults sat down less frequently to eat with their children. As for cooking the Oxo advert meal, the idea of preparing a roast dinner from scratch was considered by advertisers as a bridge too far for the majority of modern Britons. Even making up an instant gravy from granules or cubes was asking too much. The 'mother' in Oxo's campaign, actress Lynda Bellingham, lamented the trend. 'I think people buy pre-cooked meals now and I don't actually think it is realistic, people cooking gravy.'

Throughout the 1990s, it had become evident that the writing was on the wall for family meals. A 1997 poll found that two-thirds of British families had given up traditional dinnertime for eating in front of the television. The following year, another survey flagged up the extent to which this British institution was dying out. It was not just a case of waiting until the baby was settled in bed so that everyone else could eat in peace a little later. An *Observer* survey found that almost half of all children aged 7–14 did not eat a regular evening meal around the table with their parents. In *The Times*, journalist Jonathan Meades devised a special 'note' for younger readers: 'A "table" is an inanimate quadruped where people ate in the olden days. It has been replaced by street, couch, car (when not picking nose).'

By 2004, a survey for the charity Raisingkids found that 20 per cent of families only ate together once a week, or even less. It also underlined just how 'normal' it had become to watch television while eating: 75 per cent of families watched television while they ate. By 2005, the instant gravy brand Bisto – presumably concerned with its sales – launched a TV advertising campaign to encourage British households to share a home-cooked meal one night a week. One day out of seven seemed to be as strong a 'back to the table' message as the country could take. The weekly rite of an almost ceremonial meal paid homage to the desirability of communal eating while leaving room for lapses. Although Britons still feel a lingering sentimental attachment to the idea of eating together, most are deserting it at a rate of knots: 89 per cent of parents say they agree with the statement that 'families are missing out by not eating together', yet communal family meals have become so infrequent that now one in every four homes no longer has a table that can accommodate everyone. As one market analyst put it: 'We have reached the situation [in Britain] where people no longer even buy dining tables because they have effectively become redundant.'

Britain's chosen mode of eating for the 21st century increasingly consists of consuming a reheated factory-made meal on the lap, in front of a flickering screen. Once more this puts us in the same company as the United States, but sets us apart from every other country on the planet where shared meals continue to be a cornerstone of daily life. 'In Denmark, people with kids would be really embarrassed if they didn't cook for the kids or ate in front of the TV,' one Danish woman told me. 'They expect to spend time round the dinner table, but in the UK I've been in several houses that have no dinner table. One friend was doing up his living room and I asked him where the table would go. He said he didn't need one. I find it quite weird that people in the UK eat on a sofa. How do you use a knife and fork sitting on a sofa?' The columnist Mimi Spencer has pointed out that in France the favourite place to eat both lunch and dinner is in the home: 75 per cent of French people eat at the family table. Conversely, 'In the UK, by contrast, we like to eat our meals a) standing up, b) in front of *Coronation*

Street, c) at a desk while catching up with e-mails, or d) by the side of the M40.'

Family and childcare experts are united in their dismay at the breakdown of British family meals. A substantial body of research suggests that they can potentially bestow a whole clutch of non-food benefits. They strengthen communication between family members and help build relationships on a daily basis: children talk more to parents and this strengthens their linguistic skills, making them more articulate and personable, so giving them an edge in the classroom and job market; they learn social skills such as how to share things and listen to other people; they develop good manners. Basic skills, such as learning how to use a knife and fork, or holding a simple conversation with an adult, are much less readily acquired by children who eat on their own.

On the food front, family meals come as close as anyone can expect to get to finding a panacea for Britain's eating problems. Shared household meals are associated with better nutrition because adults have more control over the quality and quantity of what their children eat. The discipline of cooking a meal that everyone will eat – albeit in relays or at staggered intervals as people arrive home – means that the standard of the main meal is higher if for no other reason than that the parents have a vested interest because they know that they themselves will eat it. Researchers at Cancer Research UK's Health Behaviour Unit have found that regular family meals are related to healthier dietary patterns and higher intakes of fruit and vegetables in older children. 'This research clearly shows what a key role parents play in influencing their children's eating habits. If the grown-ups opt for fast-food TV dinners they cannot expect children to relish regular helpings of fruit and vegetables.' Quite simply, families that eat together tend to eat better food.

By contrast, in most households where a shared meal is the exception, rather than the rule, parents routinely find themselves buying a radically different range of food for children than that which they buy for themselves. Perversely, they end up feeding children food that they would never consider eating themselves. This is usually food that is less healthy and less nutritious, but because feeding children such food is a common practice in the UK, they see this as almost inevitable. In this respect, Britain is, yet again, the cultural exception. In most other countries, children are given the best food, not the worst.

You might think that in Britain the custodians of public health would be promoting shared meals, if nothing else, as a solution to the growing problem of the country's bulging waistband. But over the last two decades, the concept that eating together is a desirable goal has become controversial. Anyone who becomes too vocal in promoting its benefits risks triggering hostility and outright opposition. The columnist Julie Burchill, a self-confessed 'latchkey' child raised on Vesta paella, consumed while watching *Crossroads*, mounted a spirited defence of modern British eating habits and an attack on those who seek to revive the traditional family meal:

'He who eats on the hoof is a fleet-footed, self-reliant citizen, refusing to stuff when he's not hungry or deny himself when he is. He does not seek the stultifying comfort of fellow cud-chewers ... but sees his body as a mere engine to power his immortal soul. He seeks neither the strong man of fascism nor the matriarch of the kitchen to tell him what to do. What's so wrong with our kiddies growing up like that? Something weird is going on in households where too much emphasis is placed on eating together; all sorts of power games and control freakery, a breeding ground for anorexia and bulimia as teenagers seek to establish control over their bodies. The sort of man who demands that his daughters, especially, sit down to eat whether they want to or not strikes me as the sort of patriarchal perv who will also seek to control their dress, dating habits and, eventually, sex lives – probably because he wants to have sex with them himself.'

Julie Burchill is never one to moderate an argument for the sake of being reasonable, but extreme though these sentiments are, they are guaranteed to strike a chord with many Britons because they seek to excuse our national ineptitude with food – albeit under a trendy, modern veneer. But all the emotional baggage of Britain's troubled relationship with food is there. Food is fuel, as important as filling your car up with petrol. Fascism and matriarchs? Anyone who tries to get you to think about what you eat is a tyrannical despot interfering with your civil right to eat yourself into an early grave if you so choose. Anorexia and bulimia? People who think too much about food aren't right in the head and if you give them elbow room, they'll start passing their sick complexes to everyone else in the form of obsessive eating habits. The current interest in what we eat isn't doing anything good at all, just making girls more neurotic about what they eat. So lay off, stop making a meal of food, and just let everyone eat what they fancy, when they fancy it.

Behind this elaborate smokescreen lurks the British antipathy to awarding food any importance in life, a beginner's defensiveness born out of inadequacy and lack of experience. British people know that most cultures appreciate the pleasures of the table but we can't quite work out what all the fuss is about. A recurring theme in British television advertising for food is images of the extended foreign family, revelling in a joyous communal meal of a traditional sort, whisked up from prime, fresh ingredients by a benevolent grandmother. We find this novel foreign idea entrancing, and rather seductive, but we are anxious to be handed the comforting reassurance at the end of the advert that no one seriously imagines that we will take a leaf out of their book and follow suit. Instead, all we are expected to do is to buy a jar of industrial gloop that purports to taste just like what that silver-haired mamma in the advert used to make.

The concept of the lingering family meal of the foreign variety does not chime with deep-rooted British patterns of socializing. It is problematical because it combines the moderate leisurely consumption of alcohol with the process of eating, and that is an alien thought for many people in Britain, a country where alcohol and food were traditionally separated into distinct zones. You ate your evening meal early, efficiently, and with no great ceremony, so you could line your stomach for spending the evening down the pub with your mates. The modern equivalent is drinking yourself legless on cut-price cocktails during a Happy Hour then staggering out in search of some takeaway fast food soon to be regurgitated onto the pavement. As Raymond Blanc remarked: 'In all Latin countries, we drink with food; we hardly ever drink without food. That is an English invention.'

In 2005, changes in British licensing hours provoked a national debate about the growing phenomenon of binge drinking, particularly amongst the nation's youth. At weekends, and many other nights of the week, Britain's town centres are zones of alcohol-fuelled violence and vomit as pubs and bars empty. Police forces up and down the land do their best to keep a lid on the situation while regulators examine more fundamental solutions. But, as always in Britain, discussions about alcohol are conducted almost exclusively without any reference to food, yet bad food and bad boozing are two sides of the same coin. The British have never been persuaded of the benefits of integrating food and alcohol consumption around a communal table and have yet to see that their problem with alcohol is rooted in their difficult relationship with food.

Nowadays, although it is increasingly apparent that communal meals might be good for family cohesion, for socializing children, keeping them healthy and so on, we still find difficulty in understanding how lingering over food can be a pleasurable experience, particularly in a family context. Research in 2005 found that stress levels rose and enjoyment fell when children were around the dining table. The number of people who felt 'unhappy about eating' rose from 7 to 17 per cent. The journalist Christopher Gilmour dismissed out of hand the notion that family meals could be happy; in a *Daily Telegraph* article entitled 'Sitting down to wage war', he wrote: 'The closest my family get to a communal Happy Meal is at McDonald's, and as for sitting down as a family, the only thing this teaches them is how to score points off each other and brush up on their bickering skills.' This is yet another expression of the British view that a mealtime is merely an occasion to fulfil a basic biological need for food that is more or less appetizing. In Britain, the act of eating has never been backed up by a round-the-table culture of conviviality. Contrast this with the French attitude as expressed by Gérard Depardieu: 'I am at my happiest when I am preparing a meal for family or friends. For cooking is all about love . . . The art of cooking and preparing a meal for those you care about is also, for me, a means of communicating that love and friendship without necessarily having to utter a single word.' Many British people would consider these sentiments to be nauseatingly mawkish. As a country we seem largely unconvinced of the emotional gratification that sitting around a table sharing good food with family or friends can bring. In fact, the idea that the everyday act of eating can bring with it the possibility of pleasure is the single biggest missing factor in British discussions of food.

Another problem the British have with a meal eaten sitting down with others is that it inevitably takes longer than one eaten on the hoof, and Britain likes to get out its stop watch when it comes both to cooking and eating. The British seem perpetually in a hurry to get their food eaten, over and done with, as if it has nothing much other than calories to offer. Whether it is bolting down a microwaved sausage roll and chips before rushing out to play football, or shivering on a cold street corner eating a fish supper, or clearing up the dinner plates before they even have time to get cold, we are rushing to get on with something else. We choose food that is quickly prepared and eat it just as quickly, so missing out on the ceremony and ritual of the table and the conviviality and companionship of eating together. And when we start feeling like eating some more food a couple of hours later, it rarely occurs to us that this is a sort of psychological hunger, an expression of the emotionally unsatisfying and solitary way in which we have eaten.

Until recently, eating on your own carried a stigma because it was seen universally as nowhere near as much fun as eating together with someone else. A sage piece of advice once commonly given to elderly people who were living on their own and who were considered in danger of neglecting themselves, was to take the time to cook themselves a proper meal, however simple. Carers and health visitors would remind them that the minimal effort of choosing a pretty plate, setting the table with cutlery, a napkin, even a tablecloth and making a small ceremony out of the daily need to eat, was a way of showing to yourself that you still mattered, a means to prevent premature vegetation in front of the TV.

Naturally, as people live longer and more relationships break up, there are more single-person households in Britain and consequently people must eat on their own out of necessity, not preference. But not all solitary eaters in Britain are elderly or single. Many people have got into the anarchic rhythm of 'staggered eating' where everyone in a household eats different food at different times. Our eating habits have become atomized. A growing number of Britons exist on an ad lib diet of convenience food designed for one isolated individual even though they live with others. Nearly half the meals eaten in the UK are now eaten alone. Once upon a time that would have been considered rather sad. Now it is considered normal.

7

'THIS IS NOT JUST FOOD . . .'

In every European country, consumers can buy processed, ready-made meals in one form or other. In countries other than Britain, consumers view them as a lacklustre and unexciting category. Generally frozen or tinned, their main selling point is that they can be stowed away at the back of a freezer or pantry and forgotten about until the desperate day when there is nothing else to eat in the house. This is not the sort of food which you are meant to buy frequently, or look forward to, thinking 'Yum, yum, can't wait to eat that tonight!'; it is just a back-up for occasions when fresh food runs out, like candles kept for a power cut. A search for anything resembling a British-style chilled ready meal in a European supermarket requires persistence. Less than a quarter of Polish households and less than a third of Italian households, for example, possess a microwave. It is a different story in Britain where almost 90 per cent of households possess one, and aisle after aisle of supermarket space is dedicated to ready meals, purporting to offer the finest global cuisine, all conveniently pre-prepared in a microwavable container.

Amongst European nations, the French show the most potential interest in chilled ready meals after the British. Over the last few years, French food processors have made valiant efforts to help catch the eye of the discerning consumer by enlisting the services of distinguished chefs. Alain Senderens has put his name to Carrefour's 'hachis Parmentier' (the French equivalent of cottage pie), Paul Bocuse lends his seal of approval to Leclerc's 'sauté de veau', and Antoine Westermann has whipped up a 'cuisse de canard, sauce au poivre vert' to 'delight gourmets' who shop at Super U. They look pretty much like British ready meals when you unwrap them and contain a similar, if slightly shorter roll-call of industrial additives. Such meals come either in plastic trays, or – for the non-microwave-owning majority of the population – in little plastic sachets to be steamed or reheated in water. But blink and you will miss them because the shelf space allotted to them is small.

Companies manufacturing these 'plats cuisinés' do need their association with figurehead chefs to build sales. Although such products are more prominent than before, and are a growing category in which processors consider it is worth investing – even to the extent of coughing up the princely sums such celebrated chefs command – their presence in French supermarkets is insignificant when judged against the sheer weight of more traditional foods requiring some form of cooking from scratch.

The British, meanwhile, continue to be by far and away the most enthusiastic consumers of ready meals. Demand for them grew by 70 per cent between 1994 and 2004 – a much faster rate than other European countries. By the end of 2003, Britain already had the distinction of eating 49 per cent of all the ready meals eaten in Europe, and it is predicted that our voracious appetite for them will see us devouring more than half the total market for them by 2007. They are consumed enthusiastically by everyone from judges to refuse collectors, with only a very slight variation in sales 'penetration' according to social class. In 2004, Britons ate a staggering £900 million worth of ready meals, and the market for them is growing at 6 per cent a year. We simply can't get enough of them.

Britain is always proud to say that it is at the very forefront of developments in processed food. The British food industry does not like to talk in terms of 'convenience food' because that term has down-market connotations: TV dinners, airline meals, army rations, long-life camping packs, boil-in-the-bag – all that sort of thing. Increasingly, it prefers to talk in terms of 'meal solutions'. This term implies that consumers have a problem with every meal they contemplate – which may indeed be the case in Bad Food Britain – and that dedicated food processors have come to the rescue. Marketed this way, meal solutions sound as though they are the fruits of the food industry doing the jaded consumer a favour. True to form, the Institute of Grocery Distribution, the body that represents big retailers, likes to use heroic language to describe them. Meal solutions, it says, reflect 'many years of effort and commitment by the industry . . . endeavouring to make life simpler for consumers by taking processing out of the home and onto the factory production line'. Home cooking, just scaled-up a bit. What could be less intimidating than that?

The British food industry now classifies meal solutions into four types, according to the 'level of consumer participation' (effort) required. 'Ready to eat meal solutions' are 'immediates' or 'hand snacks' such as sandwiches, sausage rolls and pasties that can be eaten, either hot or cold, on the move. There is no consumer participation required here, other than removing the wrapper. 'Ready to heat meal solutions' include the standard chilled or frozen ready meal, which are usually fully, or at least part-cooked and simply require reheating; 20 per cent consumer participation is required with these.

We then move on to largely pre-cooked products that breathe a sense of real cooking into the 'meal solutions' category. These 'ready to prepare meal solutions' include 'ambient light meals', such as baked beans on toast with grated cheese, a tin of spaghetti and meatballs, or 'meal components', products such as beefburgers, oven chips or pasta with pasta sauce. Some individual elements of these meals may be raw or require some cooking time, hence 60 per cent 'consumer participation' may be called for, but 'most of the preparation is undertaken by the manufacturer', so this involvement comes down to opening jars, boiling water or switching on the microwave.

Sensing the money to be made from this category, the furniture retailer, Ikea, has decided to move into this area. It has coined the phrase 'assemble and dine' to describe its new extended range of individual items that are positioned together – such as frozen meatballs, mashed potato and sauces – and designed to add up to a complete meal. First it was flat-pack furniture, now it is flat-pack food.

Finally, there is the 'ready to make meal solution', where raw or only partially cooked products are grouped together to lead the consumer to a particular meal idea – say, raw, seasoned chicken sold alongside a 'cook-in' sauce, ready-prepared vegetable batons and a tub of microwavable potato gratin – that requires some form of cooking. In British food industry terms, this counts as 100 per cent participation, so any consumers who are still capable of thinking up a meal for themselves and assembling disparate scratch ingredients for cooking at home are seen as creatures from another planet, displaying superhuman levels of involvement with food.

As recently as the late 1990s, food processors' efforts were focused on the complete, one-person, zero-effort ready meal that you only have to microwave. However, it stands to reason that after a while even British consumers would tire of this functional, yet joyless category. Clever marketing only works for so long, and more people, even the young and impressionable, begin to notice that far from resembling the mouth-watering picture on the box, the actual contents of most ready meals look reminiscent of something you would swerve to avoid if spotted lying on a pavement on a post-pub Saturday night. A 15-year-old girl described her disillusionment to the charity, Barnardo's:

> 'One day I saw a curry on telly that they were advertising and I said, "We have got to get that it looks really nice", and a couple of days later when I went to the supermarket with my mum I looked and I thought it looked really nice on the front of the box and I brought it home and when I took it out to cook it, it looked disgusting, I didn't like it and when I served it up it didn't look the same.'

A further potential spanner in the works for food processors is that most Britons have long since heard the message that ready meals may be bad for you. The more food-aware amongst us know that most of them are complex techno-foods, so whether a ready meal purports to be Peking duck, lamb Jalfrezi, luxury ocean pie, or plain old sausage and mash, there is an odds on chance that it will consist of just another variant on the versatile and profitable, food industry formula of cheaply-sourced ingredients reassembled with salt, sugar and fat bound together by emulsifiers, additives and water.

Such revelations are common in the UK media. In 2005, a *Daily Telegraph* survey of ready meals found that even the simplest-looking chilled ready meals from supermarket chains often contained in excess of 50 different ingredients. It spotlighted a Waitrose Chinese meal with 59 ingredients, and a Marks & Spencer shepherd's pie with 52. David Gregory, Marks & Spencer's head of food technology, insisted – not very convincingly – that their product was modelled on home cooking. 'I recently got out an old university cookbook and the list of ingredients hasn't changed a great deal,' he said, leaving a number of British home cooks somewhat perplexed as to what recipe he could be referring. Marks & Spencer subsequently reformulated the pie to contain 25 ingredients. Later that year, the *Guardian* pointed out that Sainsbury's Taste the Difference Luxury Shepherd's Pie, 'based on the famous Ivy restaurant's recipe', had an even lengthier catalogue of 69 ingredients, prominently featuring chemical flavourings, preservatives, hardened fats and science laboratory additions like wheat gluten and dextrin, not generally associated with any domestic or restaurant kitchen.

Some Britons have also seen documentaries which offer a through-the-keyhole peep at the reality of industrial food production: freezers filled with food bought years earlier; gargantuan thawing machines; massive steaming vats; taps, sprays, hoses and peristaltic pumps spurting anonymous slurry; ingredients churned up in what appear to be concrete mixers; stuff belched out of pipes onto plastic trays and chugged down gyrating assembly lines before being embalmed in plastic and entombed in blast chillers; the whole process staffed by zombie-like operatives with glazed eyes, mentally calculating how long until the next tea break. It doesn't look much like anything that goes on in a domestic kitchen.

Yet it seems that frequent and disquieting revelations about the production methods and the quality of ready meals do little to blunt Britain's appetite for them. While we can fully appreciate that homemade food is likely to be better for us, we are so out of the habit of cooking, and so conscious of being short of time, that we can't be bothered to do anything about it. So we say one thing and do another. When surveyed in 2005, some 71 per cent of British shoppers said that they bought ready meals, yet 70 per cent also said that they try to buy as much fresh quality produce as possible. In other words, we want to think that we are buying fresh, high-quality food even when we are not. British consumers, poorly educated in food, de-skilled in cooking, and traditionally indifferent or even resistant to the idea that food is important in life, have effectively entered into a complicit pact with the food industry: 'You sell me processed food, tarted up to look and sound as good as homemade, and I'll buy it.'

The challenge for British food processors is now to make complex, overcooked, industrial food constructions appear like good, straightforward, home-cooked food. Their task is to keep one step ahead of consumers, anticipating their growing ennui with taste and chronic anxieties about provenance, with a new stream of products plausible enough to allow them to drop their guard. The processors have been spectacularly successful in doing this. As one market analyst put it: 'In the UK, the ready meal has undergone a change of image from being deemed as unhealthy, lazy food, to being repositioned as a premium, indulgent option, and retailers have further enhanced the image of chilled meals by using premium packaging and premium positioning.'

The first strategy used by the food industry to bring about this shift in perception was its concentration on developing chilled ready meals, which in Britain have come to represent the acceptable face of processed food. If you are one of the growing number of Britons who cannot quite hack real cooking, but you still want to think of yourself as more than an opener of tins or defroster of freezer boxes, then chilled convenience foods seem to let you off the hook. Any item that comes from a chiller cabinet – as opposed to a freezer, tin or packet – tends to cost more and has an instant cachet, an aura of freshness and superiority about it. We tend to assume (trustingly but wrongly) that chilled products are automatically more like homemade, less tampered with, less additive-laden because they have a shorter 'use-by' date and feel cool to the touch. Many Britons who would turn up their noses at a frozen pizza will happily go for the chilled equivalent, naively believing that they are getting enhanced freshness and superior quality, even purchasing chilled in preference to frozen when they fully intend to freeze the pizza at home.

The second winning strategy has been the establishment of an internal hierarchy in the chilled ready meals category, a sort of British class system, only applied to processed food, that can be endlessly reinvented in multiple cloned forms – Indian, Thai, Italian, Mexican, French Bistro, Café Society, Healthy Eating, Low Glycaemic Index, Chef's Special, Perfectly Balanced, and so on – to create the illusion of a whole world of choice and diversity.

At the bottom of the heap there is the cheap and honest, no-nonsense, 'value' product which does not try to look any better than it really is: essentially an economy-class airline meal. These come with minimal accompanying marketing patter. Next there is the mid-range ready meal in slightly more aspirational packaging. It looks superficially better than the economy version. It might come in a smarter plastic carton – black, lacquered-looking, with an oriental shape, perhaps – or in fresher-looking 'steam in the carton' packaging with a few strategically-placed vegetables on top to give it a halo of health. For consumers too indolent to decant the contents onto a plate, it feels more chic to eat it straight from the carton. Consequently, it costs a bit more, but it contains much the same mix of core ingredients of basic industrial standard, and the usual battery of additives. Finally, there is the up-market, deluxe-looking, much more expensive ready meal which promises sophistication and hints at enhanced quality. This fulfils a vital function for the British processed food industry because it pulls the whole processed food category upwards. It dispenses with the troublesome prejudice that might linger on amongst sections of the British population that convenience meals are a second-best, stand-by alternative to homemade food, best purchased only occasionally. This marketing pitch is encapsulated in the strapline for Morrison's 'The Best' range: 'Exceptional food for every day.' Top-end ready meals feed Britain's mass delusion that there is no longer any need to cook because food processed in factories can be as good, or even better than the homemade article or anything you might eat in a restaurant. All the consumer need do is seek out the most superior model.

Nowadays in Britain, if you want to subscribe to this delusion then there are ample effortless meals to encourage you, a positive cornucopia of products to make you feel ever more comfortable with the idea of eating ready-made, factory food. Morrison's stock 'Pure & Pronto' ready meals which proudly proclaim that they are organic, vegetarian, not genetically-modified and low fat. These come with an endorsement from TV presenter Carol Vorderman as being 'ideal for detox'. This brand's mission statement talks of 'convenience without compromise' and promises ready meals which are 'pure and always healthy as well as tasty' with 'a deliciously homemade taste'.

The Co-op now stocks Martha and Lawrence, a range of ready meals for children, developed by a former Nestlé food scientist. 'I'm sure the ideal for parents is to go to the farmers' market and cook meals for their kids from scratch, but there are times when you need something quick and good quality. We only use stuff you can find in your cupboard at home, and there are no nasties such as hydrogenated fats. The vegetables also count towards the recommended Five-A-Day,' she told *The Grocer*.

Waitrose, grocer to the affluent middle and upper classes, has come up with a range of 'restaurant quality food to eat at home' which is 'as good as going out'. Each dish, Waitrose assures its customers, is 'prepared using the finest quality ingredients from our own specialist meat, poultry and fish suppliers, allowing for seasonal changes in our range'. Buzz words like 'specialist' and 'seasonal' play to the notional concerns of the more thoughtful consumer.

Products in this range are as seductively presented as a professionally-wrapped gift box of chocolates. The descriptions are stiff with the florid vocabulary that might grace the pages of a Barbara Cartland bodice-ripper. Moussaka comes in melting 'layers', beef stroganoff is 'velvet', navarin of lamb is 'tender', 'creamy' mash is 'lovingly blended', 'hand-finished' flaky filo parcels are filled with a 'melt in the mouth goat's cheese sauce'.

But nothing that Waitrose can come up with by way of food description hyperbole can cap the market leader, Marks & Spencer, with its breathy, drooling adverts: 'This is not just food, this is Marks & Spencer's food.' Pioneer of the original British ready meal, and silky-smooth ambassador for the 'why bother cooking?' school of thinking, Marks & Spencer has lent the whole British convenience food category a cachet that it does not merit. It represents the gold standard for expensive processed food that other chains ape with their more up-market, in-house ranges, such as Sainsbury's 'Taste the Difference', Tesco's 'Finest', Asda's 'Extra Special' and Morrison's

'The Best'. Marks & Spencer has made heavily processed, pre-cooked, reheatable factory food highly desirable in Britain, a status that they have never gained anywhere else in Europe.

Although it continues to sell huge volumes of the standard ready-meal offering, Marks & Spencer has recently put much of its effort into allaying consumers' worries about additives and ingredient quality by coming up with up-market ranges such as 'Gastropub' which contain no artificial colours, flavours or hydrogenated fats, or 'Eat Well', which is free from artificial flavourings, colours and sweeteners. Marks & Spencer also started the trend amongst British retailers to spotlight – albeit selectively – any ingredients in its prepared foods with a superior pedigree, such as Welsh hill lamb and Aberdeen Angus beef.

The classier supermarket ready-meal ranges are now studded with boutique ingredients: everything from Camargue rice and Chantenay carrots to Sicilian lemon oil and sunblush tomatoes. A ready-meal description will never say 'wine' when it could specify 'Chianti' or 'Beaujolais'. Pastry is no longer just 'pastry', but 'butter-enriched' or 'hand-crimped' pastry. Prosaic coleslaw undergoes a smart transformation courtesy of the addition of trendy celeriac. Supermarket potato salad sounds more enticing when it is a 'new' potato salad. Anything foreign and exotic adds a gloss of sophistication and authenticity. Kebabs become 'brochettes' or 'koftas'. Undistinguished farmed salmon looks exciting when wrapped in banana leaves.

With other chains running to catch up, Marks &
Spencer, always ahead of the pack, has decided to go a
step further and radically subvert the definition of what
it means to cook in Britain with its new 'Cook!' range.
This range is completely additive-free, classily packaged
in stylish aluminium trays and reassuringly expensive
enough to convince the food-concerned but time-
strapped shopper that surely it must be the Rolls Royce
of all factory food. More to the point, each product comes
with the number of minutes it takes to prepare prominently emblazoned on it – clearly a selling point for Marks
& Spencer customers:

> 'Life gets so busy that, sometimes, it's temptingly easy
> to pick up some convenience food – but there's no
> need to short change your health and well-being. The
> new Cook! range uses fantastic, good quality, natural
> ingredients and takes all the hard work out of cooking,
> so instead of chopping away, you can put your energies
> into perfecting your chosen meal.'

The irony of this range, given its title, is that it does not
require Marks & Spencer's customers to cook from
scratch in the traditional sense, let alone devise a meal,
since this is the culinary equivalent of painting by
numbers. All they have to do is pick up mix 'n' match
components and carry out a few, straightforward kitchen
operations – the most complicated of which is frying or
roasting – by following simple instructions. So 'cooking'

a meal might come down to, for example, frying two pre-made, smoked haddock fishcakes and teaming them up with vegetables and new potatoes all prepped up in a microwavable plastic carton with a pat of herb butter.

Waitrose's 'Easy' range is in the same vein, described by the chain as 'the next best thing to having your own sous chef. We do the preparation, you cook and serve.' It sounds promising, but food writer Lynda Brown was not impressed:

> 'This range seems designed to seduce top of the range foodies, people who ought to know better, who can cook. The copy reassures you that it's food you can trust – select this, prime that, British the other, high standards of animal welfare and so on. But slide off the packaging with its soft focus restaurant picture of the finished dish and you're in for a disappointment. Sad looking, pale or dull pieces of meat, often squashed about, with packets of sickly-looking gloop, or meat encrusted so you can't see the meat itself, or meat with bits smeared over it, all with a shelf life of up to one week.'

Viewed positively, Cook! and Easy represent a less adulterated improvement on the drab ready-meal ranges that crowd British supermarkets, with the public paying a sizeable premium for the privilege of finishing off partially prepared dishes at home, dishes which are arguably more time-consuming to prepare – not to mention the washing-up generated – than a simple home-cooked meal prepared from scratch. Viewed cynically, in an insidious way they blur the distinction between true cooking – in all its fascinating, diverse and highly personal forms – and the uniform consumption of superior factory food.

Cook! and Easy are the most aspirational of British convenience food ranges, catering for a population of affluent people with dream kitchens that they do not know how to use, people who are chronically fretful about the provenance of their food. They represent a further dumbing down of what passes for food culture in Britain, but show the direction in which Britain's food is going. Consumers must be convinced that they can give up cooking and risk nothing, no taste penalty, no food quality penalty, nothing.

For some years, a central plank in this marketing strategy has been propagating the idea that top-end factory food can be passed off as homemade and no one will be any the wiser. Witness the Waitrose 'morality tale for today'-style advert that appeared in weekend supplements towards the end of 2005.

> ### 'A *sweet story of subterfuge and the disappearing soufflé packet*'
> The central character in this tale, Saskia (a suitably Waitrosian name – it was never going to be a Tracey) decides to invite some special friends round for a meal and cannot decide what to serve for pudding. 'Inspiration came in her local

supermarket. She spotted some wonderful small chocolate soufflés, each in its own pretty ramekin glass. They looked marvellous, they just needed heating and – who knows – her guests might even assume she'd prepared them herself.' To cut a long story short, Saskia throws out the cooking instructions by mistake but is saved by a heroic Waitrose manager who reads them out to her husband over the phone. And so the story concludes: 'Even though Saskia was tempted to regale her guests with this little tale as she served the soufflés, she knew she couldn't. For if she did they would know she hadn't made them herself.'

This is an advert that could only work in Britain. While on the continent it is quite common to buy a dessert to serve to guests, it is only acceptable if it is well-chosen, and that means from a widely-respected specialist patisserie, konditorei or similar outlet. There would be no attempt to pass such a purchase off as homemade. In fact, it would be made quite explicit that it was bought. Guests would applaud and approve the discerning judgement of the person serving it for selecting a top-quality, craft-made item. If, however, a host or hostess tried to serve up a supermarket pannacotta or factory cheesecake and pass it off as homemade, no one would be fooled because most Europeans can tell the difference between the two and do not confound their very different qualities and character. Fewer and fewer Britons, on the other hand, have benchmarks for either good home-cooked food, or high-quality bought food against which to measure what they eat from the supermarket, so they cannot tell the difference.

Britain's food illiteracy has allowed us to be brainwashed into accepting technological interventions with our food that commonsense should tell us are bad in terms of food taste and quality. Mashed potatoes quickly become stale and take on an off-flavour, even when stored in the refrigerator, and this is why traditional recipes for leftover mash usually recommend frying it up with something strong-tasting, such as bacon. But affluent Britons happily stump up record amounts of money for microwavable, long-life mash with a best-before date of five days in the future. While an experienced home cook might marinade meat for a barbecue overnight, aspirational barbecue ranges encourage us to believe that kebabs made from microbiologically dodgy meat, such as the basic broiler chicken, can be slicked in an industrial spicy gloop then stored in the fridge for another week. We are prepared to believe that a ham and pineapple factory pizza, bought chilled, frozen, defrosted then microwaved is as good as the fresh article, straight from a Neapolitan wood-fired oven. Even though our eyes tell us differently, we still see that chilly disc of dough smeared with red pulp as something as desirable as the marketing pitch on its packaging. Few Britons would consider making up a sandwich and then putting it in the fridge for a few days before eating it, because we would think that it would become old and stale. But we will willingly pay £3 for the privilege of buying precisely that.

British supermarkets have successfully eroded the fundamental distinction between fresh, homemade food and over-processed, over-handled, industrial food that has been touched by many pairs of hands and passed through many bits of machinery before being trucked around the country to a shelf near you. That achieved, they now play, quite overtly, to the traditional British reluctance towards taking any time or effort with food. In the run-up to Christmas 2005, for example, Tesco ran large adverts in weekend supplements in its 'Every Little Helps' campaign, targeting the Christmas meal – the last bastion of home cooking in Britain, and perhaps the only remaining occasion where significant sections of the population still have some residual expectations of home cooking:

> ***Stuffing parcels.***
> Pork, almond and apricot, wrapped in bacon.
>
> Okay, it's lazy, but you'll probably be wrapping enough things this Christmas.

And that, in a nutshell, sums up Britain's increasingly cavalier attitude towards food and cooking. This advert tells us that it is no big deal to drop cooking to make time for anything else you fancy doing because you don't need to cook to eat well, so cooking represents a pointless waste of effort. It hints that cooking is an oppressive burden easily and painlessly dispensed with. This prevalent mentality serves the interests of large food processors and retailers. Processed food for lazy, clueless consumers is a licence to print money. There's no end to what you can charge for 'hand-whipped, silken mash' and it beats the profit margins on a bag of spuds hands down. They have us hooked on a constant stream of processed food novelties, and the pity of it is that we believe that they are giving us something that is fresh, authentic and worth eating.

8

GOOD FOOD IS POSH

When British politicians want to stress that they are 'one of the people' and demonstrate that they are just like Mr and Mrs Average, one of their strategies is to highlight the unthreatening ordinariness of what they eat. This is why Tony Blair and John Prescott make a point of being photographed eating fish and chips, while Gordon Brown grasps any opportunity to stress his political credentials as 'a beer, football and pizza man [who] seems to regard food in the way that motorists regard petrol'. During the 2005 General Election campaign, in an attempt to dispel the prevalent notion that there was a rift between the Chancellor and the Prime Minister, arrangements were made for a media photo opportunity showing them both eating a 'Mr Whippy'-style ice cream bought from a van, thus demonstrating male bonding over a cheap, industrial ice cream. Cherie Blair gave the Labour campaign a further boost by 'divulging' that she couldn't get her husband to 'eat his broccoli'. On average the British consume under three portions of fruit and vegetables a day – less than half that eaten by Mediterranean populations – while only 14 per cent eat the recommended minimum five portions required for good health.

Also during that election, former Lib-Dem leader Charles Kennedy conducted a key newspaper interview 'while munching through crisps and a Mars bar'. Meanwhile, in a bid to boost Conservative chances, Tory bon viveur Boris Johnson sought to quell any idea that either he or his party were snobbish with a picture showing him apparently enjoying a meal in McDonald's in Oxford. As one political commentator observed: 'Nowadays, most TV-conscious politicians watch their waist line and their blood pressure. During elections, however, the rules change . . . They spontaneously eat for the TV cameras when the non-controversial takeaway is de rigueur.'

Why is this? You would not find Silvio Berlusconi or Dominique de Villepin agreeing to a photo call in McDonald's, but in Britain such an image would earn the politician brownie points with the electorate, because he would be shown to be an enthusiastic, unsnooty upholder of Britain's bad food consensus. Mainstream Britain feels comfortable with bad food, and the routine consumption of junk is an entrenched British habit. A 'no-nonsense' pragmatic approach to food is taken as a sign of normality and solid, feet-on-the-ground Britishness. For most Britons, food is well down the pecking order of life's priorities. According to one survey, just under 3 out of every 10 Britons say that food plays an important part in their lives. For the majority, food is more a matter of fuel than pleasure, so everyday eating, as opposed to dining out, is widely viewed as an essential but uninteresting functional activity, part of life's unwelcome routine. A bit like going to the toilet, eating is something to be got over with in private and as quickly as possible. Consequently, any serious interest in food, or the allocation of time to its sourcing or preparation, is commonly perceived as a time-wasting, finance-draining and an unnecessarily fussy preoccupation; it is widely interpreted as an elitist pursuit.

This mindset makes Britain something of a cultural exception. In nearly every country in the world where the population is not on the brink of starvation, the selection and preparation of food is seen as a fundamental life-enhancing activity, a zone of existence where it is within every individual's grasp to make each day that bit more pleasurable. Good food is seen as a democratic entitle-ment, so a labourer expects to sit down to much the same food as the business executive. The ingredients may vary in quality, but the menu structure and choice of dishes is essentially the same. The Spanish labourer's cured ham might be a more workaday 'jamon', while the Spanish executive feasts on a well-matured, rare breed 'pata negra' version, but they both eat broadly the same sort of ham. The French labourer and executive, like all French people, consider cassoulet, bavette à l'échalote, assiètte de crudités and tarte Tatin as their birthright because these dishes are all part of the country's culinary 'patrimoine', the shared food heritage that everyone enjoys, irrespective of class position. Throughout mainland Europe, restaurants fill up at lunchtime, with ordinary working men and women who expect to eat a decent meal. As one British visitor to Greece reported:

'We went to this very basic-looking basement restaurant in central Athens and couldn't get over the mix of its clientele. On the one hand you had smartly-dressed professionals, like lawyers from the courts, on the other, butchers in blood-spattered overalls from the nearby market. They all ate from the same menu. I can't imagine ever seeing that in Britain.'

In France, many larger employers without a staff canteen give employees vouchers that can be used in local restaurants, which is one reason why France is full of neighbourhood restaurants filled at lunchtime with workers tucking into cheap, good-value meals. In healthy food cultures on every continent, there is a prevailing food literacy at all levels of society which enables people from all social classes to feel at ease in restaurants and to think about and discuss what is on their plates as an unremarkable matter of course. Which local baker makes the best bread? Are the melons ripe enough yet? Was that new recipe variant in this month's cookery magazine better than the old one? Who makes the best noodle soup in town?

Not so in Britain where what you eat is one of the

clearest expressions of your social standing. As Margarette Driscoll wrote in the *Sunday Times*:

> 'In a mixed area such as Hackney, East London, where I live, the trolley loaded with fresh coriander, fruit and Parma ham is fairly certainly headed toward a Volvo estate and thence a £500,000 Victorian townhouse in a quiet street. Alongside it, the one laden with Coco Pops, long-life white bread, Chicken Tonight and jumbo bottles of Tango is destined for one of the shabbier blocks of flats.'

In Britain, your class is not just shown by what foods you eat but where you shop for them. The discerning and moneyed of the South favour the posh person's grocer – Waitrose. Nationwide, the bourgeoisie settles for Sainsbury's along with the more blue collar Tesco, while the working classes go for Morrison's, Asda or Co-op, or alternatively they flock to foreign discount stores such as Aldi and Lidl because they seem to sell much the same as the smarter-looking chains, but at a much lower price. In Britain, where people do their food shopping says more about their class than almost any other social indicator.

The charity Barnardo's showed just how polarized Britain's attitudes to food are when its researchers showed two photographs to children of mixed ages – one showing burger and chips with cola, the other showing a healthy meal featuring an open sandwich, salad vegetables, fruit and milk – and asked them to describe the sort of person of their age who would eat each meal. Irrespective of their geographical background, the children found it hard to believe that anyone their age would go for the healthy meal. If such a person did exist, the children thought that 'only a posh person would eat such a posh meal' and that she would be a 'sporty girl', a 'goody-goody' who lived in a 'posh house', possibly, as one respondent suggested, a 'big house near David Beckham'. Her parents were described as rich, but very strict and health conscious people, who would work in an office and eat similarly healthy food. The family would enjoy activity holidays in far away places such as Spain, Australia and Barbados. Their stereotyped picture of the consumer eating the burger meal was no less revealing: a 'burger boy' was associated with poverty, laziness, junk food and anti-social behaviour. He was characterized as living in a 'scruffy and messy' house, with parents who 'could not be bothered to cook proper food', and who might be 'drug addicts, unemployed or working at Burger King'.

In Britain, there does not seem to be any common territory where good food is every citizen's birthright. On the contrary, good food is something you find in intimidating, stiff-backed, country house, 'fine dining' restaurants with incomprehensible French menus that are playing at being mini-Bridesheads. Good food is something you buy in prestigious shops like Harrods or up-market delicatessens, where the very name on the bag radiates cachet. A liking for good food instantly makes you not just any old member of the public with a reasonable appetite, but a 'gastronome', a 'foodie', an 'epicurean', a 'hedonist' or, at any rate, somewhat unusual.

Good food is dressed up in special livery, possibly with 'heritage' packing, evoking the rarefied tastes of long-dead or sometimes mythical aristocrats, or in an ultra-modern, futurist presentation complete with a largely unintelligible foreign label. For habitués of the super-market, it seems to come dressed up in 'Better Than The Rest' ready-meal ranges which, though they might come out of the very same food factory, appear to be a million miles apart from the cheap and uncheerful 'economy' and 'value' ranges reserved for the demographer's C and D classes. How different from countries such as Italy where some of the best food is to be found in the most unassuming-looking eating places, or Portugal where people of very different means all use the same, typically small and quite ordinary shops, and buy more or less the same food while they are there.

There is probably no other country in the world where a love of eating, or interest in food, is considered to be the exclusive currency of the upper and middle classes, or where whole categories of food – such as game or artisan cheese – are only consumed by the moneyed. And yet, perhaps ironically, these classes are not that comfortable in this role. Along with the less affluent, well-heeled people in Britain do not know much about where food comes from or how it is produced, and they view any deeper interest in it with profound suspicion. They may even find it embarrassing because it exposes their food illiteracy. As late as the 1980s, it was still quite uncommon to comment on what is on the table when invited out to dinner. A simple 'Thank you, that was lovely' would suffice, but questions such as 'How did you make that sauce?' or 'Where did you buy that chicken?' might have come over as food-obsessed. Even now, in an age of ostensibly sophisticated dinner parties, anyone who savours food or wants to talk about it at any length – especially in a way that demonstrates some food know-ledge – is liable to be seen as a food bore or, at the least, insensitive by exposing the relative ignorance of others. Boris Johnson MP summed up the patrician resistance to what is construed as harping on about food:

'For lunch I eat any old thing. I go for lunch in res-taurants quite a lot, but I don't care where I go ... There is no bigger fan of food than me, but I can't stand people writing about it. It must be some puritan streak in me, but I find the detailed discussion of tastes and sensations nauseating and very distressing to read. Like a sex scene, I want to get it over with.'

Britain's inability to find an easy lingua franca for dis-cussions around food provides the fodder for BBC 2's comedy *Posh Nosh*, which features Richard E Grant and Arabella Weir as Simon and Minty Marchmont, two affected food snobs and would-be chefs. *Posh Nosh* satir-ized what the BBC called 'the pretentious language of TV cookery shows'. The running joke is that Simon and

Minty look down their noses at lower class, fat people shopping in the Co-op who 'waddle up and down the aisles buying a UHT cream-filled sponge'. Instead, they promote their Posh Nosh range which consists of their own hand-picked, esoteric delights such as polenta-free Venetian parmesan melts, Provençal capers in a wild monkfish and red onion marmalade, and dried John Dory thins in basil aioli. In one memorable episode, they spot the builder, Barry, 'off to stuff his pre-pub belly with "Builder's fish and chips"', a working class speciality described by Simon as 'cod in crispy orange gunk and black-eyed chips as mushy and squat as fat people's fingers'. So they produce their own posh version of this beloved British dish and reinvent it as up-market 'Architect's fish and chips', transforming it into 'everything that food should be, expensive, complex and utterly architectural in its use of light and space'.

Posh Nosh cleverly lampooned the Great British Food Divide, exposing the disparity between the aspirational recipes that appear in glossy newspaper supplements and cookbooks read by the moneyed classes, and the food that most people of all social classes actually eat. The theme was taken up with relish by viewers who sent in their own suitably pretentious parodies of posh food. One such recipe was 'haricots au pain grillé', otherwise known as beans on toast, which amongst other instructions involved 'coaxing the bread into overt tranches' before topping it with 'Highgrove [the Prince of Wales's organic farm] organic, slow-baked, hickory-smoked haricot beans dans a Mediterranean sun-caressed, tomato and pure pressed olive dressing'.

Irrespective of what food fashion is in the air, Britain faithfully upholds the bad food dynamic which dictates that rich and poor people must, at any given point in time, eat very different food. In the 1950s and 1960s, when the British middle classes were distancing themselves from post-war austerity, embracing the foreign food introduced to them by tutors such as Elizabeth David was one way to gain status; it was a device to show that you were coming up in the world and becoming a better class of person. As columnist Zoe Williams put it:

'It has always been a very middle class characteristic to attempt to individuate oneself through food. When aubergines and garlic were exotic, and un-English, that's what we all ate . . . The message now is still one of adventure, but now foreign food is too common. Anyone, anywhere will eat a curry.'

In the 1960s and 1970s, the British bourgeoisie had no time for peasant or working class food unless it was foreign, preferring to immerse itself in patrician recipes for dishes such as Charlotte Russe and beef Wellington. Cheap cuts and thrifty indigenous dishes were for the poor. Nowadays, the more well-heeled you are, the more likely you are to eat items like tripe and sweetbreads, and enthuse about the new-found British sport of eating offal – providing that it is served in expensive restaurants. A 'salade paysanne' served at the Chez Bruce restaurant in London as part of a £37.50 fixed-price menu, for instance, contains a generous amount of pricy foie gras alongside more peasanty ingredients such as ham hock and lentils. The working classes, meanwhile, are having none of it – nutritious, economical or otherwise – preferring to stick to mystery meat products which, although they may well contain offal, do not broadcast that fact.

Since good food in Britain has come to be considered posh, it has bred a counter-reaction, a sort of sniping philistinism that cuts down to size any attempt to im-prove the way the nation eats. The *Guardian*'s food and drink editor, Matthew Fort, provoked precisely this response when he wrote an article suggesting healthier, less pedestrian ideas for the school lunch box. 'I don't know where Matthew Fort sends his daughter to school, but if my son turned up with mushroom risotto, I'm sure he'd get a right kicking,' wrote Alex Perry, a reader in Leeds. Despite the much-trumpeted British culinary revo-lution, Middle Britain still remains hostile to anyone with a passion for eating or anything that challenges Britain's bad food comfort zone. Mr Perry was merely voicing the entrenched British notion that good food is an indulgent luxury enjoyed only by small, rarefied sections of the population, probably residing in the effete south of England. Meanwhile, up North, in a more typically tra-ditional British landscape, a liking for mushroom risotto could be a dangerous and isolating proclivity.

A similar kneejerk reaction is frequently experienced

by battling parents throughout Britain who attempt, through school boards and parents' organizations, to improve the quality of the food served to children. One parent told me:

'Even to suggest that the After School Club should serve fruit rather than crisps and sweets made other parents and some teachers quite uncomfortable. People would oppose it on the grounds that such a change would be patronizing to poorer parents and that it could upset the social cohesion of the school community. The response was basically, "We don't want to hear about that. You are being a snob." Improving food was a no-go area. If I had persisted, I would have been totally ostracized.'

All too quickly in Britain, good food becomes dislocated from its rightful place as an unremarkable cornerstone of daily life and becomes an exclusive hobby that allows you to flaunt your Marie Antoinette-style indifference to the masses. You don't have to scrape far below the surface to find that discussions of good or healthy food provoke extreme defensiveness because they are so intimately tied up with class. The columnist Julie Burchill, for one, seems to see any discussion of British food quality as an outright attack on the proletariat:

'The usual suspects were banging on about us endangering our poor ickle kiddies by stuffing them full of junk and leaving them to fester on the sofa. When columnists use "us" in this context, of course, they mean "the working class", but they can't say that because they're meant to be liberals and that would sound snooty. So they cover themselves in communal guilt while covertly making the best of this fine opportunity to give the proles a good kicking.'

One recent phenomenon that really gets up the nose of the British 'Good Food is Posh' lobby is the emergence of farmers' markets. Unlike Britain's much-reduced traditional outdoor markets which often struggle to keep going, farmers' markets are bucking the trend and growing in popularity. Their appeal is obvious: they are an alternative to mass-produced, uniform supermarket food of dubious provenance. A minority of British consumers who want less industrial, more local, and more seasonal food are sufficiently motivated to shop at them. All over the world, outdoor food markets have a 'producers only' section and there is no sense at all that these are exclusive, marginal, or pandering to a foodie elite. On the contrary, they are seen as entirely normal, an obvious outlet for small producers in the area, and another shopping asset for the majority of the population who know that good shopping is the key to good eating. But in Britain, where bad and homogenous food has been the status quo for as long as anyone can remember, this classic form of food retailing is considered by some to be rarefied and elitist by the majority of Britons who mistake an oligopoly of large retail chains for genuine food democracy. Few Britons have sufficient experience of eating good food to see the deficiencies in what is on offer in supermarkets, so they assume that supermarket refusniks are simply cultivating airs and graces – an attitude articulated by one correspondent in *The Grocer*:

'Farmers' markets aren't like traditional fruit and vegetable markets. They are not a substitute for supermarkets; rather they're an opportunity for small-scale producers to sell premium foods at premium prices. Good on them. It's no surprise that some happily trek 200 miles to Borough Market and back every week. Paying a premium for quality actually denotes the social cachet of farmers' markets. The food itself comes second. Go to a London dinner party on a Saturday night and the welcome chat will be about where the grouse and greengages came from. If they came from Borough, you've made it, chum.

'Similarly, a percentage of affluent consumers across the country proudly boast that they don't do supermarkets. These sectors, buoyed by the social value of success, are the lifeblood of farmers' markets. With that in mind, popularize them with convenience store prices and they'll die.'

The perception that farmers' markets are automatically more expensive than supermarket alternatives is precisely that, a perception, not a fact. In the same week that this letter was published, a survey of markets carried out by the Mayor of London's London Food Board found that a basket of goods at Marylebone farmers' market in the autumn of 2005 cost £7.90, compared with £8.90 at a local supermarket. Researchers concluded that farmers' markets are 'more price competitive than is often presumed, and as the price analysis demonstrates, can compete effectively with supermarkets'.

But is there anyone out there listening? In Bad Food Britain, no amount of empirical observation can quash the deep-rooted belief that the pursuit of better food is a phoney indulgence, reserved for the aspiring and wealthy.

9

LAWFUL PREY

British people love cheap food. It is a characteristic that unites everyone from refuse collector to aristocrat. There's nothing quite like a 'Buy One, Get One Free' offer to put a smile on the face of the British consumer. It's not that we are a nation of cheapskates – in other zones of life we are quite prepared to part with our cash. When it comes to buying cars, for instance, the British have no difficulty understanding that you get what you pay for. They can appreciate that a cheap car now might turn into a Pandora's box of mechanics' bills and personal risks later. Not so with food. One of the first things a British person wants to know about food is what it costs. This single, vital piece of information dwarfs all other considerations such as 'Does it taste good?', 'How was it produced?', 'Is it good for me and my family?', 'How can anything wholesome be produced so cheaply?' Cheap food is a national obsession.

In 2001, the Food Standards Agency asked British

consumers to list in order of importance what most influenced their grocery shopping choices. For almost half of shoppers (46%), price topped the list, way ahead of taste (18%), quality (17%), personal and family health (12%) and production method (10%). This pattern was consistent across all social groups. Any suggestion that these findings were unrepresentative was knocked on the head by a similar survey carried out two years later by the Scottish Executive which concluded: 'For consumers, the main concern is financial and value for money ... Thus, any schemes or processes that increase the price without any discernible product benefit are likely to be resented and unlikely to be taken up.' The people surveyed put animal welfare at the bottom of their list of priorities, followed by food safety and farming methods.

Of course, European consumers also like to take advantage of the latest deals, but they are more discerning. They understand that all chickens are not alike and that if you snap up a bargain broiler chicken for £2.99, it has most likely been produced in less than appetizing circumstances and will doubtless taste accordingly. They appreciate that a chicken costing £9 must have something extra going for it and that its price tag must to some extent reflect the effort, time and husbandry that went into its rearing. Countries with a thriving food culture know that there are different qualities of product within a food category, and that any type of food comes in forms which can be plotted on a scale from most to least desirable. But in Britain, traditionally we have not been encouraged to think much about what we put in our mouth. After all, why pay more for something when everything else bearing that name appears to be the same? A chicken is a chicken is a chicken, and there is only so much that we are ever prepared to pay for a chicken. As French chef Raymond Blanc put it: 'Ninety per cent of British consumers believe that supermarket food is the best in the world. And eighty per cent of British consumers buy a £2.80 chicken and still think it is the best in the world.'

This is not so much a decision forced on people because they are poor or ill-informed, but more a British point of principle. Rarely a week goes by on British television screens without a programme detailing, in disturbing detail, the unsavoury underbelly of industrial food production, or the effect that cheap, overprocessed junk food has on the nation's health. A minority – government figures suggest anything from 8 to 23 per cent of the population, depending on the nature of the revelations – is so affected by that knowledge that it changes its shopping habits instantly, boycotting this or that, and forking out more for an alternative. But within a few days after the headlines die down, it is business as usual for most British shoppers. The cheap, fatty, broiler chicken (which featured in that graphic documentary), contaminated with antibiotic residues and pathogenic bacteria, goes into the trolley again, no questions asked. In 2005, a Channel 4 *Dispatches* investigation highlighted the sordid conditions in which British broiler chickens are reared and the surprisingly high levels of fat in their flesh caused by intensive rearing methods. This was a much-discussed, high-profile documentary, but sales of chicken actually rose by 19.6 per cent in the two weeks following its broadcast. As the columnist Deborah Orr observed, '[British people] prove with their loyal purchases again and again that they don't much care what they swallow.'

Why is this? Disillusioned food producers and farmers sometimes suggest that the British just don't care whether their food is bad and possibly dangerous, or if they do care, they don't care enough in practice to act upon it. As Professor John Webster, an authority on animal welfare put it: 'Consumers pay lip service to the environment and farm animal welfare, and express a desire for higher standards, but this desire is seldom matched by demand.' The British are certainly past masters at not connecting blatantly related food facts, preferring to insulate themselves in naive feel-good fictions. Surely that dead chicken being cannibalized by its shed-mates on TV has nothing to do with the nice clean poultry breasts they buy each week in the supermarket. As the journalist Richard D North said: 'They [supermarkets] have been brilliant at delivering what their customers want, which is cheap food smothered in pictures of a long-dead countryside of straw-sucking peasants in smocks . . . We turn up and buy their stuff whatever scare is in the air.'

A 2003 government report suggested that consumers prefer not to think about factors such as animal welfare or production methods because they find it too upsetting.

'This is not to suggest uncaring respondents,' it noted, 'but more that people prefer not to think about it as it is potentially off-putting and upsetting.' In other words, it might turn my stomach or cost me more, so I'd rather not know about it, thanks very much.

Psychologically speaking, Britain is largely locked into a mindset where it views food as one of the first things on which economies can be made. It is unconvinced that money spent on food is a sound investment for future health and well-being. Although they may be poles apart on the social spectrum, the person who views 40 cigarettes a day and a subscription to satellite TV as lifestyle essentials, and the person who sacrifices everything in order to send children to private schools and run an SUV, can still agree that they can't afford to spend any more money on food. Like the majority of British people, they view food as just another consumer product or service with no special importance. By contrast, people of all income levels in European countries see food as a standalone, high order priority, up there with shelter, warmth and breathable air. A survey of eating habits in Italy described Italians as: 'attuned to the concept of eating food that is as natural as possible and more than willing to pay premium prices for it'. As Carlo Petrini, Italian founder of the international Slow Food Movement, neatly put it: 'When I wear a pair of Armani trousers, they do not become a part of me. But when I eat a slice of ham it does. That's why I spend money on food.'

But the British don't think that way. As the food writer

Hugh Fearnley-Whittingstall says: 'Even those of us for whom the food budget isn't a problem still seem unable to resist bargain food. It seems to be an area where we're happy to save money, whereas it should be the most important thing.' The proprietor of one specialist cheese shop provided this cameo of the typical British reluctance to part with money for better quality food:

'We sell a very reasonably priced farmhouse cheddar. It is made in the West Country on a family farm with years of experience using unpasteurized milk. It has been aged and cloth-wrapped so it has natural maturity and flavour. It drives me mad when we get people coming into the shop commenting on how much more expensive it is than the cheap, rubbery, tasteless block cheddar they sell in the supermarket along the road. They just aren't prepared to see that they aren't comparing similar products. The other thing we suffer from here is well-heeled middle class shoppers who tell you loudly all about their house in France or Italy and how they buy cheeses, like we stock, all the time for a fraction of the price. I used to try to explain to them that we don't really mark up our imported cheeses as much as we should because we just couldn't sell them at the right price and we want people to buy them. Then I realized that they also resent spending money on food and really just want to show off by talking about good food, rather than actually buying it.'

Our appetite for cheap food is not shrinking as our affluence and apparent food awareness grows – quite the opposite. For years, Britain has spent less on food than on transport, recreation and culture. National statistics show that we shell out more on cars, trips to the cinema or holidays than we do on food. But now the nation's collective food bill is decreasing even further. Despite the vociferous debate in Britain over how our food is produced, and despite growing levels of affluence, we are spending less on food as a proportion of income than ever before. The most recent government survey shows the largest ever decrease in the spending on food – down from 23 per cent of total spending in 1980 to 16 per cent in 2004–5. In that same period, spending on motoring has increased steadily so that now the average British household spends more on motoring than on what it eats. Some £59 of the average British household's weekly budget now goes on TVs, computers, leisure activities and holidays, while food and non-alcoholic drinks account for only £44.

A contributor to *The Times*, Martin Samuel, used the example of big-time spender and fiancée of footballer Wayne Rooney, Colleen McLoughlin, who was spotted by paparazzi shopping in Kwiksave in Liverpool, to illustrate how Britain willingly stumps up for the most fashionable and expensive brands of clothes and jewellery, but remains tight-fisted when it comes to food:

'No clue to what she was buying but it was unlikely to be the work of hot designers Viktor and Rolf or the latest Frank Muller timepiece. So a wild guess would suggest that Colleen was on the lookout for cheap food, bringing her neatly into line with the rest of modern Britain. A nation dribbling mass-produced ready meals down its designer tops. A population of bleeding hearts that want animals to be treated ethically but would rather eat a tin of condemned veal than put 2p per pound on a packet of chicken drumsticks. Have you seen the price of free-range meat? Get back into the cage the lot of you . . . The future Mrs Rooney may only have stopped for some cheap booze and a toilet duck. But no footballer's wife would be seen dead leaving H Samuel or British Home Stores.'

Sainsbury's chief executive officer, Justin King, offered another example of how well-heeled Britons are happy to trade down when buying food:

'I was in the Camden branch which you will agree is in a pretty smart area of London. One in three baskets going out contained our Basics [lowest price] crisps. There was one woman, very well dressed. In her basket was a bag of our Basics chicken nuggets. I asked her why she'd got them and she said that they were the only ones her three-year-old son would eat.'

Recognizing that food comes low down on most Britons' list of priorities, the food industry has been more than happy to appeal to its consumers on a platform of low prices. It is fond of portraying itself as the great democrat, putting good food at low prices on everyone's plate. In the words of one industry spokesperson: 'The ability of the British food chain to deliver increased choice at reduced real price has been a significant contributor to improvements in living standards.' The food industry has indulged the national fantasy that cheap food can also be good food because, paradoxically, it is a licence to print money. Britain is not a country that understands the concept of value for money in the context of food. Although we bitterly resent stumping up money for good-quality raw ingredients, we can easily be conned into parting with astronomical amounts of money for over-packaged, over-processed, added-value products that look good and appear to offer convenience. Yet, in reality, ready meals for a family of four work out much more expensive than a simple, homemade family meal, such as sausages and mash.

The over-arching goal of cheap food has given the food industry a perfect excuse for its persistent, profit-driven, self-serving tinkering with the British food supply. The English art critic and reformer, John Ruskin, once observed: 'There is scarcely anything in the world that some man cannot make a little worse and sell a little more cheaply. The person who buys on price alone is this man's lawful prey.' Were he alive today he would be sad to learn that prosperous 21st-century Britain is full of people who, through their ignorance (wilful or otherwise) of how food is produced, and their preoccupation with price, have become the food industry's lawful prey: that is, gullible consumers who will swallow marketing spin in place of quality, providing the product seems cheap. Waterlogged meats, eggs from miserable caged hens, preternaturally long-life loaves plumped up with air and artery-clogging hardened fats, squashes with a single figure percentage of real fruit juice, crispy-crumbed slaughterhouse slurry, and all those ready meals, sauces, soups and desserts constructed using the food industry's profitable formula of water, fat, salt and sugar bound together with additives – this is what our addiction to cheap food buys us.

There is, of course, a hard core of British shoppers who will look you in the eye and tell you frankly that they would not be in the least surprised if a lot of cheap, mass-produced industrial food which they routinely buy is of poor quality. They will defend their choice either by telling you that food is unimportant to them, or by insisting that they simply don't have enough money to do otherwise. But the vast majority of price-driven shoppers try to justify their decision in non-pecuniary terms. British people are quick to suspect a con when presented with a more expensive version of a food than that which they commonly buy. The very existence of such products – be they organic, free range, environmentally friendly, 'grown for flavour' or whatever – is unsettling because it implies that there might possibly be something less desirable about their cheaper lookalikes.

In 2005, for example, the *Observer* ran a front page

story, 'Britain's Organic Food Scam Exposed'. This turned out to be an exposé more fitted to a local newspaper since it consisted of two small-time frauds. A shopkeeper and a market stallholder were exposed by local trading standards officers in the London borough of Richmond for passing off conventionally-produced food as organic. The *Observer* was keen to suggest that this was just the tip of a national iceberg, not a very convincing proposition since organic food is subject to at least as much, if not more surveillance and checking than its conventional equivalent. But it was a story sure to sell a few papers in Britain's cheap food culture which holds that if you spend a bit more money on what you believe to be better food, more likely than not, you are being taken for a ride. In Britain, an interest in organic food – or, for that matter, any other food which purports to be better-produced than the cheap industrial food norm – is often seen as the food equivalent of visiting a counsellor when you are only mildly neurotic – self-indulgent, self-obsessed, more money than sense. As one outspoken organic critic put it: 'They [muck and magic farmers] believe and talk nonsense and sell at high prices often surprisingly manky food to anxiety-ridden consumers who also talk and believe nonsense.'

Cheap food defenders love to play the poverty card as a justification for manufacturing huge quantities of low-grade industrial food. Any improvement in food production standards that might make food even fractionally more expensive is dismissed as disenfranchising the poor.

This argument studiously ignores the fact that poverty has spawned some of the world's greatest cuisines, such as the southern Italian *cucina povera*, based on thrifty use of good, local, raw materials. There is no universal law that says food for poor people must be debased industrial food. Advocates of cheap food also suggest that it is positively obscene that well-heeled northern Europeans such as the British should spend time worrying about the quality of the food on their plates, stumping up ridiculous amounts on food they regard as superior, when in famine-stricken countries of Africa people are desperate for a few grains of rice or some mealie porridge. Such people, they insist, do not appreciate how lucky they are to live in a land where food is cheap and plentiful. In no time at all, the starving and needy of the world become a rod with which to beat the backs of anyone who takes anything more than a passing interest in food and who is prepared to put a bit of money where their mouth is.

This argument is, of course, simply a more politically-correct-sounding expression of Britain's long-standing food philistinism that sees money spent on fleeting pleasures such as an artisan cheese, a well-hung, patiently reared piece of meat or a unique and special bottle of wine, as money down the drain. All you have to show for your outlay at the end of a mealtime is some crumbs of cheese, a trickle of gravy and an empty glass. New trainers, a flat screen TV, another car? Now those are solid things that endure, for a while at least, and they buy you status in the eyes of friends, neighbours, colleagues and classmates. The external world sees them, unlike the everyday food you eat at home. Somehow, the starving African masses don't affect your appetite for them.

10

WE HATE SHOPPING

In all countries with healthy food cultures, food shopping is seen as an important, worthwhile and often pleasant activity. Food-aware citizens take the pragmatic view that without informed and engaged food shopping, there is no possibility of good cooking or pleasurable eating. In Europe, consumers have four tiers of food shopping possibilities at their disposal; independent specialist shops, traditional open-air or covered markets, farm or co-op outlets, and supermarkets. Unlike the British, most Europeans would never entertain the notion of doing all their shopping in a supermarket. Why indeed should they when there are much better, more attractive options on their doorstep?

Cultures that really care about what they put into their mouths know that food shopping calls for a very particular set of skills; knowledge of food quality, experience in assessing that quality, wise selection from what's on offer. To build up these skills, foreign consumers appreciate that it is advantageous to get as close to their food as possible. Self-interest, if nothing else, tells them that it helps to strike up a direct dialogue and trading relationship with the people who supply their food. They pride themselves on identifying the trader in the market with the ripest fruit, the baker with the best tasting bread, the stall with the freshest fish, or the farm with the best pressed fruit juice. The people for whom they cook generally acknowledge and respect their shopping acumen.

Most of the food on sale in countries associated with good food and gastronomy is home-produced, often regional. Shoppers walking through fresh produce markets or the zones in foreign cities that host a nexus of small food shops cannot help but be aware of the seasons, of what that region grows or rears, and get a sense of what food feels right to eat for the time of year. As food writer Tessa Kiros put it: 'They don't look for ingredients that are out of season, but use whatever is available fresh, and when it is bursting with flavour and goodness.' Their food retailing system cherishes and encourages a rotation of traditional dishes, consumed on a natural seasonal cycle which takes note of local customs, celebrations and habits: lamb at Easter, oysters at New Year, doughnuts for Mardi Gras. The consequent shopping experience acts as a constant tonic for the household cook who might otherwise reel under the pressure of dreaming up a succession of meals. Shopping in bustling fresh markets and specialist food shops is one of the simplest and cheapest sensual pleasures to be had in life. Unlike supermarket shopping, it generates enthusiasm and a desire to cook, and that enthusiasm shines through in the calibre of food that is subsequently prepared. People who shop this way look forward to the week ahead because they think of all the good things they have to eat and the appetizing meals that they will make. Shopping for interesting, good-quality, varied food is one small way, within the individual's control, to make life more enjoyable.

Most of mainland Europe is now studded with hyper-markets, vast, big-box retail sheds with a wide range of groceries, but planners – recognizing that a nation must protect all that is small, local and one-off from that which is large, cloned and uniform – have generally ensured that these are far enough out of town so as not to prejudice the town- or city-based independent sector. European consumers use hypermarkets on a routine basis, but with long intervals between visits. A monthly trip might be the norm. They use them primarily to stock up on duller, routine store-cupboard items that will last for some time. They may buy some fresh food when they are there, generally considering it to be of a good, if not exceptional standard, but when it comes to high-quality fresh food – meat, fish, fruit and vegetables – the independents win the laurels in the public's eye and are rewarded with repeat business, several times in the course of the week.

In countries such as Austria, Germany, Italy and France, town centres also tend to have a small-format, rather lacklustre supermarket with a pedestrian stock of everyday foods. These coexist alongside independent outlets and markets without jeopardizing their existence, largely because it is obvious that the independents sell fresher, higher quality food. This forces the chains to raise their game, which is one reason why supermarkets on the continent sell better quality, fresher and more local food than their British counterparts whose shelves groan under the weight of ready-made food, global brands and imports.

In fact, Britain offers one of the dullest and most monolithic food shopping experiences to be had anywhere on the planet, largely because there is little real choice of shopping outlets. Here you will never hear the term 'retail therapy' applied to food shopping. Farmers' markets provide the equivalent of a happy pill for the near comatose, resentful, under-stimulated British food shopper, but even in their currently buoyant state, less than 1 per cent of all retail food spend is being channelled through them. Many traditional open-air food markets are either struggling or in chronic decline. There is the odd town, such as Ludlow in the Marches, or Abergavenny in South Wales, which by virtue of a number of felicitous factors manages to retain a portfolio of independent outlets that allow for the possibility of a richer food shopping experience. In larger cities, there are still some pockets of food shopping diversity, thanks to the odd tenacious greengrocer, butcher or fishmonger of the traditional British type and the efforts of settled immigrants whose culture instils in them an innate feeling for fresh food. In Marylebone in London, the enlightened

Howard de Walden Estates which owns most of the area, has offered attractive leases to encourage small, independent shops, so offering the motivated food shopper a more stimulating and original range of shopping options. But such centres are small, rare treasures. As the journalist Jonathan Meades put it: 'There are as many decent food suppliers in a single Paris arrondissement as there are in the whole of London.'

In the main, British planning authorities have taken an accommodating attitude to the perpetual expansion of cloned branches of large retail chains because they hold a short-sighted view of these as an indicator of economic development. Discussions around food shopping in British planning circles are routinely conducted in a framework of 'survival of the fittest' thinking. The near obliteration in many areas of anything resembling an independent food sector in the wake of perpetual supermarket expansion is viewed as an unfortunate, but necessary casualty of the momentum of food retailing progress and the unstoppable, breakneck pace of our workaholic lives. As a result, three-quarters of the food we eat is supplied by three large supermarket chains. Tesco alone gobbles up 30 per cent of the nation's food spend. By 2005, it had the biggest share of food sales in 57 per cent of Britain. In certain 'Tescotowns' such as Inverness and Milton Keynes, the company supplies around 50 per cent of all food purchased. In many parts of the UK, consumers' food shopping 'choice' is a huge Tesco, a big Tesco and a handful of smaller Tescos.

As supermarkets go, Britain has some of the most sophisticated chains in the world, with a product range of over 30,000 different lines. On paper, this might sound as though it makes for a bigger and better food choice, but apart from the odd product here and there, they all sell the same thing: vast quantities of profitable industrially-produced, intensively-farmed food presented in many chameleon forms to give a phoney illusion of variety and value.

Britain's plummeting interest in cooking is a direct consequence of this miserable shopping experience. There is so little to fire up the enthusiasm of anyone pushing a trolley around a British supermarket. Any regional sense of place is totally missing because they offer a standard range of food in every store, up and down the land, 365 days of the year. Any genuine sense of seasonality that might enliven periods of the year with character and special interest has been ruthlessly removed to make way for globally-sourced imports. Fresh foods are retailed in such a mechanical, sanitized manner that the buzz that foreign shoppers get from being in a market and seeing abundant displays of raw, fresh, local produce is almost totally absent.

A shopping experience that centres on small independent shops and markets, either at home or abroad, has built-in diversity that recharges the batteries of the food shopper and catalyses the urge to cook. Walk through a good market and certain purchases will positively stand up and shout 'Buy me!' Grey-green bunches of tight-headed broccoli with the ice still dripping off them. Fish still stiff and gleaming. The sustaining, chewy crust on a loaf of patiently-made bread. Products like these generate ideas for dishes and meals. The British supermarket shopping trip, on the other hand, kills any such urge stone dead because there is so little produce with any sensual appeal, nothing to fire a spontaneous, enthusiastic, pleasure response.

For most Britons, food shopping is an exercise in chronic alienation best endured on auto-pilot, made more bearable because it can be crammed into a once-a-week trip. As chef Antonio Carluccio sees it: 'They [the British] go into the supermarket, they load their trolley, but they are not critical, they are not looking, they do not compare. In Italy, the importance of food is such that one goes to any lengths to get very good food.' Shoppers are funnelled into making a robotic tour where the only food shopping skill to be honed is spotting the 'Buy One, Get One Free' offers while not banging your trolley into the ankles of the person in front of you. Increasingly, as British supermarkets relegate displays of fresh, unprocessed raw ingredients to make way for wall-to-wall aisles of fizzy drinks, boxed convenience foods and labour-saving snacks, Britons are so insulated from fresh food that flashes of inspiration are few and far between. The only possible highlight of a supermarket trip is getting up close and personal with the carefully manicured, made-over pictures of food on the sleeves of ready meals. We are increasingly resistant to the idea of shopping for fresh food every two or three days as Europeans do. Instead, we favour the weekly one-stop shop to stock up with products bearing 'use by' dates well in the future. Every meal becomes a problem to which supermarkets provide a solution in the form of functional convenience food that performs the joyless, utilitarian task of keeping household members fed and any blatant nutrient deficiency at bay.

British shoppers are reporting high levels of alienation. In 2005, new food industry research revealed the extent of Britain's apathy and confirmed how, for most Britons, shopping, cooking and eating are only peripheral concerns. It warned that most British consumers consider food shopping to be 'a monotonous but necessary chore' triggering high levels of irritation and frustration. Those classified by the research as 'foodies' – people with at least some passing interest in food – were vastly outnumbered by 'fuelies', those who saw food as fuel, an essential commodity to be bought only on the basis of price. Most British shoppers, it found, are now more excited by the non-food items on sale in supermarkets than any of the food or drink.

The dreary homogeneity of the British supermarket shopping experience is so commonplace and meshed into the fabric of British life that relatively few consumers question it, except when they travel abroad and find themselves making invidious comparisons with inspiring foreign markets. Nicholas Cooper, the British captain of a container ship, was so struck by the appetite-crushing dullness of British shopping that he catalogued the differences between his UK base, Banbury in Oxfordshire, and two other towns he frequently visits, the Calabrian port of Gioia Tauro in southern Italy and the Normandy town of Pont Audemer in France.

'Banbury typifies the whole supermarket slash and burn strategy. There is a large Tesco on the north side of Banbury where all the council estates are. They targeted that market perfectly. There is a large Sainsbury's on the south side of town and their catchment area includes the half dozen or so middle-class villages scattered around the region. Again, perfect targeting. Morrisons built a large store a short walking distance from the town centre, there is a small Somerfield and Marks & Spencers in the shopping mall and an Aldi near Tesco. Banbury has two McDonalds, a Burger King, Pizza Hut, Domino's, Baskin Robbins, Haagen Dazs, Thornton's, Tchibo, Café Costa, Café Nero and half a dozen local copies and clones of these multinational chains, as well as three or four of those giant "theme" pubs selling food and drink all day and night.

'And there's the crunch; we would like to patronize small local businesses but there aren't any. The fruit and vegetable shop only sells what you can buy in the supermarkets, while the family butcher next door, although they butcher and pack their own meat, sells only bright red beef and cheap quality poultry, lamb and pork. We have a twice weekly market, but again all the fruit and vegetables are what you could buy in any of the supermarkets, most of it is imported and nothing local. There are no fishmongers anywhere near Banbury. Our only saving grace is the monthly farmers' market, where we can stock up on fresh and smoked trout, and buy dirty, mis-shapen, locally-produced, or at least British vegetables. A new stall sells properly hung beef which is marbled in fat and looks almost mahogany in colour. Lamb, pork and poultry are also available.

'Gioia Tauro – what a contrast! – is one third of the size of Banbury, but there the comparison ends. Here, roughly, is a list of what this small, provincial and working class town has to offer:

- Six bread shops, all artisan;
- At least six pastry shops, all artisan, selling homemade or locally-made pastries, cakes, sweets, chocolates and ice cream;
- Four delicatessens;
- Five or six greengrocers;
- Two fishmongers in town, and at least half a dozen near the sea front;
- Three butchers – one shop selling local Calabrese specialities;
- One fresh pasta shop;
- Ten or more local bar/cafés, all selling a small selection of pastries, cakes and ice creams;
- Three or four small supermarkets on the fringes of the town centre, but no multinationals;

- No McDonalds, no Burger king, Pizza Hut, or any other multinational fast-food outlets.

'Pont Audemer is a small market town. We know it well, and come away thoroughly depressed every time we have to return to Banbury. This small town has one high street, perhaps four or five hundred metres long, but on it you will find two fishmongers, three butchers, two or three boulangeries, at least two delicatessens, a cheese shop where Monsieur will select a dozen cheeses for you to take home to be eaten within two, three, five and seven days. There are also three patisseries. And that's just the high street. There is also a twice weekly morning market where the very best of French local and country produce is sold; fish and meats, fresh cheese of every variety, live and hung game and poultry, fruit, vegetables, herbs and the whole gamut of the French pantry. We have been reduced to tears at seeing all this wonderful produce on display in the shops and on the market, but perhaps the tears were for what now masquerades as shopping in Britain, and for the dread of returning to it.'

Britain's ennui with grocery shopping has became so pervasive that even the food industry is becoming worried that it might be bad for business as people simply rush to get it over and done with in as little time as possible. 'Supermarkets, food manufacturers and suppliers need to find new ways to change shoppers' views of food from filling up to something they fancy for a fantastic dinner,' the chief executive of the Institute of Grocery Distribution, Joanne Denney-Finch, has warned. The British food industry likes having a trusting base of passive, de-skilled, unaware shoppers who will fatten themselves up prodigiously on its latest value-added, super-processed fodder, but it does not want one so lethargic and demotivated that it can barely be bothered to shop. 'There is a real danger,' wrote Müller Dairy's UK sales director, David Potts, 'that food will be sidelined and that meals will become little more than in-flight refuelling stops, to be completed quickly and with as little investment in time and money as possible.' Even the boss of Asda, Andy Bond, sounds worried: 'It's no wonder so many people hate shopping these days. It's boring. If there is nothing to differentiate one store from another, the chain with the most outlets [a thinly disguised dig at Tesco] will always win.' By the end of 2005, a survey found that 70 per cent of the buyers who purchase food for retail chains agreed with Mr Bond that British supermarkets were guilty of 'bland, amorphous sameness'.

This is the current state of Britain's food shopping. There is a battle amongst giant chains as to which of them will grab the national licence to provision the masses by establishing de facto supremacy over retail food supply; it is a battle waged in full view of the regulators, and with their apparent blessing. Meanwhile, a tiny, food-aware minority keeps alive a vision of a different kind of shopping by supporting farmers' markets and the few plucky independent shops that refuse to call it a day.

Belatedly, there is a sense that something has gone wrong, albeit in country circles. In 2005, the Cornwall Federation of Women's Institutes – in what was subsequently dubbed 'the housewives' rebellion' – voted overwhelmingly to support a motion calling on members to make every effort to use small, local shops rather than supermarkets. The motion also called on members to consult their local shopkeepers so they could lobby councils for systems that would support them, such as free parking for customers or discretionary rate adjustments. The motion is due to go to the 2006 annual general meeting of the National Federation of Women's Institutes. Also in 2005, the incoming chair of the Countryside Alliance, Kate Hoey MP, made a plea to consumers to think about the connection between their food and where it has been reared, to buy as close to the farm gate as possible, and to boycott supermarkets.

Any prevailing pattern of routine supermarket shopping connives to downgrade the importance of food in life and to conceal the sensual pleasure it has to offer. This much is obvious to nationalities who enjoy eating and cooking, but because most Britons now have little or no vision of a shopping experience outside a supermarket, they infer wrongly that all food shopping is necessarily tedious, mechanical and boring. From there, the logical conclusion is that food in itself is necessarily tedious, mechanical and boring also.

The British refuse to give food status, time or respect, and our lack of food shopping alternatives reflects this. In Britain, food shopping is now seen as a national burden, a black, oppressive manacle on the ankle of a nation rushing around purposefully trying to improve itself. Everything other than food is automatically seen as more important. The saddest thing of all is that few of us now get any pleasure from choosing food. In *The Kitchen Diaries*, Nigel Slater wrote that for the most part he shopped in small, local shops and farmers' markets. 'This book is very much a gentle plea to buy something, however small, each day, to take time to shop, to treat it as a pleasure rather than a chore.' But the millions of Britons locked into the British supermarket nightmare simply cannot see that food shopping could ever brighten up their lives in any way, so they just grit their teeth and get on with it.

11

FEAR OF FOOD

For the vast majority of Britons, choosing food is a simple exercise. The drill is as follows. You buy all your food in your preferred supermarket – usually the nearest to home. You routinely select the same best-selling brands as most other consumers. You do not think too much about what goes into your trolley, other than you expect that it should be cheap (because cheapness is Britain's paramount food shopping goal). Your habits are fairly constant; the odd food scare here or scandal there does not bother you much because you share a herd mentality, a safety in numbers philosophy. Sudan 1 and Bird flu are mere storms in a teacup that will blow over sooner or later, just like mad cow disease and salmonella before them, leaving you to get on with eating what you did before. Eating the same as everyone else makes you feel secure. You subscribe to the dominant British bad food consensus, so you will consume pretty much anything, providing it is cheap and ubiquitous, because to do so is considered middle of the road and normal. For you, food shopping may be mind-numbingly boring, but at least it is relatively stress-free and undemanding. No mental effort goes into your shopping decisions. The physical challenge is getting round the supermarket and out again as quickly as possible.

The same cannot be said for the minority of Britons who try to engage more actively with issues surrounding what they eat. They are high on a volatile, stress-inducing cocktail of food scares, conflicting health claims and contradictory diet advice. As journalist Mimi Spencer wrote:

'We are, it seems, a Mad Food Nation – in a state of constant anxiety. If it's not E. coli, it's E numbers. If it's not pesticides, it's food miles. If it's not dairy, it's dioxins. Or danger diets. Or Ronald McDonald. We're frightened of everything. Turkey Twizzlers. Tanzanian sugar snap peas. Evil salt. Evil sugar. Evil antibiotic-resistant campylobacter. In this climate of fear, little wonder that we're feeling a trifle bilious.'

The more Britons hear about food, the more complicated their food shopping becomes. They shop defensively, trying to protect themselves and their families from suspect, unhealthy products. If they are not fretting about additives in their children's lunchboxes or puzzling over what mayonnaise is doing in their chocolate brownie, or worrying about whether dairy products can cause breast cancer, then they are trying to shut out nightmare footage of slaughterhouse slurry spurting into their sausages. Some of these defensive shoppers also aspire to shop ethically, at least on a piecemeal basis. They seek the comfort of knowing that they are not trashing the planet, or contributing unknowingly to the unnecessary suffering of animals, or aiding and abetting the exploitation of food producers in some far-flung place, and this gives them even more to worry about. One way or other, their food shopping trip has turned into a minefield, with automatic cautionary notices popping up in their heads that read 'Don't buy X, oh and while you're at it, worry about whether you should still be buying Y and Z'. *The Times* columnist Kate Muir summed up the modern British food shopper's dilemma:

'I suddenly realized, as I hauled myself through Sainsbury's the other day, that my main feeling now while food shopping is not joy but nagging guilt and worry, coupled with attempts to recall vague scientific factoids about various superfoods. How active is the *bifidus* in this dinky drinking yogurt? Are blueberries still all-powerful? Are they still powerful imported from Poland and coated in chemicals? Or is raw ginger now the thing? Is it on the Eat-Me-Or-Die-Sucker list provided by the national media? Plus, there's the regulation: thou shall eat oily fish (but not in tins since the Omega 3s appear to die in tins, and you can't eat fish anyway because it's so full of mercury or magnesium or plutonium or whatever, and all fish are endangered or sterile or lesbians now because of the Pill hormones in the water). Worried? I felt a panic attack at the wet fish counter and fell to the floor frothing at the mouth, screaming "Bring back Birds Eye".'

The penalty for those Britons who actually think about what they eat, is that food seems to have become dizzyingly complicated. Their food decisions are increasingly made against a backdrop of worries, limitations and even fears. When they are not brooding over the macro food issues of the day, they are struggling to accommodate the shrinking list of foods that they and friends and family feel able to eat. As one woman put it:

'I've gone off having people for dinner because I just can't think what to serve. Last time I was going to cook pasta or a shallot tarte Tatin because one friend is a vegetarian, but another person was on a low carb diet because she suffers from yeast infections and she is also avoiding sugar. I thought of making a Mediterranean vegetable dish but another guest's husband has a number of food allergies including raw, but not cooked, tomatoes and aubergines. The final killer was having someone else who couldn't eat or drink anything with a strong colour like carrots or red wine because she was undergoing tooth whitening treatment.'

The sheer amount of time and effort that goes into the thinking Briton's food shopping these days makes for mental exhaustion. Being on a perpetual quest for that elusive safe, wholesome food that will appeal to everyone does tend to shrink the appetite. And then there is the question of weight: 77 per cent of British women say that they worry about their weight and the average British woman has dieted seven times by the age of 30. Worrying about getting fat makes food choice even more vexed – a phenomenon observed by *Independent* columnist Deborah Orr:

'I've been troubled for ages by the behaviour around some of the most attractive middle-aged women I know. Slender, toned, with the boyish bodies of teen-agers, they are never happier than browsing through the shelves of health food stores. Constantly absolutely starving, and ever on the look-out for "healthy snacks", they're never actually on something as naff as a diet – though they might embark on a "detox". But they're never in much danger of putting on weight either, because virtually all food is off limits due to its unhealthiness. Cutting out sugar, caffeine, alcohol, wheat, gluten, yeast and dairy is usually just the start.'

Or as one professional woman in her mid-fifties put it:

'I've noticed that many women of my age, and of my kind of background, have sort of given up eating. They are often single, so they have no one else to cook for, and they are fighting middle-age spread. They have found the easiest thing is to eat as little food, and have as little to do with food, as possible. It's not that they eat rubbish, because they understand healthy eating, just that a meal for them will consist of something like two crispbreads and an orange. It's as if they can't allow themselves to associate food with pleasure.'

In Britain, dietary dilemmas are becoming regular problem-page fodder in women's magazines, along the following lines:

Q: 'My girlfriend has become incredibly fussy about what she eats. No wheat, no caffeine, an occasional glass of red wine. Food was one of our shared passions. I feel frustrated that this part of our life is over. Am I being unreasonable?'

A: 'Not at all! Oh, the horror of having to sit with them in restaurants while they talk through the menu options with the waiter, merrily chirping, "Oh yes, if you can take the yolks out, an omelette would be lovely!" when clearly it wouldn't. Why don't you try inviting other, less macrobiotically challenged people to dine with you both? Extol the virtues of the girls who aren't afraid to eat cheese often enough and she might get the message.'

One of the more recent words to make it into 21st-century English language dictionaries is 'orthorexia', defined as 'an extreme obsession with eating healthy foods' or 'an obsessive concern with eating only health-giving food'. The word is modelled on the term for the well-known eating disorder anorexia, where *orexis* is the Greek word for 'appetite' and the prefix *an-* indicates 'without'. In place of the *an-*, the prefix *ortho-* is substituted from the Greek word *orthos*, meaning 'correct' or 'right'. The coinage of this term in 1997 is attributed to Dr Steve Bratman, a Californian organic farmer turned practitioner in alternative medicine, who published a book on the subject, using the more accessible title, *Health Food Junkies*. He wrote:

'Orthorexia bears many similarities to the two well-known eating disorders anorexia and bulimia. Where the bulimic and anorexic focus on the quantity of food, the orthorexic fixates on its quality. All three give food an excessive place in the scheme of life . . . It's great to eat healthy food, and most of us could benefit by paying a little more attention to what we eat. However, some people have the opposite problem: they take the concept of healthy eating to such an extreme that it becomes an obsession. I call this state of mind orthorexia nervosa, literally, "fixation on righteous eating".'

It is not surprising that such a condition was first identified in the US. America is the world's cheerleader for fast food and an extreme reaction against it is only to be expected. When the rest of the country is getting stuck into Kentucky Fried and super-sized Big Macs, it is understandable why an alfalfa sprout and wheatgrass movement would flourish. In countries where people lack food, there is no such problem because being 'picky' or nervous about food is a luxury that no one can afford. In affluent countries with a sound food culture, such as Italy, France or Sweden, any tendency to 'orthorexia' amongst the population is checked by the fact that most people, although eternally suspicious of the machinations of the food industry, still overwhelmingly trust their food not to do them any harm. Furthermore, they view it as a constant source of pleasure.

In Britain, a country that has long stumbled over the word 'enjoyable' when attached to the word 'food', two decades of food scares have irrevocably shaken our trust in what we eat. Orthorexia, in its extreme form, may still be extremely rare, but it is prevalent in a diluted, chronic form. There is a persistent, low-level anxiety amongst certain sections of the population about food provenance. It grows prolifically like pathogenic bacteria on neutral agar jelly because there is no positive counter-influence to inhibit it. Unlike Europe, our tradition of celebrating food and revelling in its pleasures is weak and showing signs of being close to moribund. Britons, in company with Americans, feel more out of control of their food because – unlike Europeans, who maintain a sense of sovereignty over their food since they still prepare the bulk of it at home – they have less and less hands-on contact with basic ingredients in a natural form. The British have devolved much of the responsibility for what they eat to the food industry, and so it does not take much to get them worried about what that industry might get up to in those windowless 'farm' sheds and Brave New World processing plants.

In Britain, the voices worrying us about the food we eat resonate much louder and further than those with a positive story to tell. Reporters dishing the dirt on food production methods never lack material, and they are guaranteed prominent headlines, such is the nation's urge to pick away at the scab of its unhappy relationship with food. Well-intentioned activists campaigning against junk food are more to the fore, and are granted a more receptive audience with the public, than in any other country, bar the United States. They are bearers of an urgent message to the British consumer: 'Here is how bad the food you are eating is. Now what are you going to do about it?' They act as a much-needed counterweight to the towering might of the food industry, but judged in terms of how much they inspire Britons with a vision of pleasing, natural food that might actually galvanize them into changing their eating habits, their cumulative effect is almost certainly negative. Despite their best intentions, they give Britons yet another reason for not liking food, and so contribute to the creation of what the food writer Tamasin Day-Lewis identified as 'a population of faddists and neurotics'.

Britain has raised the business of communicating bad

news about food to an art form. A buoyant new industry which exists to inform people what is wrong with what they are eating and what they can do about it. Watching families, even whole streets of wayward eaters, enduring behaviour modification training from 'size 6' dieticians who can't stop jogging on the spot, has now become prime-time viewing in the UK. This industry feeds off Britain's troubled relationship with its food, and it is largely composed of self-appointed gurus who look as though they would get more lit up at the prospect of swallowing a Smarties-sized tube of vitamin pills or undergoing colonic irrigation than trimming off the oozing sides of a perfectly ripe cheese or nibbling on a particularly crisp morsel of pork crackling.

Such people are evangelists who seek to convert flabby, nutritionally-challenged Brits to the shining path of betterment through righteous food and a Spartan commitment to physical exercise. This movement's torchbearer is Gillian McKeith, star of Channel 4 TV's *You Are What You Eat*. Her programme refers to her as the 'Shock Doc of Nutrition'. In her book, she confesses that she is 'an unrepentant nutritionist, a food freak obsessed with natural foods and married to a health nut'. One interviewer, noting her extremely slight figure, described her as 'oddly emaciated'. Her eponymous magazine appeals to readers with that heady mix of hope, certainty and fear more usually associated with fundamentalist religions. It pitches in with fear – 'The food hazards you cannot ignore' – and then dangles the promise of improvement

– 'Exclusive! Inside Dr Gillian promises you a better life.'

In her television programmes, the hectoring, finger-wagging Ms McKeith drops in on a household of 'food offenders' and lets rip at the residents' eating habits. As lumbering Britons are paraded before the cameras, *You Are What You Eat* comes uncomfortably close to being a freak show, an exercise in public humiliation, but its leitmotif – the table laden with brown-beige, packaged, over-processed junk – does offer a graphic snapshot of everything that is wrong with the typical British diet.

Britons who consider that they eat better may watch it smugly. They can enjoy being revolted by the food choices of the less nutritionally enlightened and feel superior about their own. But voyeuristic light entertainment apart, *You Are What You Eat* does nothing to promote any sort of democratic, accessible, common ground of healthy, appetizing eating. The food regimen advocated, strong as it is on miso soup, tofu and seaweed, and reliant on unseasonal imported fruits and vegetables, would be more appropriate for the neurotic, weight-obsessed inmates of an Asian fat farm than any significant segment of the British public. As the journalist Rachel Cooke observed:

'The real problem with her [Gillian McKeith] is that she is so anti-life. Food is about history, and culture, and ritual. Not for her the artisan cheesemaker, or the fifth-generation baker, or the man with the ancient vine. Many of the foods she recommends are not even indigenous to these islands; flying them literally costs the earth. Most of all, though, it bothers me that there is so little that is celebratory – or even vaguely pleasurable – about her regimes.'

A programme such as *You Are What You Eat* could only flourish in a country like Britain. Try telling the Swiss, the Belgians, the French, the Italians or any other country with a track record in making fine chocolate that Ms McKeith's 'carob fudge brownie delight' – ingredients: dates, raisins, flax seeds and carob powder – is a more toothsome treat than real chocolate, and you would be laughed out of court. But in Britain, a country locked into a long and abusive relationship with a milky, fatty brown substance that would more accurately be labelled 'vegelate', the hypothesis appears plausible to the growing ranks of nervous, fretful eaters.

Each week, Britons hear more bad news about what they eat. Pundits have hailed the emergence of a new British breed, a so-called 'Super Consumer' who can take on board limitless amounts of dietary and nutritional advice, wisely plotting their own personal course through it. But for most Britons, the more information they get, the less they know what to do with it. Simply trying to keep up with what they should (or should not) eat is complicated and dispiriting. Unless they are people who are hooked on being worried and do not want to have fun in life, then the temptation is to adopt a 'what the hell, we've all got to die sometime anyway' attitude. Julian Hunt, editor of *The Grocer*, put it this way:

'This week they were telling us that soya should join the long list of products they have decided are bad for us, because it can harm a woman's fertility. But not that long ago, we were being bombarded with scientific messages about the many health benefits of soya. And only last week, another group of experts was telling us that red meat caused cancer. Before that there were those in the scientific community warning farmed salmon was dangerous and we should eat less, until others amongst them insisted it was not and we should eat more. Devour your greens, cries another group. Then their colleagues go 'tsk, tsk', you must beware the veg you buy because it has been sprayed with poison. One week those people are telling you to eat more chocolate and swig more red wine; the next they are warning how the very fabric of society is being ripped apart by obesity and alcoholism. Is it any wonder that most normal folk are now completely turned off by the, usually contradictory, messages and "insights" put out by the boffin community?'

In 1998, research carried out by the food industry found that British consumers had already become 'slightly desensitized' to food scares. People explained that the first time they heard a scare on the news, they listened to it, but when it was repeated over and over in a day, they tended to switch off. Most people saw scares as cyclical and contradictory, so they did not alter their shopping habits in the long term. 'For short spells it stops you, but then something else happens and they say it [the food in question] is safe again, so you go back to eating whatever . . .' one shopper explained.

By 2005, a survey by Mintel found that the British were in active revolt over healthy-eating advice. Nearly half of all Britons were suffering from 'do-gooder fatigue' and were fed up with being told what to eat by government ministers and charities. Yet despite the weight of diet advice coming their way, 69 per cent complained that it was still hard to work out what was good for them. As one market analyst commented: 'Today there is a wealth of information which bombards the public in matters of health and given the complexity of many of these issues, it is hardly surprising that so many consumers feel confused. It seems that they may now be in switch off mode.' Some may even be determined to distrust every new nugget of information that comes their way. The *Guardian*'s Lucy Mangan spoke up for the growing number of Britons 'who are sick of being harangued by Quorn-filled, carbless freaks intent on using their rapidly diminishing physical resources to suck the little remaining joy from the lives of everyone acquainted with them' and expressed a growing British cynicism about food health revelations. 'Perhaps if we get enough scientists to put their heads down and concentrate, the greatest triumph of all will come to pass. The headline will read: "Pork Scratchings Cure Cancer – Sunflower Seeds Do Sod All".'

Britain's Bad Food information machine helps make what should be a relatively simple pleasure – eating –

into a complex problem. The bulk of food-indifferent citizens ignore it studiously, or treat it with extreme scepticism. Those who listen are condemned to live in a permanent state of food paranoia, or even fear. No wonder only 50 per cent of Britons say that they really like eating.

12

THE YUCK FACTOR

In 2005, the French actor, Gérard Depardieu, published a cookbook celebrating his love of eating and cooking. In it, a passion for ingredients in their raw form loomed as large as the actor himself. Though Monsieur Depardieu doubtless has a British fan base for his cinematic persona, Depardieu the cook was overly strong meat for the British palate. 'My eye will roam with equal pleasure over the face of a beautiful woman as over the meat in a butcher's shop window,' he wrote, an observation sure to make many British readers recoil. Enjoy looking at raw meat? How revolting! Surely only a typical Frenchman would slobber over something repellent in such a lascivious way? How French to obsess about food in such a ridiculous manner that grossly exaggerates its importance in life.

But the truth of the matter is that it is the British who are out of kilter with the rest of the world here, not the French. Most countries are able to look food production in the eye without losing their appetite, but in Britain we live in a barely controlled state of panic about the origins of our food. Like an excitable class of primary children who can be rendered hysterical by the arrival of a bee, we are fearful of food in its raw state. We flinch at the ripe aromas that greet us in a good cheesemonger's shop; avert our gaze when passing a traditional butcher's shop for fear of catching a glimpse of anything red, fleshy or visceral; worry that garlic might make our breath smell, or that asparagus might make our urine stink.

The British like to think that they have a civilized Anglo-Saxon attitude to food while other countries live in the barbaric dark ages, turning pet ponies into steak haché and stir-frying puppies at the drop of a hat. When the presenters of British television food programmes are sent abroad, there is an odds on chance that an event will be engineered where they are obliged to eat something foreign and taxing; tripe tapas in Spain, pork intestine soup in Malaysia, grubs in the Australian outback, donkey salumi in Italy, durian in Vietnam, snails in Portugal, grasshoppers in Mexico. The drill is that presenters should a) confess to viewers how challenged they feel by the prospect of what's been offered to them, b) hold their nose while sampling the tiniest amount before c) smile wanly at assembled locals like good sports, then d) spit out the suspect substance in partial view of the cameras. The whole point of this exercise is to highlight the near depravity of foreign eating habits and the normality of Britain's own eating mores, where food in its raw and primitive form is well and truly refined or 'tamed' before it is allowed anywhere near our tables. Like watching a gory crime series featuring serial killers and psychopaths, we actively enjoy being shocked and entertained by arm's length encounters with savage, primordial food. When Gordon Ramsay insisted that trainees in *Hell's Kitchen* had to kill a lobster, using the humane, but graphic method of a heavy knife through the head, it was no surprise that it provoked upset letters to Channel 4 and complaints to Ofcom. And when Jamie Oliver slaughtered a lamb on television, Britain, in the words of one *Times* commentator, had 'a collective seizure'. He pointed out that there was nothing gratuitous or macho about the footage, it just showed 'death as a part of life … the weirdness was in the public reaction'. Such candid camera insights into the realities of food production easily trigger the 'yuck' reaction that comes as second nature to many Britons. This reaction is a reflection of how, at some basic level, we do not like food very much, and so if our exposure to it is too full on, we simply cannot hack it.

The best food, for a growing number of Britons, would be one that betrays no connection with any living organism, an immaculate conception that just landed miraculously in the supermarket chiller cabinet, gift-wrapped in shiny, clean packaging. Most countries harbour a healthy suspicion of processed food, viewing it as second best to the home-cooked equivalent prepared from scratch. Somewhat unusually, the British are positively happy to buy food heavily processed and over-wrapped to a profligate extent because it makes it less real. Less real means less chance of it having any natural characteristic that we might find unpleasant.

The list of what we fear is long and detailed. Anything carnal tops it: blood, skin, bone, sinew, marrow, muscle, membrane, connective tissue. *The Times*'s television reviewer spoke for millions of viewers when he flagged up a forthcoming episode of Hugh Fearnley-Whittingstall's *View From River Cottage* which showed buckets of blood destined for black pudding production: 'This could easily develop into a cult horror film based on a true story, along the lines of Nightmare At River Cottage.' Never present us with anything with eyes, ears, snout or tail unless the smelling salts are handy. As for miscellaneous shuddery offal bits, they are Britain's gastronomic equivalent of a snuff movie.

The average British person tolerates fish as long as it is completely free from bone and is assiduously skinned and filleted so it looks as harmless and pappy as a slice of white bread with the crusts cut off, but then again we would really rather have it in a 'crispy crumb' coating because that makes it look even less like fish. Things piscine with tentacles, shells or an obvious central nervous system, are of minority appeal. Anything with a pungent smell – ripe cheese, salumi, garlic, boiling cauliflower – is treated with instant suspicion. Odour in food is taken as a sign of abnormality, an indicator of matter that is past its best. A stray caterpillar or slug on a lettuce can send us running for the kitchen door. Plums with sticky, sappy bits on the skin; carrots with dirt on them;

sprouting potatoes; black spots on bananas; mould on marmalade; blue veining in cheese; russeting on an apple; clots of cream on unhomogenized milk; red flecks in an egg – Help! Our ignorance of food leads us to interpret these as signs of morbidity, disease and decay. A butcher told me:

'This lady came into the shop one day and she was lifting the lids on the egg boxes as you do to check that none were cracked. Then she called me over and pointed out to me, almost conspiratorially, as though she had spotted a major problem, that one of the eggs had a little bit of dirt on it. I said that I was sorry, but every now and then, some muck or feather on eggs was unavoidable. Then she said to me, without a trace of irony, "You know, I think the hen must have sat on it". It made me want to ask her where she thought eggs came from.'

One of the most obvious manifestations of British squeamishness about food is our dilettante affair with vegetarianism. Clearly, vegetarianism has a noble intellectual and religious tradition in countries such as India, so it can co-exist with a healthy, vibrant food culture. But in Bad Food Britain, vegetarianism dovetails nicely with our problematical relationship with food and it gives us yet another reason to narrow down the catalogue of foods that we are prepared to eat. Britain's vociferous vegetarians pack a bigger punch in formulating British perception of food than their numbers would seem to merit. Although only five per cent of Britons describe themselves as vegetarians, this is high compared to southern European countries where the figure is around two per cent and eastern Europe, where they account for a mere one per cent of the population, but it is lower than more northern countries such as Germany and Sweden where they account for eight and seven per cent respectively. Within that British five per cent, there are a small minority of hard-line vegans who think it is wrong to eat any animal product, so they avoid not only meat and poultry but also dairy products and eggs. Most British vegetarians, however, are satisfied with the more moderate line that it is wrong to eat a food that has caused the death of an animal.

Since the 1950s, British vegetarians of all inclinations have drawn moral justification from the indisputable animal suffering involved in intensive factory farming. Animal welfare resonates very widely in Britain. The British, vegetarian or otherwise, like to think they are kind to animals and are fond of having them as pets. We prefer to use them for leisure (horse riding), or pleasure (companionship) and like to turn a blind eye to our baser interest in them: that we quite fancy eating them. Our tendency towards anthropomorphism is well-documented. While a Turk looks at a sheep and thinks of kofta, a Greek contemplates moussaka, a Sardinian imagines spit-roast joints 'alla brace', and an Indian sees mutton pulau, the British think of Mary's Little Lamb with a ribbon bow around its neck, and any jokes about mint sauce are considered in rather poor taste. British vegetarians do not only think of animals as sentient creatures, capable of having emotions and feeling pain, but they also see them as people, subscribing to Bernard Shaw's dictum, 'Animals are my friends and I don't eat my friends'. Hence, this opening verse from the poem 'Talking Turkeys', written by the vegetarian poet Benjamin Zephaniah:

> Be nice to yu turkeys dis christmas
> Cos' turkeys just wanna hav fun
> Turkeys are cool, turkeys are wicked
> An every turkey has a Mum
> Be nice to yu turkeys dis christmas,
> Don't eat it, keep it alive.
> It could be yu mate, an not on your plate
> Say, Yo! Turkey I'm on your side.

Whether or not you relate to this typically British variant of anthropomorphic vegetarianism, it evidently has some internal coherence. Many of its adherents are sincere, thoughtful and consistent in applying their beliefs, but Britain also seems to breed the world's most confused demi- or semi-vegetarians, providing a spiritual home for the self-declared 'vegetarian' who makes up the rules as they go along – the sort of person who tells you 'I'm basically a vegetarian but I do eat fish, although I'm not very keen on mussels or squid but I do like prawns if they are shelled'. British food attitudes positively nurture the obliging 'vegetarian' who shuns anything red and bloody, the person who is in a quandary over pork (is it red or white meat?) but who will accommodatingly eat chicken, as long as it's white meat only. There are even larger numbers of people who claim to have 'vegetarian leanings' but who will happily eat meat, just as long as they don't have to see or handle it in its raw state. Even most self-styled meat eaters only really appreciate meat when it is presented as a firm, dry piece of protein, free from any hint of the farmyard, the slaughterhouse, or its animal origins. One chef summed up the winning formula for meat in British restaurants as follows:

'As a chef in this area [an industrial area near a provincial capital] you get pretty disillusioned. You put steak on the menu because that's what they all expect and nearly everyone wants it well done. It has to be cremated so that you can't tell that it's bloody good beef to start with. If there's a little bit of pink juice coming out of it, they will send it back. It breaks my heart but at least I've made some progress. We only used to be able to sell fillet as a steak. If you put on sirloin it would hardly shift because it's a more irregular shape and comes with a bit of fat around it. But I've gradually had some success with rib eye steak, probably because I trim it generously and put it on the menu at about two-thirds of the price of fillet. You have to watch out for anything with a bone in it, even something like lamb chops can stick. We had lamb on [the menu] but

eventually we had to take it off. Some customers think
it tastes too strongly of sheep. Round here it's basically
got to be fillet steak, chicken breast or salmon escalope
. . . something you can eat easily with no effort.'

If British children were tested with the simple task of
matching the name of a meat (beef, lamb, pork) to an
animal, many would fail. Increasingly, British adults also
want the connection between the two glossed over. Food
industry research carried out by the Institute of Grocery
Distribution into consumers' attitudes towards buying
meat found that most British supermarket shoppers want
their meat 'presented in a sterile, packaged format, with
minimal reminders of the animal from which it was
derived'. Consumers said that they liked meat 'looking
clean' and that blood on chicken would put them off.
Others were put off by 'too many veins' or 'seeing the
bits' on meat and found that the smell of a butcher's
shop made them 'physically sick'. In 2005, the Advertising
Standards Agency received a flurry of complaints about
a Burger King advert because it showed a live cow wearing
a blanket with the Burger King logo. The complainants
considered the link between the product and the cow to
be offensive. The advertising agency responsible for the
advert defended it, saying that it was intended to be
humorous and that it had never intended to draw a direct
parallel between the product and the animal. The complaints were subsequently dismissed.

Knowing that the British don't like to face up to the fact

that meat comes from a dead animal, retailers encourage British consumers to think forward to a meal, not back to a cow, sheep or bird. The name of the game is to prevent them from thinking about animals at all. By the time that raw meat is on sale in British supermarkets, it has been cut up and wrapped in a way that belies any animal origins. Nothing must appear on a supermarket shelf that might distress British shoppers. When it comes to raw, unprocessed meat, retailers have more or less liquidated from their shelves anything other than prime, lean cuts. Cheaper, less neat and tidy cuts are taboo, unless – like pork belly and lamb shank – they are currently undergoing a heritage meat revival amongst the country's foodie minority.

For shoppers who might freak out at the prospect of handling any raw meat offering, however unlike meat it looks, there are ready-made meals which require no hands-on cooking, only reheating. Processed meat products cater for the hypocrisy of the vast majority of British shoppers whose meat purchases are selected on an 'out of sight, out of mind' basis. Although in theory they may have scruples about eating meat, they are happy to overlook them if the meat is presented cleansed of any prior history. The same people who squirm at the very idea of eating offal will consume it when it is mulched up inside an economy sausage. The processing of factory-farmed meat into anonymous cheap meat products plumped up with water and an arsenal of additives is a profitable industry in the UK. It feeds off the self-serving, selective ignorance that afflicts many so-called ethical shoppers when they get behind a shopping trolley. The antiseptic supermarket has a crucial advantage over the more visceral butcher's shop in the British consumer's mind because it allows us to shut out any thoughts about where our meat comes from and abdicate the responsibility for doing so to the retailer on the dubious and naive assumption that supermarkets would only tolerate the highest standards.

Unlike true, principled vegetarians, there is only so far most Britons are prepared to go in their daily lives to stop animal suffering. The IGD research concluded that although British consumers found images of cows and sheep in green fields positive and reassuring, 'overall it seemed that these consumers didn't really want to know too much about where their meat comes from'. When it came to chicken, the country's most popular meat, the research found little understanding of rearing methods. There was a general impression that chickens were kept in battery cages (a confusion with egg-laying hens). Some more informed consumers knew that table chicken is reared in sheds. Either way, many people had the impression that they were kept in extremely overcrowded circumstances. 'Despite this rather negative perception,' the survey reported, 'none of the consumers implied that it was a real concern.' So much for British compassion for animals.

And yet British voices dominate European debates around animal welfare. Britain has a few well-informed animal welfare organizations that mount an articulate critique of factory farming and that are active in campaigning for their principles. But once again, their arguments are picked up selectively by the larger mass of Britons who claim to be concerned about animal suffering. The British find it easy to be outraged by foie gras – foie gras is French and we love any opportunity to feel superior to the French – but being angry about foie gras does not challenge any British domestic industry. Is foie gras the cruellest of all meats? Ducks and geese are migratory birds with the biological capacity to overeat and lay down the excess fat in their livers to sustain them over lean winters. Afterwards, their livers return to normal size and the birds show no physiological side effects. Arguably, foie gras production merely takes advantage of this natural propensity. Force feeding of ducks and geese is traditional in France and there are two different models for it, one is labour-intensive and small-scale where the birds are patiently fed, the other is large-scale and industrial (the 'Hungarian system'). Whichever way they are fattened, ducks and geese reared for foie gras generally have much better quality, longer lives than your average factory-farmed broiler chicken, since they spend most of their lives outdoors until the final fattening period.

Britons are inconsistent and illogical in reviling foie gras production unless they also object to the shocking animal abuses that occur in everyday British factory farming; the artificial insemination of turkeys that are so overfed they are incapable of copulating, the de-beaking of hens, the 'tail-trimming' of piglets, the listless sow condemned to the farrowing crate where she must give birth and feed her young without the space even to turn around, the cannibalization of dead birds in the broiler shed, the default cruelty to millions of British farm animals who never feel the sun on their backs in the course of their short, brutish and unnatural lives.

Britain's confused and partial intake of animal welfare information is exemplified by its attitude to veal. The British food consensus is that it is an intrinsically cruel meat and that it should be shunned. Once again, it is easy for Britons to disapprove of veal because we have almost no tradition of eating it and very little is now reared in the UK. Veal owes its negative image to the notorious system whereby calves were taken away from their mothers at birth and kept indoors in a small crate without any bedding. Fed only powdered milk made up with water, this made them anaemic but it produced that tender, white, tasteless meat that was once highly prized for escalopes. As a result of campaigning by animal welfare organizations, this type of production will be banned throughout Europe by 2007.

It is possible, however, to raise 'welfare-conscious' veal, often referred to as 'rosé' veal. In this system calves are suckled by their mothers or other lactating cows acting as wet nurses. They are given free access to natural feedstuffs providing the full range of vitamins they need. Their meat takes on a slightly rosy hue and a slightly more meaty flavour due to this natural diet. The calves live outdoors in summer, or stay inside in family groups in winter in comfortable barns with generous straw bedding. But British consumers still won't countenance eating it because they have decided that all veal, like other nasty foreign foods, is cruel, however it is produced. Yet most of them, apart from the odd vegan, see no contradiction in boycotting veal but drinking milk and eating dairy products. This is yet another example of Britain's inability to get to grips with the realities of food production. In order to supply milk, dairy cows are kept either pregnant or lactating. When they produce male calves, who clearly cannot give milk, the only use for these calves is to be reared for veal. But because we eat so little veal, male calves in the UK are usually shot at birth, even on organic farms, because they have almost no commercial value.

If you buy milk, it is illogical and wasteful to avoid veal, but the British blanket prejudice against veal is so strong that any humane farmer who sees veal production as preferable to culling calves can barely manage to sell it. 'We try to point out that it is different, labelling it as pasture-reared, pink veal and we have leaflets explaining how it is farmed,' one farmer told me. 'Even so, we toil to sell it and may have to give up because we keep coming up against this British "veal is cruel" reaction.'

Much of what drives Britain's confused and inconsistent attitude towards meat eating is not concern over the welfare of farm animals but the modern horror of coming too close to food in anything but a transformed, prettified state. Our grandparents prepared and ate tripe, liver, rabbit and pig's trotters in the company of the rest of the world without making a song and dance about it. We feasted on living creatures from the land and sea making good economic use of every bit of edible protein. Nowadays most Britons live in a more affluent world sanitized from any experience of food production. We prefer to be at a distance from elementary foods, keeping nature at a distance, only handling it with a metaphorical pair of protective gloves once it has been transformed from its original state. The dominant British Anglo-Saxon Protestant mindset – not shared by immigrant communities which still allocate food a central position in their daily lives – sees any direct contact with the raw version of what we will eventually eat as something to be minimized, or better still, eliminated. It smacks of peasantry and poverty, of everything that is base and unevolved. Our mechanistic 'food is fuel' way of thinking relegates primary producers who have daily contact with muck and gore to a lower rung of the progress ladder. We think that we have made it when we have devolved responsibility for food production and, increasingly, cooking, to someone else.

This is one reason why our collective stock of food skills, knowledge and expertise is running so low. Nowadays, it is a rare Briton who can tell if a fish is fresh from looking at its eyes and gills, or size up the maturity and provenance of a joint of beef by looking at the colour of its flesh and the marbling of fat. Thrifty, inventive cooks who could always think of something edible to make with sour milk, day-old bread, cold cooked potatoes, giblets or bones are an endangered species. The less experience we have of smelling, tasting or handling a wide variety of foods in natural, primary forms, the less stomach we have for doing so. This collective food ignorance breeds fear, so any hint of what might or might not be going on behind the curtains of food production can trigger our revulsion. The origins of what we eat have become a mystery to us and, if we are honest, we rather like it that way.

13

SAFETY FIRST

At the beginning of December 2004, the children of Springbank Primary School (not the real name) were looking forward to the fun and glitter of the festive season. A letter to parents came home in the children's satchels, reminding parents of holiday dates and advising them of the timing of Christmas parties. It included an important request from the head teacher: 'As in previous years, donations of food would be most welcome. However, it would be appreciated if the donations were not of the homemade variety as current thinking on food safety suggests this approach.' Having read the letter twice to make sure that he had understood the tortured wording correctly, one parent was incensed enough to put pen to paper:

'No homemade food for a children's Christmas party? Is this official policy? Surely this is a joke? It certainly flies in the face of what the government is trying to achieve in respect of healthy eating and the war against obesity. I refuse to send my children to school with processed muck, the contents of which would be more familiar to a chemist than a home economist. We have brought up our two children to eat and know how to prepare good wholesome food made from fresh, natural ingredients. That's how it is and that's how we will continue, policy or not.'

Meanwhile, parents in another school 150 miles away were experiencing similar difficulties. Each year, Ingrid was in the habit of making a stollen, the traditional German Christmas cake, for the end of term party. Being German, she thought that this was the obvious seasonal treat to bake. The stollen had been well received in previous years – although, admittedly, only by other parents and teachers because the children preferred iced biscuits and fondant fancies out of a packet. Then she also was informed that food donations could no longer be home-made. She regarded this as deeply misguided but decided to acquiesce for the sake of a quiet life. Would it be all right, she asked, to buy a stollen and bring it to school instead? After some deliberation, an answer came back: No, a stollen would not be acceptable if it came in one continuous piece and would have to be sliced with a knife. Such a knife might contain germs and contaminate the stollen. Ingrid could only bring in a stollen if she could find one that was pre-sliced in a bakery with each slice individually wrapped in a sealed plastic sleeve.

These Yuletide battles marked the end of a year where paranoia about the food poisoning potential of that most innocent of commodities – home baking – had spread through Britain like head lice through a nursery. In July, spirits plummeted amongst the elderly patients at Saffron Walden Community Hospital when they learnt that the exemplary home-baked cakes they had been enjoying at afternoon tea, courtesy of local Women's Institute volunteers, were now banned. The spectre of the MRSA superbug was stalking hospital patients up and down the land, and campaign groups were complaining about the sub-standard nature of hospital food – it subsequently emerged that some 17 million hospital meals were being thrown away untouched and that some 40 per cent of patients leaving British hospitals had malnutrition – and yet hygiene officials at the local care trust had decided that home-baked cakes were dangerous enough to outlaw. 'We have to adhere to strict hygiene criteria and without inspecting the kitchens of Women's Institute members who prepare the cakes we cannot eliminate all potential risks. The hospital treats very vulnerable elderly patients, many of whom have special dietary requirements. Patient safety is our top priority,' said a trust spokesperson.

But the patients were not persuaded. Far from killing them off, it was the comforting prospect of a nice cup of tea accompanied by home-baked cake that was keeping them going. The president of the Radwinter Women's Institute was having none of it either. 'What dangers lurk inside a Victoria sandwich or fruit cake?' she asked. 'We are sure our baking was more tasty and healthy than National Health Service-purchased cakes with their artificial colours and preservatives.' The Women's Institute pointed out that their cakes had never killed anybody and that many Women's Institute members had been baking for years and years with great care and dedication. Anyone who knew anything about food hygiene appreciated that because cakes are thoroughly baked at a high temperature, the risk of food poisoning is almost non-existent. The Women's Institute refused to back down, the press got involved and the local trust overturned the ban. Having reconsidered its decision, it now took the view that 'the negligible risk to patients is greatly outweighed by the pleasure they can give'.

A victory for the sensible Women's Institute, then, but not all branches were so resilient. By November, two Women's Institute markets in Norfolk had no option but to close. The problem they faced was twofold. 'Everyone involved is of pensionable age. Young women don't want to get involved and cook. We rarely get any young people coming to buy produce … I think people now prefer supermarkets and ready meals. And we have been overwhelmed by hygiene regulations. We have to sit and re-sit hygiene exams even though we are only making jams and chutneys on a very small scale,' said their chairwoman, Barbara Twigg. Jams and chutneys, like cakes, pose a negligible food poisoning risk because of the high amount of sugar and vinegar they contain.

By the following year, the paranoia seemed to have

extended not just to food, but also to its packaging. The press got hold of a story that a Lewes school had banned the use of egg boxes for craft work saying that there was a risk of salmonella being passed on through handling them. An eminent professor commented that he had never heard of an example of an egg box posing a risk of salmonella. 'There's no realistic risk of that ever happening,' he said. East Sussex Council quickly responded, saying that it had never banned them, but the head teacher in question was insistent that he had been told by the council that egg boxes were unsafe. 'It [this advice] is the sort of thing we get all the time these days,' he complained.

Such sentiments are widespread in Britain among well-intentioned people whose job imposes on them some responsibility for the health of the public. Confusion is rife concerning food hygiene regulations and what they do, or do not, allow. And anyone with a home-spun food project in mind who consulted the Food Standards Agency's guidance looking for elucidation would be left none the wiser.

'If you provide food to members of a club, or at events such as fêtes, then you might have to comply with food hygiene regulations. This is still the case if you don't charge for food. There isn't any straightforward answer to whether you need to comply with the regulations or not, because this could depend on a number of things, such as whether this is something you do regularly or a one-off. Get in touch with the environ-

mental health service at your local authority to find
out if regulations apply to you.'

Up and down Britain, anyone who wants to produce food
on a small scale, either on an amateur or professional
basis, is slowly but surely getting the discouraging message that this is a minority, fringe activity that might be
cause for concern. This is not the case in other European
countries where homemade offerings continue to provide
sustenance at everything from school fairs to community
festivals, and small food producers are valued, respected,
and even revered. But you can count on Britain to latch
on with gusto to any theoretical food safety concern relat-
ing to small-scale food. In Britain, there is a deep-seated
belief that industrial food equals safer food. A large mass
of European consumers of all social classes understand
that artisans who uphold food traditions – the small-scale
cheesemaker, fish curer, fruit grower – provide both diversity and some of the highest quality of food to be had.
Most Britons – give or take some 20 per cent of the
population that still has some lingering intellectual
attachment to the idea of artisan food – like their food
to look manufactured and processed. We find it reassuring to think that our food comes from large, modern
industrial factories, kitted out with cutting edge technology, staffed with men in white coats and policed by earn-
est inspectors with clipboards and lengthy checklists. We
are impressed that it is transported in nice clean lorries
to shiny, sterile supermarkets. The more packaged, the

more antiseptic our food looks, the safer we think it will be. In a country that industrialized early, where a mutual sea of incomprehension lies between the urban and the rural, relatively few Britons have any intuitive feel for food. Divorced from any first-hand knowledge of production, food is a big mystery to us, and a potentially black and sinister one at that. Our anxiety is fed with a daily diet of food horror stories and the drip, drip of negative propaganda from the food hygiene establishment. Dr Richard North, a former leading food safety adviser, describes the current situation as follows:

'Food hygiene in Britain these days is not a science, but a religion. The dogma is handed down by high priests and implemented by their servants, grey little apparatchiks called environmental health officers, who have been schooled as administrators, not inspectors. They have a total obsession with purity and whiteness. Their paradigm is that they see the food as one heaving, contaminated morass. They like food locked away in a sealed environment and they have a morbid fear of fresh air. They look on small food producers or artisans making a traditional product with unrestrained horror and revulsion and see them as dangerous businesses to be eliminated in their mission to root out all contamination.'

Britain's fear of food is fed from a very early age. The government, through the Food Standards Agency, has developed an 'interactive resource' for children aged as young as seven, and their teachers, called 'Food Hygiene Mission Control'. Cartoon characters called the 'Safe-T' and the 'H-Squad' (safety and the hygiene squad) are on a fun 'mission' – note the evangelical language – to impress upon children the dangers that lurk in food. They are invited to 'join Safe-T and the H-Squad on their special mission to exterminate Pathogens [with a capital P] and save the human race from food poisoning!' The text is stiff with exclamation marks and flashing red light words such as 'risk', 'poisoning', 'contamination' and 'danger'. Its catchy jingle goes 'Stop! Wipe that surface throughout the day, if you want to keep the pathogens away!' Primary school children find out how pathogens 'wait in hiding' and how they can 'double their numbers in just a short space of time'. Before starting any food activity, teachers are warned to carry out a full 'risk assessment' and cover all surfaces with 'non-permeable covers'. One learning outcome is that children should understand that their hands are 'lethal weapons' and carry out hand-washing experiments to 'to find effective ways of removing dirt and bacteria'.

With these lurid images being fed to British children at an age when most are already deeply suspicious about anything other than chicken nuggets, pizza, plain pasta, crisps and sweets, is it any wonder that we are breeding generations of children who are scared of food and cooking and who crave the apparent security of a ready-made product? As the *Guardian* columnist Ros Coward pointed out:

'What is being whipped up here is anxiety about food as dangerous, promoting the idea that the only safe food is wrapped in plastic and drenched in cleansing agents . . . I sympathize with the importance of basic hygiene . . . But teaching kids to wash their hands is simple and straightforward. It shouldn't involve teaching them that handling food is like handling radioactive waste.'

The Food Hygiene Mission Control is just the most infantile version of the food hygiene gospel that now drives regulatory thinking. It is based on a system of food safety management known as 'Hazard Analysis Critical Control Point' (HACCP) that focuses on identifying the 'critical points' in a process where food safety problems – 'hazards' – could arise and attempts to put practices in place to prevent things going wrong. What HACCP boils down to is a system of checklists, form filling and record keeping. A company might be asked, for example, to keep a note of every time an employee cleans down tables, and be encouraged to write down a comment about the state of the table at that time. The glaring flaw is that saying you are doing something is not the same as actually doing it, but it looks good, even though what is recorded may have no bearing on the reality. This system creates a paper trail so that in the event of a problem, the companies or producers implicated can demonstrate that they did their bit, and walk away blameless, plausibly denying responsibility. Like naughty children in the school playground, it allows them to say 'It wasn't me sir!' A supermarket that poisoned customers by selling contaminated chicken – bear in mind that over half of British chickens on supermarket shelves are contaminated with multi-drug-resistant strains of the potentially deadly *E. coli* bug – could use HACCP to show that its suppliers followed correct procedures so it was not at fault.

HACCP should not be confused with a really tough inspection regime of spot checks and surveillance that rigorously polices the food we eat or one that attempts to tackle the roots of food poisoning that lie overwhelmingly in large-scale food processing and factory farming. It was designed for large industrial food manufacturers and has limited relevance outside that factory system. In fact, it has been criticized for distorting the focus of the traditional premises inspection, so that the environmental health officer now makes a fleeting 'royal tour' surrounded by company top brass, examines paperwork, ticks boxes and sends out a standardized, computerized report on the basis of that. At best this system is an irrelevance to small food producers. At worst it fails to pick up hazards or even creates new ones. It most certainly acts as a positive disincentive to smaller food producers because it imposes a disproportionate burden on them. Like the disheartened ladies of the Norfolk Women's Institute, they feel unloved and undervalued. It seems to them that they never have the hygiene police off their backs with some ridiculous, unnecessary and often expensive requirement which is simply not applicable to their modus operandi.

The HACCP system is now enshrined in EU law, so all artisan producers in Europe must conform to it, along with a rag-bag of labelling regulations and other safety-driven requirements, most of which involve outlays that are relatively insignificant for large players, but major considerations for smaller ones. In other European countries, however, small food producers may be slightly more insulated from the full force of this. In Germany and Austria, state authorities have subsidized small, local slaughterhouses. In France, technical institutes support small producers and French producer cooperatives benefit from very substantial tax breaks. In Holland, there is free technical support advice for small farmers and growers, unlike in Britain, where they must pay for the privilege. Informally, Europeans are good at bending the rules to aid smaller, more vulnerable food businesses. In Spain, the relevant authorities will send out invoices for health inspections, but they may be prepared to turn a blind eye to whether they are ever paid or not. In France, small abattoirs were reclassified as something else so that new hygiene regulations did not apply to them.

Even more important, European artisans can count on some loyalty and support from the general public, and from those charged with surveillance because they are consumers of their products. A hygiene inspector in Greece, Finland, Poland or any other European country likes to eat traditional, small-scale food, and knows a lot of other people who do, and so has a vested gastronomic interest in encouraging it. Meanwhile, in Britain, the local environmental health officer most probably lunches on a factory sandwich, a packet of extruded snacks and a can of cola, and looks forward to a supermarket ready meal for supper. This is one small producer's assessment, based on practical experience, of the typical environmental health officer:

> 'Most of them are tossers. They are not familiar with an artisan product and therefore are conservative about anything they don't recognize. But you have to play along with them. It starts with threats. You get a lot of "I don't make the rules, I'm only following them", so even if what they are telling you to do is rubbish, you have to play ball. Their decisions are arbitrary and there's no point appealing to their boss because they all sing from the same song sheet. If you tell them where to go, you can win. You can make them back off if you do more research, if you stand your ground. But most people just find the pressure too much and throw in the towel.'

One traditional British delicacy that was put under the spotlight by a local environmental health department was Cornish salt pilchards, a rare and unique speciality of which any country wishing to preserve taste and regional identity would surely feel proud and protective. Predictably, the market for them was more foreign than domestic. Cornish pilchards have only a dedicated minority following in the UK because they are salted and pressed whole, so they have eyes and tails. Their guts are not removed, and it is the enzymes in them that give the final product its mature, complex flavour. They are too strongly flavoured and visceral to appeal to the typical British palate. They offend against the British principle that the best food is one that looks as if it has nothing whatsoever to do with anything that was ever alive. Northern Italians, on the other hand, love them. Drop into a small 'gastronomia' or 'alimentari' grocer's shop in a town such as Lucca or Florence and you may find these amber beauties from the traditional wooden barrel or from smaller circular wooden boxes, wherein the gleaming fish lie fanned out attractively, almost like slices of fruit on a baker's tart. Italians call them 'Salacche Inglesi' or simply 'Salate'. These intense little fish, whose flavour is thought to be akin to the ancient Roman 'garum' or fish sauce, traditionally had a strong following amongst the poor rural communities of northern Italy. They use these pilchards frugally, almost as a seasoning rather than an ingredient, grilling them first to intensify the flavour, then flaking them over polenta.

Historians record that this trade between England and northern Italy has been going on since 1555, and since 1905, the 'pilchard works' in Newlyn, where they used the traditional screw presses, had been the centre of this commerce. Then, in 1992, it hit a problem. Local environmental health officers decided that they wanted the pilchards to be gutted because they might contain pathogenic (food poisoning) bacteria. Nick Howell, who ran the pilchard works, remonstrated with them, pointing out that according to the Public Analyst, no Cornish pilchard, or salted fish similar to it, had ever been implicated in any food poisoning incident on record. The high levels of salt used in the process acted as a preservative, stopping any potential pathogens or food spoilage bacteria in their tracks. The environmental health officers had no evidence to the contrary, and had to back down, but they were still not happy. They then found another potential problem. They did not like the fact that the pilchards were packed in wood. They liked the hessian mat that lay between the fish and the wood even less. Wood and hessian did not conform to modern hygiene standards with their fondness for impervious surfaces, plastics and chemical disinfectants. The fact that this packaging had proven to be a sound, workable method to soak up surplus fish oil and brine for over four centuries cut no ice with them. They were insistent that the hessian should be removed, and replaced with a supermarket-style absorbent 'soak up' mat. They also wanted the boxes sealed to exclude air.

Mr Howell had no choice but to go along with their demands or risk seeing the whole operation closed down. Very quickly, it became clear that the new packaging was a disaster. This supposedly superior, super-hygienic, modern packaging had altered the balance of humidity and salinity. A rather unpleasant looking mould began to grow on the outside of the pilchards. 'They looked,' said Mr Howell, 'as though someone had taken a flour shaker with soot and sprinkled it all over them.' Abandoning the new packaging it had advocated, Mr Howell presented the environmental health department with a bill for £9,000, which represented the cost of the whole repackaging experiment and refunding unhappy customers. The department declined to pay up, leaving Mr Howell to bear the expense.

In Britain, it can cost a food producer dear to cross swords with health authorities. In 1999, the distinguished craft cheesemaker, James Aldridge – who made a specially matured, raw milk Caerphilly called Tornegus – was brought to the point of ruin by the Department of Health. To cut a long story short, he had £44,000 of cheese seized, was prohibited from selling any more, and lost approaching £100,000 in legal fees, even though the authorities had to finally admit that his cheese had never posed a health risk.

The Aldridge case illustrated how British public hygiene authorities often act heavy-handedly on the basis of shaky science. A central plank in their conviction is the assumption that anything shiny, modern and high-tech is safer than something that is tried, tested and traditional, even in the face of evidence to the contrary. In 1994, researchers at the University of Wisconsin-Madison conducted an experiment comparing the relative safety of the traditional wooden chopping board and the modern plastic equivalent. They inoculated each type with toxic bacteria and left them at humid room temperature overnight. The next day the bugs had multiplied on the plastic but not on the wood. It emerged that wooden chopping boards had bactericidal properties and were safer than plastic boards, particularly when the plastic ones were scored with knives; they trapped contamination in their grooves, even when put through a dishwasher. Yet more than a decade on, the British hygiene establishment is still so wedded to the notion that wood equals old and dangerous, while plastic equals modern and safe, that environmental health officers continue to recommend, and frequently require, that food producers and handlers use only plastic chopping boards.

Back in the 1980s and 1990s, there was a sense of a renaissance (some would say naissance) of craft food in Britain, but it was always vulnerable in the midst of an industrial food economy whose norms are dictated by huge corporations and where only a small minority of consumers were persuaded of its value. The small independent food sector is healthier elsewhere. To encourage small-scale products, the European Union has a scheme where their makers can apply for Protected Designation of Origin (PDO) or Protected Geographical Indication (PGI) status. In 2005, Italy had 149 such items, France had 143, Portugal had 93, Spain had 91, Greece had 84. The UK had a paltry 29, including items such as Whitstable oysters, Cornish clotted cream, Arbroath smokies and Jersey Royals. As Richard Burge, chief executive of the Countryside Alliance, put it: 'Most European countries have thriving food cultures based around the preparation and consumption of excellent regional produce, and good food and good health is simply a way of life. Yet in Britain, despite having excellent local produce, our farming is dying and our food culture is dominated by low-nutrition, high-fat convenience junk food.'

In a domestic market which is largely immune or indifferent to the charms of its products, Britons who go into small-scale food production do so because it is something they enjoy and believe in, not because they expect to make much money. But when they find themselves drowning in controls, paperwork and pressure, that marginal living stops being agreeable, there is no economic incentive to continue and they begin to feel that it is just not worth the time and hassle involved. The people in Britain who produce that special cheese, high welfare meat, distinctive local pie, traditional variety of apple juice or any other small-scale product with particular character that offers relief from the standard industrial norm, are getting fed up. Some keep going by adjusting their methods, say by using pasteurized rather than raw milk, or by vacuum packing their product perhaps, while others simply give up and do something else. It is Britain's loss, and our food is the poorer for it.

14

KIDS IN WHITE COATS

In countries with a healthy food culture, children learn about food and cooking at home. Like little dry grains of rice plumping up in water and steam, they simply learn by absorption from watching food being prepared then eating it, slowly accumulating experience through observation and participation. As they grow older, they learn to help guide the pasta through the teeth of the pasta machine. They help with podding peas, or peeling potatoes. They are sent to check if something is burning in the oven. They pick up ideas about what you can do with a glut of seasonal fruit. They watch adults, usually mothers and grandmothers, turning out a family meal almost every day. And they have the experience of sitting down around a table and enjoying communal food alongside adults who know more about food than they do. In most societies, food appreciation and cooking is an effortless chain of knowledge, passed on in a domestic setting through the generations, informally and without any fuss.

This is precisely how young British people used to learn to cook, but not any more. Now that we have become a 'no time to cook' culture, parents are unable to fulfil this natural educational function because they themselves have become steadily de-skilled and reliant on ready-made foods. In the UK it can no longer be taken for granted that children learn even the most basic cooking skills at home. The hope is that they pick up some at school, but given the current British thinking in food education, that remains a faint prospect.

Back in the days when most people still cooked from scratch at home, the complementary subject known as 'Domestic Science' or, more recently, 'Home Economics', was widely on offer and practical cookery lessons were a major component within it. But, consistent with Britain's historical tendency to see food as unimportant, even then it was a low-status subject, and this was a state of affairs not unrelated to the fact that it was taught exclusively by women. Home Economics was always a subject that could be used to fill up the timetables of younger years and less academic pupils.

In the 1990s, in keeping with the educational dogma of the time that stressed the importance of a more scientific and technological approach, food education was given a makeover and reinvented as 'Food Technology', an altogether more impressive-sounding discipline wherein children were encouraged to learn the ins and outs of food processing and 'interact successfully with materials, tools and resources' rather than being given straightforward cooking lessons. As Ali Farrell, a leading food education specialist, put it:

'The domestic context is no longer the only relevant one. A great deal happens to food before it reaches our homes, which impacts on its quality, and there are more food options available to us than in the past . . . It is just as important for today's young people to be conversant with the issues surrounding food as it is to be able to boil an egg.'

This argument has a ring of plausibility about it until you take a look at the Food Technology curriculum. Where once children learned that the 'rubbing-in method' was the basis of scones, pastry and crumble, or discovered that a roux was the progenitor of any hot soufflé, white sauce, or macaroni cheese, contemporary Food Technology has turned British children into white-coated, net-capped, miniature food industry technologists whose key tool is not an oven, but a computer.

In GCSE 'Food Technology', for example, pupils have to 'design and make' a commercial product – anything from an airline vegan meal to a low-calorie dessert, demonstrating that they can use 'Information Communication Technology' (ICT), 'Computer Aided Design' (CAD), 'Computer Aided Manufacture' (CAM) and Computer Integrated Manufacture (CIM) to see their product idea through from the conceptual stage to its finished form, all ready for the supermarket shelves.

Where once they learned to bake a fillet of fish in one lesson, they now take a term to design a new battered fish product to meet a hypothetical retailer's specification. Instead of being taught how to cook, Britain's food illiterate pupils spend most of their timetabled hours on lengthy projects based around designing an industrial product. As one teacher put it: 'They spend months producing a 20-page project on designing a muffin. Why can't they just bake the bloody muffins?'

The vocabulary of British food education used to centre around words like sieve, scales, wooden spoon, chopping board, washing up and oven gloves. Now the language that a pupil should master and use to ensure exam success consists of a whole new lexicon of key words, such as 'prototype', 'mouthfeel', 'sensory profiling', 'test kitchen', 'accelerated freeze drying', 'conveyor belt', 'unit cost', 'designated tolerance', 'best before', 'dextrinization', 'calibration', 'bar codes', and 'non-enzymatic browning'.

A classic project for pupils taking Food Technology would be to draw up a computerized model process flow chart showing the Hazard Analysis and Critical Control Point system for a product such as 'Saucy Chicken Animals'. In the context of a cook-chill factory, a diligent student would be expected to show every production stage of this delightful convenience food from the preparation of ingredients through to the filling of heat-proof containers, the reheating to a core temperature of 65°C, the adding of 'standard components' like previously 'stripped' chicken, the rapid cooling and blast freezing to

−18°C, ending with the product's storage and final despatch in freezer container lorries. Alternatively, they might draw up a computer model for manufacturing coleslaw, showing understanding of the use of sensors to detect weight, colour, thickness or temperature changes and the role of various industrial gizmos that fulfil key roles in industrial processing, such as flow rate devices for adding fillings, and magnetic metal detectors. Or they could opt to design packaging for 'novelty birthday cakes' or focus on how to prolong the life of food by storing it in special 'Modified Atmosphere Packaging'.

By the end of the course, they should be so thoroughly schooled in food manufacturing and all its related jargon that they can answer exam questions such as:

- Complete the five point specification for a cake or biscuit vending machine.
- What are the advantages of irradiation as a method of preservation?
- During a production run, why would a food manufacturer use the triangle test for the sensory analysis of custard cream biscuits?
- What are the advantages of continuous flow production?
- Draw a flow diagram for the production of a chicken curry.

Obviously, the more the nation comes to rely on highly processed convenience food, the more this syllabus has some relevance, if for no other reason than it draws back the veil of commercial secrecy behind which the food industry generally hides and it gives an insight into the many interventions to which raw materials are subjected. But the most disturbing thing about the tenor of Food Technology is that it encourages the idea that normal British food is made in factories by new product developers wearing hair nets and white coats. As a consequence of its narrow frame of reference, where every food is manufactured industrially rather than prepared simply and practically at home, it sends out the message that home cooking is no longer relevant. Food education becomes a question of evaluating labels on processed ready meals, rather than buying raw ingredients and cooking them for yourself. It encourages a mindset that craves the apparent security of prepared food with a 'use by' date and it breeds suspicion of natural, fresh foods that have not been industrially transformed. A prevailing 'Gee whizz . . . isn't it wonderful?' tone sets any debate arising from the curriculum. The question becomes not 'Is it necessary to always buy processed food?' but 'Which processed foods should I buy?' Pupils are not encouraged to ask themselves, for example, whether a product with an extensive list of additives is good or bad, or whether most additives are even necessary, but whether the additives are portrayed as a useful technological tool to preserve food and ensure its safety. The knock-on effects of this approach are now being reflected in the shopping patterns of younger consumers. A government survey in

2003 found that consumers in their early twenties were reluctant to use greengrocers, butchers or farmers' markets because: 'They express anxiety about entering environments that do not have pre-packed produce available.' The result is that one out of every two young 'housewives' aged 17–24 do not cook anything from scratch.

Home Economics continues to be offered in some schools as a separate certificate subject. Here again the syllabus sidelines cooking. Although it allows at least the possibility of some practical cooking experience with tasks such as planning, preparing and making a special family meal on a budget, the subject matter is probably more suited to those who want to become social workers, clothes designers, dieticians or health visitors than anyone who just needs to learn to cook, since pupils study subject areas such as: the nutritional requirements of certain age groups, how to cut down salt intake, how to complain about consumer products, food chemistry, fashion design, dietary and demographic trends, the welfare state and poverty.

So just exactly how much practical cooking might a typical schoolchild do? The curriculum for English primary schools specifies that children have to 'work with food as a material', but it doesn't say that they have to cook. 'Working with food as a material' can, and often does, boil down to simple tasks such as assembling fruit kebabs or sandwiches due to a lack of facilities and equipment for making anything more demanding. Most British primary schools would be fortunate to have one oven, or a sink with running water nearby, let alone have enough facilities for up to 30 children to carry out any real hands-on cooking. Anita Cormac, director of Focus on Food, a charity which campaigns to strengthen the profile of cooking in the curriculum, estimates that it is an unusual teenager who leaves secondary school with more than ten practical cookery lessons under his or her belt. The extent of most school leavers' cooking skills is reheating something pre-cooked or boiling pasta. Hardly any can make a finished dish.

Focus on Food pluckily champions the cause of cooking in schools. It has two well-equipped Cooking Buses that tour around the UK, giving children the opportunity to do some real cooking and training teachers to do the same in their schools. There is a seven-year waiting list for a visit. Focus on Food also publishes a stimulating *Cook School* magazine which provides interesting and imaginative materials for teachers starved of practical support for cooking while drowning in a sea of ICT, CAD, CAM, CIM and assorted Food Technology ideologies.

When Focus on Food was founded by the Royal Society for the Encouragement of Arts, Manufacture and Commerce in 1998, it was accused by sections of the educational establishment of turning the clock back by stressing the importance of practical cooking skills as the cornerstone of food education. Nowadays, Britain is waking up to the growing food illiteracy and consequent obesity among its children. The National Farmers' Union published a disturbing survey in 1999 which showed that younger generations were worryingly ignorant about the origins of food. Nearly half of the children surveyed thought that margarine came from cows, a third believed that oranges grew in Britain and nearly a quarter did not know that the main ingredient in bread was flour. Around one in five children did not know that ham came from pigs – as opposed to a tin or a packet – and they offered colourful suggestions for its origins such as cows, chicken, sheep, and even deer. In 2005, Jamie Oliver exposed British children's ignorance of food in *Jamie's School Dinners* when he asked a class of children to identify certain common fruits and vegetables such as rhubarb and leek, and found that most were unable to do so. Any notion that these less affluent city schoolchildren were unrepresentative of the country as a whole was shattered when later that year, a survey by the British Heart Foundation found that 36 per cent of children aged 8–14 could not identify the main ingredient in chips, with answers including oil, egg and apples. The same research found that 37 per cent did not know that cheese was made from milk. As the Foundation's director general, Peter Hollins, commented: 'Kids have lost touch with the most basic foods and no longer understand what they are eating.' A further survey by the British Potato Council subsequently found that 60 per cent of schoolchildren thought that potatoes grew on trees.

Food 'education' in schools is now predicated on the notion that you can dispense with cooking and still pick up the basics of food. This is an outlandish idea. All countries with healthy food cultures appreciate that cooking is the key to wider food appreciation. If you do not ever make a shepherd's pie, and then a retailer informs you that its ready-meal versions are simply the best around, and easily as good as you would make at home or encounter in a restaurant, then how would you be able to know any different if you have no homemade benchmarks against which to judge? Cooking is also the missing link in health education. The bombardment of children with healthy eating messages at school is destined to be a futile exercise if they cannot put them into practice because they are unable to cook.

More schools are becoming disillusioned with the Food Technology approach and are beginning to see the value of traditional Home Economics which stressed cooking skills as the best way to get future generations to take control of their food lives by intelligently planning, buying, preparing, cooking and sharing simple but good quality food with others. But such schools are often hobbled by the run-down state of their kitchens, the large size of classes, and a lack of teachers who want to go into the field because of its Cinderella image. The average Home Economics teacher of the 'old school' is now a 53-year-old female, near the end of her career. Within a decade, her replacement is likely to be a younger teacher thoroughly imbued with the Food Technology mindset who may not see the value of cooking, let alone being a competent cook herself.

British children are picking up less and less about

cooking at home and little or nothing of practical use at school. As one MORI survey into the UK's eating habits concluded: 'Most adults of today learnt to cook from their parents, however parents of today are passing less of their cooking skills on. Findings also indicate that the school currently plays a small role in teaching children to cook.'

So if they don't learn to cook either at home or at school, how are future generations going to be equipped to feed themselves in a way that is independent of the food industry? If you asked most Britons if they think that the food industry should have control over what ends up on our plates, the answer would be a resounding 'no'. But when younger generations can no longer cook even at the most elementary level, that is precisely what will happen.

15

KIDDIE FOOD

Most British people would be amazed to learn what foreign children eat for school lunch. Primary school children in the Lombardian city of Vigevano in Italy, for example, might sit down to vegetable soup, followed by braised beef with polenta, and a yogurt. On another day it might be meat ravioli with sage, or pumpkin soup, followed by a vegetable fritatta (omelette) served with raw fennel salad, or on a Friday, baked fish with a green salad. Further south, their compatriots in primary schools in Genoa might be tucking into rice with peas (a risotto), followed by a soft fresh 'stracchino' cheese and carrot salad, rounded off by fresh seasonal fruit. Another typical day's offering might be pasta with tomato sauce, followed by tuna with boiled potatoes and, once again, seasonal fruit for dessert.

In France, primary school meals commonly run to four courses, because the French always consider a small cheese course to be essential. For instance, the schools in

Limours, just south of Paris, might serve up a lunch consisting of a starter of saucisson with gherkins, a main course of sautéed chicken with mixed vegetables, a small piece of cheese – Brie, Tomme, fromage blanc or goat cheese, perhaps – with fresh fruit for dessert. Other days the children eat meals such as tomatoes dressed with vinaigrette, followed by fish in a tarragon sauce with rice, some cheese and a portion of apple compote. In Paris itself, schoolchildren in the 13th Arrondissement assemble in the dining room to eat meals such as taboulé (couscous with vegetables), chicken breast with lemon and green beans, then a wedge of Camembert and a kiwi fruit. Other days' menus might be lettuce salad, pasta baked in a white sauce with spinach and chicken, a mild, unsweetened natural yogurt, and seasonal fruit, or combinations like fresh radishes and butter, followed by herby roast ham served with a gratin of cauliflower and potatoes, then a yogurt with a waffle to dip into it. Children in Helsinki dine on lunches such as barley porridge or sausage soup followed by spinach pancakes and ham and potato casserole served with lingonberries.

Viewed from Britain, Land of the Turkey Twizzler, such menus are entirely alien and almost unthinkable. This is not only because some of the ingredients and dishes are not indigenous to British shores, but also because they offend against one of Britain's deep-seated bad food beliefs – the notion that you cannot expect children to like, and therefore eat, the same food as adults. None of the French or Italian menus above is hugely different from the lunches that their parents might themselves eat at home, in a canteen or in a restaurant. As in most parts of the world, with the exception of the United States, children are expected to eat more or less the same as adults from a very early age and this is reflected in menus which, although changed daily, are set and offer no choice. Most countries believe that given a reasonable amount of time to sit down around a table, and perhaps with a little encouragement from canteen staff, children will eat what is put before them. Assuming that they are hungry to start with, the expectation is that they will end up eating what is on offer.

How different from Britain where children's food or 'kiddie food' is as distinct from adults' food as from cat food or 'kittie food'. School meals have become a totemic example of Britain's inability to feed itself properly, a situation made all the more strange given the nation's affluence. Jamie Oliver put his finger on it when he visited the poorest township in Johannesburg in South Africa and tasted school meals that were healthier than those in Britain. He watched as a group of women created a school lunch out of the freshest ingredients they could find – a mutton stew with fresh, locally grown carrots and cabbage, with fruit for pudding:

> 'It completely astounded me that in a place of unbelievable poverty, the love and care put into children's meals was greater than in inner London, and resulted in a more nutritionally balanced lunch . . . Our friends

across the world are amazed that a proud country such as ours can have such little regard for the health and well-being of its children.'

Mr Oliver is quite correct. If you assembled an international jury and briefed it on the state of Britain's school meals, you would be met with total incomprehension. In a rich G8 country – one that can afford to build grandiose public projects such as the Millennium Dome, and finance a costly war in Iraq – the average amount spent on food ingredients for a primary school meal, last time it was systematically reviewed in 2003, was 35 pence. That is half what was then spent on lunch for residents in Her Majesty's Prisons, and a quarter of the sum allocated to feeding an army dog. This pitiful sum appears all the more mysterious when we learn that British parents fork out a not insubstantial £1.40–£1.70 for a meal. How is this possible? School meals are not seen by the powers that be as an ideal opportunity to improve child nutrition, nor as a particularly deserving candidate for subsidies. On the contrary, not only are local authorities obliged to source food as economically as possible to meet the government's 'Best Value' requirements, many of them also look on school meals as a revenue raiser to subsidize other parts of their education budget. Hence the striking disparity between what British parents pay and what their children actually get. It would not be difficult to reach the conclusion that Britain must either be a country that hates children, or one which in some twisted way wants to undermine their health by failing to feed its younger generations properly.

So what do Britain's schoolchildren eat? For at least two decades, many British parents have preferred not to ask the question 'And what did you have for lunch today?' for fear of the answer. The answer is not always illuminating as children reel off brand names not recognizable as basic foods. Such novel products arrive fresh from the freezer van, 'breadcrumbed', 'coated' or 'battered', formed into shapes and given fanciful names that are designed to appeal to children. Whether they are nominally fish, meat or fowl, such products characteristically consist of processed protein mulch – frequently not much more than 50 per cent of the product. The rest is bulk filler, water and additives. To keep the cost down and the manufacturers' profits high, the meat component may have been sourced, perfectly legally, from countries such as Thailand or Brazil where animals are reared even more intensively than in the UK. If it is fish, forget whole fillets or even flakes and expect 'dematerialized' fish paste, recovered from filleted bones.

A traditional 'roast dinner' still features prominently on many school menus, but even this promising-sounding dish can be made using reconstituted meat cuts, plumped up with water and polyphosphates then pressed back into something that resembles a whole joint. A British roast is always popular with hard-pushed catering staff who are short of time, because it can be prepared in the favoured British institutional way – cooked the day before, sliced super-thin when cold, then reheated in a gravy made up with water from a packet mix. Well, nothing's too good for our kids, is it?

Post BSE, there is little in the way of beef on 21st-century British school menus but that still leaves plenty of burger and sausage offerings, along with their vegetarian lookalikes, that all share a strangely similar bouncy texture, thanks to their winning combination of low-grade protein or carbohydrate mush and generous amounts of water, all laced with artificial flavourings, preservatives, colours and emulsifiers. Such offerings are served up with stodge – such as sugary, salty, tinned spaghetti, garlic bread or potato waffles – and some token boiled, previously frozen, vegetables, of such spectacular tastelessness that they are destined for the brimming waste bins. Round that off with an iced bun, a sweetened fruit 'flavoured' milk shake, jelly or mousse with no real fruit in it, or perhaps an 'ambient' yogurt that doesn't need to be refrigerated because it is stiff with additives, and you have the formula for a British school meal, all served up on an airline-style plastic 'flight tray'.

Even this provision has proved too much for some cash-strapped councils with school kitchens now so run down and sub-standard after decades of under-investment that they do not allow for real cooking. Many British primary schools have now gone over to a 'sandwich only' service, where even in the depths of winter, the tiniest pupils are handed a chilled petrol station sandwich, a sticky fruit 'drink' with precious little fruit juice in it, a packet of crisps and a 'healthy' cereal bar, stuck together with fat and sugar – an instant 'Grab-A-Bag' of sustenance.

One Yorkshire parent explained how her daughter's school had dispensed with hot meals entirely: 'The lunch break is only 35 minutes and the headteacher doesn't like hot meals because they take too long to eat. She thinks it is more important that the children get out to play in the playground. So she has gone over to the "Grab-A-Bag" system and only allows the children 10 minutes to eat it.'

In many British schools, children now bolt down the food, such as it is, in record time, or, alternatively, dump it in the waste bins after a few bites. It is a far cry from school meals in Europe where children sit down calmly and take their time to eat a square meal, served on a ceramic plate, while socializing with their class mates. In many secondary schools in Britain, actually getting a meal is quite a struggle, and it is characterized by long queues and shortages, as one teenager explained to researchers from the University of Edinburgh:

Interviewer: 'What do you do at lunchtime?'
Pupil: 'I run to the dinner hall and get a tuna salad sandwich and then talk to my friends outside the dinner hall.'

Interviewer: 'Why do you have to run to the dinner hall?'
Pupil: 'Cause they are all taken. There's a big line and they're usually all gone.'

Many secondary pupils have given up on their school canteens entirely, grazing on a host of bad food opportunities in nearby shopping parades: a deep-fried half pizza and chips from the chip shop, a carton of rice with sweet and sour sauce from the Chinese takeaway, some cheese dip and crackers from the convenience store, liberally washed down with soft drinks. One teenager described his lunch-break routine as follows:

'We usually run to try to beat all the queues for the food [on the high street] and then go down to the pigeon bit [an area frequented by pigeons just outside the school grounds], sit, eat our lunch and then probably have about two fags and then go back up to school.'

Back in 2000, the government looked as though it might be taking the situation in hand when it introduced new nutritional standards. These specified that certain foods – such as fresh or tinned fruit – should be available every day and they restricted the number of days on which items such as chips could be served. But they did not limit the amount of fat, sugar and salt a lunch could contain, nor did they set levels for vitamins and minerals. Consequently, many school caterers managed to conform to the guidelines while continuing to serve nutritionally inadequate food to balance the books. They developed a technique known as 'menu opposition' where you restrict the uptake of the more costly healthy choice – say fresh fruit – by serving it as an alternative to chocolate sponge and custard, knowing that children will go for the latter over the former if they are offered simultaneously.

Menu opposition conforms to the British viewpoint that schoolchildren must be offered a choice of food because it would be too dictatorial to do otherwise. It also, rather conveniently, allows local authorities to say they are offering healthy options but the children do not like them. Vested interests in the catering industry and cynical cost-conscious local authorities like to make out that they are only responding to their 'young consumers', not to hungry, growing children who deserve a decent meal. Suggestions that children should either go home for lunch, or be kept at school at lunch time as is the case in many European countries, so that they have no option of popping out the school gates for junky alternatives, are likewise dismissed as too prescriptive and undermining the sacrosanct marketplace principle of consumer choice.

The net effect of this mantra of choice is that most British children eat extremely badly at school. As Professor Kevin Morgan of Cardiff University, who has made a study of the school meals served in countries such as Italy, puts it, '[the government] is obsessed with choice, but in the area of school meals this is a mistake. It is sometimes better to have a restricted choice so you learn what is good for you.' The charity Barnardo's stressed this point after carrying out research into school food. 'The more choice children and young people have,' it pointed out, 'the less likely they are to eat a healthy, nutritionally-balanced meal' – particularly when the healthier option is more expensive. It noted that in one typical secondary school visited by its researchers, a jacket potato with one filling and a salad cost more than twice as much as a burger and chips, while a bottle of water was double the price of a can of cola.

In 2003, when the Soil Association carried out a major survey into British school meals, it labelled the food on offer in most schools as 'muck off a truck' and showed how most children would be unable to make a healthy choice, even if they wanted to. It summed up the dismal food on offer as follows:

'The "regeneration" of ready prepared and highly processed convenience mass catered food items has replaced, if not eliminated, real cooking with real ingredients. Skilled and highly motivated school cooks are rare. In many areas poorly paid "food service operatives" prepare food. Where they do cook, ingredients are of poor quality and of questionable or unknown provenance. Some do virtually no fresh food preparation, many do little more than reheat "cook-chill" dishes made previously and shipped hundreds of miles to the school. Most do little more than add water to sauce powders or cake mixes, defrost and reheat frozen meat or vegetable "shapes", reheat frozen vegetables, reconstitute dried potatoes and "assemble" other ready prepared foods. In doing so they produce meals that contain little or no fresh food but large amounts of salt, fat, sugar, colorants, flavourings or preservatives.'

As one 14-year old put it: 'They are saying that we are going to be the generation that are going to be overweight and that, but we can't help it, what's in our canteen.'

The Soil Association subsequently carried out a thorough nutritional analysis and found that a primary school child eating the typical British school meal would be consuming way over the government's recommended limits for fat, sugar and salt and receiving inadequate amounts of vital nutrients like iron and zinc. It also flagged up how uptake of school meals had dropped to under 50 per cent, with a majority of primary school pupils bringing packed lunches. The dire state of these was reported by the Food Standards Agency in 2004, when it found that three out of every four lunchboxes surveyed would not meet the government's minimum standards for primary school meals. Nine out of ten lunchboxes surveyed contained food that was too high in fat, had twice the recommended amount of sugar and supplied close to half of a child's recommended salt intake. The typical British school lunchbox consisted of a white bread sandwich, a packet of crisps, a piece of chocolate confectionery and sometimes a sweetened yogurt or fromage frais.

Just how long will it be before Britain is brought to court over its failure to ensure a nutritious school meal for its children? After all, the right to food is a binding right under international law, featuring in the Universal Declaration on Human Rights and numerous other commitments that the British government has signed. It is defined as: 'The right of every man, woman and child alone and in the community with others to have physical and economic access at all times to adequate food or means for its procurement in ways consistent with human dignity.' It is questionable whether British school meals fit that bill.

Following the Soil Association's report and the screening of Channel 4's *Jamie's School Dinners* in 2005, a wave of concern flowed through Britain about what the nation's young were eating, with the now infamous Turkey Twizzler, and products of that ilk, coming in for widespread condemnation. In the autumn of 2005, there was a sense of 'and about time too' when Education Secretary, Ruth Kelly, announced extra funding to double the government spending on school dinners to ensure that they 'will be able to cook freshly prepared ingredients'. This would allow cooks to spend 50 pence on ingredients, instead of 35 pence, a sum still far short of other European countries such as France and Italy where anything between 60 and 90 pence is allowed. It then emerged that a quarter of new schools being built in England under private finance initiative contracts were to be built without kitchens in which fresh food could be prepared. Instead, they were only to be equipped with 'regeneration kitchens' designed to reheat pre-cooked and chilled or frozen food, previously prepared elsewhere.

In the autumn of the same year, Ruth Kelly also backed recommendations from the School Meals Review Panel – set up after the screening of *Jamie's School Dinners* – for an effective ban on low-quality foods high in salt, sugar and fat, both in school meals and in school vending machines. Optimistic headlines read 'Junk food to be banned in school'. It sounded great. Problem sorted, in England at least. What was not made clear was that the proposals would be subject to a consultation period in which interest groups, such as food manufacturers and caterers, would be given the chance to bend the government's ear. Ms Kelly's undertakings were greeted by a chorus of rancorous voices predicting all the reasons why they would not work. Teachers' leaders came up with the usual 'it's not as easy as all that' arguments: 'Pupils will continue to eat unhealthy packed lunches and visit the local chip shop. Schools, especially those in private finance initiatives, may be locked into long-term contracts with caterers and vending suppliers.' Some British schools are signed up to catering contracts covering 30 years at a time. One major private catering contractor warned ominously that tougher school food guidelines would make it harder for schools to balance their books:

'If schools ban chips at lunchtime, or sweets from vending machines, then that money will leak out of the school to the local chip shop or newsagent and £10,000 to £20,000 will have to be found elsewhere to make the meals service viable.'

In a classic case of shooting the messenger, Jamie Oliver was attacked by the Local Authority Caterers Association which blamed him for a 9 per cent reduction in take-up of school meals since *Jamie's School Dinners* was broadcast: 'The perception in the public arena now is that school dinners are very poor. That is not manifestly the case.' Jamie Oliver was bound to get it in the neck for upsetting the preconception that British school food is bad, and always will be, because no one seems sufficiently bothered to do anything about it.

Whether or not the current indignation over school meals results in a real overhaul of the food on offer remains to be seen. In Britain, a gloomy fatalism hangs over all discussions of the state of children's food. There is a perceived wisdom that children are supposed to prefer unhealthy food, and that to wean them off that is well nigh impossible – an attitude that many other nations would find incomprehensible. When British nursery school children were asked by Barnardo's what they would choose for lunch, even at that early stage they went unhesitatingly for junk foods – chips, burgers, hot dogs, pizza, cakes, ice cream, doughnuts and crisps – the only ray of light being that they also chose fruit and fruit juices.

Although Britain is a country that fully appreciates the benefits of compelling children to sit at a desk and learn English, mathematics, and any other life and career-improving subject, it balks at requiring children to sit down at a table to learn how to eat decent, life-sustaining food, because good food – for children or anyone else – is simply not a British priority. In 2003, when *Which?* magazine asked children to keep a food diary, it singled out this example as 'fairly typical' of what British children eat:

> 'For breakfast, Zoe, aged 15, has a slice of white toast and butter, washed down with a couple of mugs of milky tea. During the morning she has a bag of crisps with a soft drink, and in the canteen at lunch she eats a plate of chips and gravy with a Turkey Twizzler. In the afternoon she buys a lolly and her second bag of crisps. Tea is more chips and gravy, this time with chicken nuggets, mushy peas and a soft drink. Before bed, she eats two chocolate bars.'

When the charity Barnardo's researched children's attitudes towards food, it noted that 'very few children are subject to family rules in the home concerning food' and that most children of all ages are allowed by their parents to 'eat more or less what they like'. This illustrates just how unimportant the British consider food to be. So what if the kids eat junk at school and home – it really doesn't matter, does it?

16

BRITAIN MAKES YOU FAT

It is terribly easy to become fat in Britain. Bar the United States, there is no other developed country in the world where, if you go with the flow, you will end up eating quite so badly. In Britain, you have to go out of your way, and make a special effort, to find good food. Healthy food is the exception, rather than the rule. If you just eat what everyone else eats, and take advantage of the popular food options that are regularly presented to you, then there is a strong chance that, as the years roll on, you'll be joining that growing band of compatriots who struggle to fit into last year's wardrobe, or worse, who can't see their toes for their bellies.

Up and down the British Isles, bad food is omnipresent, and more wholesome alternatives are elusive. It is as if there is a national conspiracy to get the population to eat fattening junk. Bad food is woven into the structure of daily life. Going for a swim or a workout at the fitness centre is good for your health – as long as you ignore the vending machine loaded with fizzy drinks and sweets. If you want to read a newspaper and keep abreast of national and world events like a participating citizen, then you'll probably need to walk into a shop with a wall of confectionery, crisps and garish liquids called 'juice'. You might even be waylaid by confectionery sitting right next to the till when all you wanted was the *Financial Times*. It's up to you to exercise your willpower and say 'No thank you!' assertively. As the Conservative Party leader, David Cameron, put it: 'Try and buy a newspaper at the train station and, as you queue to pay, you're surrounded, you're inundated by cut price offers for giant chocolate bars.'

If you're popping into a high street off-licence to buy a bottle of wine, it's made easy for you to pick up some confectionery as you pay. Forget wine and olives – in Britain it's wine and sweeties. Filling up on petrol? Go on, treat yourself to something from that monumental display of chocolate confectionery, sticky gums, boiled sweets, crisps and extruded snacks – after all, you're worth it – and throw in a long-life, mini-salami while you are there. Or what about a more substantial snack, a 'meal replacement' – or 'smeal' (a play on snack and meal) as the industry likes to call it? A big, fatty, salty burger or deep dish steak pie perhaps, carefully microwaved just for you by the languid youth at the pay point? The market for these chilled, microwavable delights grew by 98 per cent between 2003 and 2005. While you are there, look out for US-style 'cup-holder cuisine', a handy range of snacks, soups, and even cooked meals, designed to be eaten with one hand while driving, that fit into car cup-holders. They'll be coming to a petrol station forecourt near you – soon! And at the weekend, if you fancy taking in a film, munching and slurping your way through the main feature is absolutely de rigueur. If you prefer a night in with a rented DVD, then you'll probably want to avail yourself of a bumper box of popcorn, or a two-for-the-price-of-one mega-offer on salty tortilla chips with 'salsa'.

The British have become so accustomed to having bad food thrust under their noses in places and situations not otherwise associated with food that they no longer notice it. But it is odd. If you were to buy a newspaper in Italy, Holland or Denmark, you might just about spot a box of Tic Tacs wedged beside the matches. If you want a work-out in Spain or Germany, then you'll need to take your own junky snacks with you to the gym, because you won't find any there. Buy petrol in Europe, and the shop may try to sell you a map, bottles of water, or a few packets of salted crackers. But if it is run by a British petroleum company, it will be stocked up with enough sweets to see a small town through a two-month world sugar shortage.

Although in Britain snack food almost always equals junk food, there is no universal rule that it must be this way. Some of the most nutritious and delicious dishes in the world are everyday, inexpensive snacks: Middle Eastern falafels, Indian vadai, Sicilian panelle, Malaysian roti canai, French galettes de sarrasin. People from other countries who come to Britain are instantly struck by how much the British seem to eat while they are out and about, going about their daily lives. More than any other nationality, bar Americans, the British people eat – or to be more accurate, snack – on the hoof, as a matter of course. There is an abundance of 'street food' in Britain, but not of the gastronomic, life-enhancing sort. Kids gulp down cans of pop and sweets on the way to and from school. City suits bolt out from offices to grab a hasty sarnie and crisps, devouring them as they dash back to close that last deal. Lethargic shoppers amble round shopping malls with a giant cookie in one hand and a can of diet cola in the other. Chewing gum-spotted pavements bear silent witness to Britain's addiction to having something sweet in its mouth for large parts of the waking day. Carriages on the London Underground rumble along, pungent with the odours of partially eaten, then abandoned, fast food and smelly sandwich debris.

Britons are given endless opportunities to snack away on food with a questionable nutritional profile, even in places where they should have a right to expect better. People who end up in hospital and miss a meal can fill the gap with a 'Snack Box', introduced in 2001 as part of the government's 'Better Hospital Food Programme'. These boxes all come with a piece of fruit, a portion of cheese and crackers – or cheese spread and bread sticks for children. But they also contain a packet of Walkers crisps and a piece of chocolate confectionery, typically a Mars bar or a Twix, and a sweet fruit 'drink'. When researchers from Barnardo's logged the food and drink offerings in one suburban secondary school, they found that the students were presented with 28 opportunities to buy different brands and flavours of chocolate and confectionery, compared with only 5 opportunities to purchase fruit or fruit salad. Furthermore there were 27 opportunities to buy different brands of sugary, soft drinks, compared with only 4 for water and 5 for fruit juice. In the words of one teenager: 'I eat about six bags of crisps a day just because they are there for us to eat and there is no healthy food.'

The British are Europe's most ardent consumers of snack foods. The average Briton eats 7.2 kg of snacks per year. Italians, by comparison, eat just 1 kg, and Russians eat even less. On the savoury front, by 2002 the United Kingdom was gobbling up 51 per cent of the European 'savoury snacks' market (crisps and their variants, salted crackers and nuts), three times more than the nearest contender, Germany. Whereas 86 per cent of Britons eat such snacks, less than half of Italians do so. In European shops, any crisps on sale tend to be of the straightforward salted variety, while extruded, savoury potato snacks are generally limited to the basic types that have been around for decades. Europeans view crisps and snacks of that ilk as an occasional purchase, a rather unimaginative nibble that might be served along with a pre-dinner aperitif, not as a staple daily alternative to real food.

No other country in the world has Britain's extraordinary, and endlessly expanding, collection of variations on the crisp and savoury snack theme, but then, as the

Savoury Snacks Information Bureau puts it: 'Snacks are indisputably an integral part of the British culture.' It estimates that the country munches its way through 6,000 million bags of crisps and 4,400 million packs of savoury snacks every year. The British consumer is positively spoilt for choice nowadays. Take your pick from prawn cocktail potato heads, aromatic lemongrass with lime flavour corn bites, thick-cut balti curry golden skins, ketchup flavoured teddy-bear-shaped potato snacks, Worcester sauce flavoured wheat crunchies, Wensleydale cheese and cranberry crisps, teriyaki rice bites, cheese Quavers, French fries, Thai red curry and coriander bites, Hula Hoops, Balti curry flavour potato skins, firecracker lobster hot chilli crisps, Wotsits, space alien-shaped corn and wheat snacks, Southern fried chicken flavoured bubbled chips, crushed sea salt and balsamic vinegar crisps, Mediterranean salsa dippers, Skips, lower fat, higher fat, skins on, skins off, ridge-cut . . . the list goes on and on. The British have more words for crisps than Eskimos do for snow.

Recent innovations include items such as Mini Pringles, the product which, according to its manufacturers Procter and Gamble, 'can go where no snack has gone before, bringing a new level of portability' to the 'snacking on-the-go' market, and Limited Edition flavours Walkers Great British Dinner crisps. The latter come in three nostalgic forms – roast beef and Yorkshire pudding, lamb and mint sauce, baked ham and mustard – and are pro-moted by none other than Britain's top chef, Gordon

Ramsay. Astounding amounts of food industry research and development effort, not to mention advertising muscle, have been invested in cultivating Britain's taste for such hi-tech mouthfuls.

Neither has any other country in Europe Britain's seemingly insatiable appetite for sweets. On the continent, sweets and chocolates are considered to be optional extras, available for people who have already sated themselves on sustaining foods – meat, fish, fruit and vegetables – but the British have come to see confectionery as a primary food source, a surrogate meal component. The British eat their way through a £6.1 billion mountain of confectionery every year. British children now consume 25 times more confectionery and 30 times more soft drinks than they did in 1950.

Confectionery manufacturers and retailers know that 70 per cent are bought on impulse, so their key task is to tempt the population at every turn. As confectionery giant, Nestlé Rowntree, puts it: 'It is essential to make it really easy for shoppers to see the products they desire.' The merchandising of confectionery in Britain has become an art form. Industry psychologists delineate three different 'motivations' that drive people to buy sweets: hunger, snack and pleasure. Any retailer who wants to maximize their sales is advised to group together an array of products according to these motivations, in order to 'optimize' sales. This way, impulse buyers might make a multiple purchase, a Picnic for hunger, a mint Aero for pleasure and a Twix as a snack to keep as a stand-by, perhaps. Shrewd retailers in the UK know that you don't just offer confectionery once in the shop, but repeatedly. 'Understanding the consumer flow around your store will help you identify the high traffic areas which are ideal for siting secondary confectionery displays and capturing impulse purchases . . . Siting confectionery in a dumpbin can provide a sales increase of 20 per cent, but add a price promotion and sales can increase by a massive 450 per cent,' explains Nestlé Rowntree.

The profits to be made from snack purchases are immense. In the words of Procter and Gamble, 'mini bites for maxi profits'. This is why the amount of aisle space given over to snack foods in British shops dwarfs that allotted to more wholesome, basic foods. Snack foods loom large in supermarket price promotions. On one day in May 2005, for instance, Sainsbury's 'cool weekend offers' – flagged up with half page adverts in newspapers – consisted of two large packets of Walkers Sensations crisps (£1.50), a Buy One Get One Free offer on Mars ice cream (£1.99) and two 2-litre bottles of Coca-Cola for £1.50. A survey by the National Consumer Council subsequently found that every supermarket, with the exception of Marks & Spencer, ran twice as many special deals on fatty and sugary products as they did on fresh fruit and vegetables.

All sorts of retail outlets, from supermarkets to corner shops, now have what is known in the trade as 'Food For Now' zones, or what Tesco refers to as 'Grab and Go' counters. Food For Now zones flourish because substantial sections of the British population cannot, or will not, make the time to eat something approximating to a square meal, so they cater to them with chiller cabinets stocked up with sandwiches, crisps, sweets and soft drinks, positioned conveniently near to the till or a fast pay point. In Britain, because it cannot be taken for granted that most citizens have eaten a proper meal, or have any prospect or intention of doing so in the near future, retailers know that a majority of people passing through the shop are almost permanently on the look-out for something to supplement the appetite that lingers from their last unsatisfactory eating experience.

In Britain, eating is an occupation that has been uncoupled from the civilizing protocols to which countries with sound food cultures still adhere. On the continent, it is widely viewed as impolite to telephone people between 7.00 pm and 8.00 pm, because it is generally assumed that they will be eating and should be left to do so in peace. But eating in Britain no longer requires a table, time out from other activities, or a certain timeframe with generally recognized limits – breakfast, lunch, dinner – in which it can be accomplished. It has become a portable skill that can be combined with other tasks. Eat what you want, when you like, when you fancy it. Have a little bit of this, and if you're still peckish – which inevitably you will be – then have a further little bit of that. Forget forward planning. Don't worry about not following any meal pattern. Just feed your appetite in a totally unevolved way: I'm hungry, I need to eat now. Don't think about what you eat, just respond to one pang of hunger after another on an ad hoc basis, depending on what is on offer. Refuel on the go.

No food institution is immune to on-the-hoof snacking. Breakfast used to be a safe bet when out and about in Britain. As the writer Somerset Maugham famously observed: 'If you want to eat well in Britain, eat three breakfasts a day.' But Maugham's strategy for surviving the rigours of British food is rarely an option nowadays since breakfast has become yet another key snacking opportunity. Britons are now officially Europe's worst breakfasters, according to market research. Despite Britain's traditional attachment to the cooked breakfast, the oft-quoted nutritional dictum that one should eat breakfast like a king, eat lunch like a lord and eat dinner like a pauper, falls increasingly on deaf ears. Busy Britain does not have time to eat breakfast like it used to. A proper breakfast is becoming something most people only consider at weekends. Our weekday stopwatches start ticking the minute the alarm goes off in the morning. In the words of one market analyst: 'More and more [people] are opting to sacrifice breakfast or substitute it for a morning snack to save time. In the UK this is becoming increasingly possible with the proliferation of products targeting such fragmented consumption.'

These days, Britain doesn't breakfast, it 'deskfasts'. En route to work we can pick up a large, and astonishingly expensive Starbucks caramel macchiato (£3.09 in 2005).

Alternatively, when passing the sandwich bar on the corner, an 'All-Day Lemon Croissant' ('tastes pretty much delicious 24–7') might be just the job. If that is too conventional, we could go for a warm 'Food To Go Breakfast Bar' which 'incorporates all the ingredients of a full English breakfast in a hand-held pastry bar'. Feeling less than thrilled at the prospect of yet another sticky cereal 'breakfast bar' – sales of these grew almost sevenfold between 1998 and 2003 – or the familiar 'All Day Breakfast' sarnie, we might be more tempted by the warmth of a pre-assembled, pre-cooked bacon bap to be heated up in the office microwave in only 50 seconds. Would-be healthier eaters can keep a cache of ready-made porridge in the office fridge, designed to be microwaved then eaten straight from the container.

At lunchtime, an occasion when most of the world still sits down to eat, restless Britain is once more on the move: buying some ready meals for instant supper perhaps, window shopping for clothes, out for a jog around the park. Three personal assistants in big British companies described their lunchtime eating habits to *The Times*:

'I spend my lunch hour with my personal trainer at the gym. I tend to eat at my desk, usually a salad or a sandwich . . .'

'At lunchtime I'll have a hazelnut cappuccino and a sandwich. Our office does have a canteen, but I find that I don't often have time to spend my lunch there . . .'

'Lunchtime? What lunchtime? My day is working around my boss's day, so I usually get his lunch in between his meetings and grab a sandwich myself at my desk most days when I can . . .'

As the managing director of one leading catering company put it: 'People have moved away from the "meat and two veg" scenario to all-day grazing. A lot of our attention goes into packaging food, so it's quick for people to take back to their desks and easy to eat when they get there.'

Such incessant activity is great news for outlets purveying the now ubiquitous British 'meal deal' – another recent concept that caters for the increase in desktop and in-vehicle dining. The British like the sound of meal deals. Those words encapsulate a promise that they find endlessly seductive – cheap food. Meal deals are now what passes for lunch for most Britons. Forget meat and two veg, that went out with the ark. Real lunch is something you eat on a Sunday – if you are lucky. Feast instead on a chilly, floppy, flavour-challenged, factory sandwich, together with a toothsome drink, and either a bag of crisps or a piece of confectionery.

At Cardiff University's coffee shop, for example, £2.50 buys you either a) a baguette with crisps, and Lucozade or Ribena, or b) selected sandwiches, crisps, and Coca

Cola. In the University of Surrey, £2.85 secures an 'Extra Big Meal Deal' which gives you the sandwich and the drink, along with both the crisps *and* the sweets. If you have £2.99 to spend on the British high street, any number of outlets will supply you with the basic sarnie/drink/crisps or sweets formula. If you fancy a healthier-looking salad for 'main course', instead of yet another soulless sandwich, a tiny carton of apple slices conspicuously studded with a couple of grapes, or anything as nutritious as a smoothie or bona fide fresh pressed juice, then you will have to dig deeper into your purse.

Slowly and insidiously, in an echo of the fast-food culture of the United States, serial snacking has usurped proper meals in Britain. In world terms, this is a cultural exception. Spaniards get by on a doughnut dipped in chocolate for breakfast, Italians and French make do with an espresso and croissant in a bar, but only because they expect to eat a real, filling meal at lunchtime, either at home, in the canteen, or in a restaurant, followed by a lighter, but nevertheless sustaining meal in the evening. The British, on the other hand, muddle through a 9–5 day munching away on hastily-bought, no-effort snacks, most looking forward to another scintillating serving of convenience food for supper. Consequently, many Britons are deprived of the emotional and physical satisfaction that a sit-down, home-prepared meal delivers. At a psychological level, they have been robbed of any enduring sensation of having eaten satisfactorily, since their food is poor and industrial in quality and devoured in a matter of minutes, without any sense of occasion or ceremony. Physically, they are likely to have had an instant, high-impact fix of empty calories that leaves them feeling hungry an hour or so later. Even would-be healthy eaters who try to select the high-fibre breakfast snack, the fat-reduced sandwich, the diet drink and the Low Cal dessert find themselves piling on the pounds. Resolve breaks down, after all, if you are never left totally satisfied by what you have eaten. Too many Britons are forever just that little bit hungry, and that makes them perpetually receptive to the next ill-considered snack that presents itself. They want to eat and eat.

Britain no longer has much that adds up to a food culture, based on home-cooking skills and regular meals using sound native ingredients. As a nation, we have tacitly agreed to outsource the lion's share of food preparation to a profit-driven industry. In so doing, we have substituted the possibility of a food culture with what Professor Mike Kelly of the Health Development Agency dubbed an 'obesogenic environment'. The professor coined this phrase in 2003, in the context of a new study by the Agency reporting the latest figures on rising childhood obesity. Professor Kelly blamed Britain's ever-expanding waistline on the proliferation of fast-food outlets and junk food advertising, as well as unhealthy lifestyles. 'We live,' he said, 'in an obesogenic environment – a plethora of fast-food outlets, reliance on cars, and offers enticing us to eat larger portions.'

Much of the rise in diet-related disease – diabetes,

stroke, heart disease, cancer – is now attributed by public health bodies to the move away from homemade food, which tends to be relatively low in fat, sugar and salt. A 100-gram serving of baked cod, for example, contains only 1.2 grams of fat. The same weight of cod fish finger served fried contains a whopping 12.7 grams.

Thanks in major part to our gradual abandonment of homemade meals, and our enthusiastic adoption of serial snacks and convenience food, Britain is lumbering towards a fat epidemic. Around two-thirds of adult males, and more than half of adult females, are now either overweight (fat) or obese (extremely fat). Obesity has grown by 300 per cent over the last 20 years. More than a fifth of Britain's adult population is obese – and that's just the grown ups. Nearly one third of British children aged 2–15 are either overweight or obese. Obesity is rising twice as fast amongst children as adults. Nowadays, nearly 16 per cent of children aged 6–15 are now officially obese – three times as many as a decade ago – and this puts them at risk. In 2002, cases of maturity-onset diabetes in obese British children were reported for the first time. Fatty deposits – one of the first signs of heart disease – have also been identified in the arteries of teenagers. Though rising obesity, particularly amongst children, is now regarded as a worldwide problem, Britain's youngsters seem to be second only to the US in piling on the pounds. In France, by comparison, though obesity is on the increase, the proportion of boys and girls who are considered obese stands at just 4 per cent. Currently, a third of the total number of obese children in Europe are British.

The outlook for the future, without any exaggeration, is terrifying. The National Audit Office forecasts that one in every four adults will be obese by 2010. This may be an underestimate. According to the International Obesity Taskforce's measures, overweight and obesity in British children shows a 'firmly embedded upward trend'. On the basis of conservative estimates, it predicts that 23.5 per cent of British boys, and 32 per cent of girls, will be either overweight or obese by 2020 if current government policies remain unchanged. It goes on to say that on current trends, 34 per cent of British men and 38 per cent of women, will be obese by that same year. British women will begin to show the record levels of fatness now recorded in some of the most overweight populations in the developed world – black Americans and Mexican Americans. The average UK dress size in 1950 was a size 12. Currently it is a size 14 but 47 per cent of British women now take a size 16 or larger. The average British woman's waistline has expanded by 6 inches since the 1950s. Slowly but surely, our bad food diet is reshaping even the way we look.

17

'NO BAD FOOD . . .'

There is, according to the British food industry, no such thing as bad food, only bad diets. The Institute of Food Science and Technology, the professional qualifying body for industry scientists and technologists, reassures the public that there is no need to get bogged down in a 'Is this a Good or Bad Food?' debate because the industry has their best interests at heart. 'Food technologists in industry take great care to ensure that food products are safe and wholesome. But eating or drinking too much of any food can be bad for you – too much water can kill you. We shouldn't think of good foods or bad foods, but of good or bad diets,' it insists. The 'no bad food' argument has picked up some academic muscle in Britain, that it could never hope to attract elsewhere. Vincent Marks, the Emeritus Professor of Clinical Biochemistry at the University of Surrey and co-editor of the book *Panic Nation: Unpicking The Myths We're Told About Food and Health*, says that the very term 'junk food' is an oxymoron:

'Food is either good – that is, it is enjoyable to eat and will sustain life – or it is good food that has gone bad, meaning that it has deteriorated or gone off . . . To label a food as "junk" is just another way of saying "I disapprove of it". There are bad diets – that is bad mixtures and quantities of food – but there are no "bad foods" except those that have become bad through contamination or deterioration.'

Such intellectual justification is music to the ears of Britain's food manufacturers. As the population becomes fatter and fatter, the finger of blame is increasingly pointed in their direction. The heat is on as independent nutritionists, and even potential regulators, start taking a longer, harder look at the composition of particular products. Since the routine, bulk consumption of such products as crisps, fizzy drinks, greasy burgers, sticky cereals, chicken nuggets and chocolate sweets is common-place and widely regarded as normal, the realization that such items are not that great for the health has been relatively slow in dawning in Britain. Europeans are much more aware that to eat such items on anything approach-ing a regular basis is to court obesity and ill health. Most nationalities would be aghast to learn the extent to which products of doubtful nutritional value have infiltrated both the public and private zones of the mainstream British diet. Not for the Germans the idea that children cannot be expected to drink plain water and must have it sweetened with diluting, fruit-flavoured squash, nor for the French the belief that a packet of crisps is an acceptable snack or 'casse-croute'. Try telling Spaniards that a pile of crackers and a runny cheese paste is an ideal lunch.

Increasingly, the British food industry is running for cover under the 'no bad food, only bad diets' blanket. Ironically, it is coming in for this criticism because it has become a victim of its own spectacular success. Countries with sounder, healthier food cultures where people base their diets around mainly home-cooked food can afford to take a more laid-back attitude because their population is food literate enough to keep the proportion of such products eaten down to a level that does not seriously jeopardize health. In Britain, however, junky snacks and fast foods are slowly but surely usurping the place of more wholesome home-cooked staples in our diet, making every such item consumed another cause for concern. One of the most significant problems with these foods is that they tend to be what nutritionists refer to as 'energy dense', that is, they pack a lot of calories for the size of the portion. A homemade spaghetti Bolognese, or a typical British roast dinner, for instance, has less than half the calories of the average meal from a fast-food chain.

The more that the British food industry is called to account for the runaway commercial success of its products, which manifest in spreading waistlines and an upward spiral in diet-related diseases, the more it tries to wriggle off the hook, to pass the buck, to muddy the dietary waters. Defence Number One is that it really isn't the industry's fault, or anything to do with its massive marketing spend (about half a billion pounds is spent on food advertising in Britain each year, 100 times more than the government spends on healthy eating campaigns), if Britons cannot keep their taste for its junk in check; rather, it is just another example of the failure of lazy citizens to balance their own diets. As Malachy Reynolds, president of the UK Biscuit, Cake and Confectionery Association, put it: 'We believe that the great majority of our consumers know that what we make are treats, a reward at the end of a long day, something to share with family and friends, a pleasure to enjoy in moderation. They are not the products of the devil incarnate, to be demonized and hounded off our shelves. As Marie Lloyd put it all those years ago: "A little of what you fancy does you good".'

Defence Number Two – which cedes some ground to health lobbyists – involves the admission that large sections of the British population are indeed confused and bamboozled by the nutritional profile of many widely available foods and need a helping hand to work out what they can wisely eat. Here the food industry can step out of the frame as the villain of the piece, and portray itself in an altogether more favourable light as the helpful interpreter. Many of the biggest food manufacturers are now reinventing themselves as 'wellness' companies. Nestlé, for instance, now describes itself as a 'research and development-driven nutrition, health and wellness company' even though its extensive product portfolio includes products such as Yorkie bars, Toffee Crisps, Kit-Kats, After Eight mints, Lion bars and Walnut Whips.

Food manufacturers are quite happy to put nutritional labels on products in the full knowledge that most people will not read them, while the few who do will be puzzled about what they mean. This is the 'Don't blame us if you get fat, we told you what was in it' defence. In the US, there have already been two (unsuccessful) law suits against food companies, and the food industry there faces the prospect of more litigation of the type that has come the way of the tobacco industry. One way for a company to limit its liability is to show that it gave clear information and so consumers know exactly what they are eating. McDonald's set the pace here amongst fast-food takeaways by announcing that by the end of 2006, some two-thirds of its outlets worldwide will label products with lists of calories, fat, carbohydrate, protein and sodium. Helpfully, this information will be on the food packaging itself, not at the point of sale, so any interested consumer will only be wise after the event. Rival chains are expected to follow suit.

Empowering the public to make healthy choices might also involve the food industry in putting prominent 'help-ful' ticklists on products to give them an aura of health. These are red herring labels, designed to send any interested consumer off the scent: statements such as 'Less than one per cent fat' on high-sugar products like sweets where fat was never an issue in the first place. Otherwise, the drill is to bombard the consumer with random bits of nutrition information that are strictly correct, but which do not give a rounded account of the product as a whole: 'Made with real fruit', 'Counts towards your Five A Day', 'Free from artificial colours', 'Contains calcium for healthy bones', 'Helps aid digestion', 'Good source of energy', 'Helps reduce cholesterol'. Product innovation consists of dreaming up ever more inventive ways to repackage processed foods and junk to give them a new lick of health paint. Bite-sized, scaled-down versions of the product can be portrayed as helping greedy consumers who just can't say 'no' to control their intake. A product can be genuinely re-formulated, even if only minimally so, but the consumer will still be impressed and reassured by those claims on the label that promise less fat, sugar and salt or flag up a 'calorie-controlled' option – in other words, 'healthy junk'. The only problem with this is that such claims represent the food manufacturer's self-serving view of what constitutes low fat, sugar and salt or calorie-controlled.

Defence Number Three, the most audacious of the lot, is to drag the whole fat and ill-health debate well away from the vexed territory of food and nutrition and dump it in the fertile terrain of physical activity. Here the script is that Britain's ever-extending girth is not primarily due to the type of food we eat, it is all down to lack of exercise. Britons are led to believe that as long as they touch their toes enough, they can safely fill up on junk. Eat junk, burn it off. No problem.

The food industry has taken up the sporty fitness angle

on obesity with gusto. Walkers Crisps – Britain's number one food brand – has enlisted the footballer Gary Lineker, who in addition to promoting their crisps in adverts, doles out nutrition advice on behalf of Walkers. Not surprisingly, Gary's view on nutrition still allows for the regular consumption of Walkers crisps. There is a lot at stake here: Walkers cheese and onion flavour crisps alone are worth £81 million a year. Here is his advice:

'My family and I always try to enjoy an active lifestyle – just doing 30 minutes of physical activity a day can help keep you fit and burn off calories. Also combining this with a healthy balanced diet is vital, but it's OK to have a few snacks along the way. My personal opinion is everything in moderation.'

Mr Lineker shares the Walkers view that the 'golden rule of food and lifestyle is balance'. In 2004, Walkers was giving away free pedometers, rebranded as 'Walkometers', to underline its philosophy. To celebrate the 2004 Olympics, McDonald's created a special Happy Meal for adults which included a salad, a diet drink and a free pedometer. A million such meals were sold within a month. McDonald's customers could not be blamed for inferring that you can fill up on a Happy Meal with impunity, as long as you walk it off. In reality, fast-food calories generally take rather a lot of walking off, as *Which?* magazine pointed out when it calculated what it would take to burn off certain popular types of meals:

Kentucky Fried Chicken Original Chicken Salad: Walk for 1.8 hours (5.5 miles)
Burger King Chicken BLT Baguette and Large Coke: Walk for 3.5 hours (10.5 miles)
Big Mac, Medium Fries and Small Vanilla Milkshake: Walk for 5.5 hours (16.5 miles)
Pizza Hut Individual Margarita Pan Pizza and Garlic Bread: Walk for 6 hours (18 miles)

Nevertheless, the counter-intuitive association between fast or junk food and sport looks sure to run and run. As Professor Gerard Hastings, who carried out a review of food advertising to children for the government, sees it: 'I predict fast-food companies will become increasingly interested in being associated with sports, to counter-balance the unhealthy image. It's something that needs to be watched carefully.'

But who is doing the watching? In Bad Food Britain, subsequent governments have traditionally taken a laissez-faire, or even positively supportive attitude to the food industry. In 2003, the sports minister, Richard Caborn, was widely criticized by health watchdogs such as the Food Commission, the Consumers' Association and teachers' unions for endorsing chocolate manufacturers Cadbury's Get Active! scheme in which school children were encouraged to purchase Cadbury's confectionery in exchange for 'free' sports equipment. Mr Caborn was quoted as saying: 'I am delighted that Cadbury is prepared to support this drive to get more young people active by providing equipment and resources for schools. In partnership we could make a real difference to the lives of young people.' The Food Commission took a somewhat dimmer view of the scheme. It calculated that a 10-year-old child eating enough chocolate to earn the school a basketball through the scheme would then need to play basketball for 90 hours to burn off the calories consumed. Cadbury's defended the scheme by saying that it was not about children single-handedly collecting sports equipment for their school, but 'about the wider community clubbing together to use their wrappers from the chocolate they're already eating'. Tessa Jowell, then Secretary of State for Culture, Media and Sport, backed her colleague's support for the Cadbury's scheme: 'It's not so much that children are getting fatter because they are eating significantly more,' she said, 'they're getting fatter because they're taking much less exercise.'

The government, along with the food and soft drink industry, likes to divert discussions about health and obesity away from food on to physical activity. Any government that starts taking a serious look at the ways in which the fast-food industry keeps the population in thrall to its products is going to have large companies breathing down its neck in an unnerving manner. Rather than restrict the industry's room to manoeuvre in any significant way, they find it more expedient to dole out sanctimonious, 'get fit' advice: telling people to be active costs the government nothing; manufacturers of sports equipment are thrilled as sales soar; and fitness centres will sign up legions of fretful fatties.

No one can disagree with the idea that it is good to be active. It shifts the burden of Britain's ever-growing bulk back into the zone of personal responsibility and well away from the state and its obligations to create an environment in which any interested, motivated citizen has a realistic chance of eating well and sticking to it without being constantly undermined at every turn. Instead of clipping the food industry's wings, politicians now seek refuge in the sport angle on obesity because they lack the principles and bottle to stand up to big food corporations.

Contemplating a looming obesity epidemic, such as Britain now faces, some might think it was time to be less accommodating to food processing barons, to give the food industry a taste of the regulation that has come the way of the tobacco industry. Populations that live on a diet of processed junk food are eating themselves into an early grave, just as surely as 20-a-day smokers are heading for heart disease and cancer. Smokers cannot taste food properly because smoking deadens the taste buds. Junk food corrupts the palate in an equally insidious way. Generations reared on a diet of chemical sweets, bone-rotting fizzy drinks, sugar-crusted cereals, sweets, crisps and poultry slurry nuggets, soon find the natural taste of unprocessed foods unpalatable. No amount of public health propaganda will then be able to wean them on to wholesome, unadulterated foods.

There is now quite a throng of individuals and organizations in Britain putting pressure on the government to take more forceful action, and turn its attention, fairly and squarely, to food. In the words of Professor Mike Lean, chair of Human Nutrition at the University of Glasgow:

'In the 1980s, the rise in obesity was mainly fuelled by people becoming less active, but through the 1990s and into the present decade, the main influence has been an increase in food provision. The food industry is providing more fat, more calories and more food to people who are now becoming fatter. There are grounds on which government should have a moral obligation to intervene.'

In 2004, the Commons Health Select Committee attacked the government, the food industry and advertisers for failing to take action on rising levels of obesity. It called for measures such as a voluntary ban by the food industry on television advertising of junk food, the reintroduction of cookery lessons in schools and annual fat tests for children. Confed – the confederation of education and children's services managers in England – has called on the Department for Education to give local authorities powers to ban vans selling chips, burgers and ice creams from areas around schools and set up exclusion zones to prevent school meals being undermined by 'Mr Whippy and Mr Chippy'. British doctors have urged the government to intervene to improve the nation's eating habits, calling for strict school meals guidelines and a ban on junk food advertising and on vending machines in schools. One South London GP, Sam Everington, warned in 2005 that children and young adults are now arriving in GPs' surgeries with the diseases of middle age. Doctors are now testing British children for Type Two diabetes, which is associated with obesity. This condition used to be seen only in adults. Other children suffer from low levels of vitamins and minerals, breathing and sleep problems, and bone disease. 'The situation is much worse than people think,' he said. 'A quarter of the children I see are overweight and blood tests show that more than 50 per cent are malnourished.'

The list of interest groups clamouring for action goes on and on. A private member's Children's Food Bill – which aims to ban the advertising of junk food to children – has been placed before Parliament. By December 2005, it was backed by 158 different organizations, including Cancer Research, the British Heart Foundation, the Royal College of Surgeons, the British Dental Health Federation and the trade union Unison. Top chefs and cooks such as Marguerite Patten OBE, Raymond Blanc, Nigel Slater, Gary Rhodes and Rick Stein have publicly called on the government to end advertising promotions aimed at children and to 'stop the scandal of children leaving school knowing only how to open a packet or tin'. The Chartered Institute of Environmental Health wants tough new measures to limit sales of unhealthy food, saying that ministers may have to take steps such as imposing extra VAT on unhealthy, pre-prepared products, banning adverts for junk food aimed at children and putting cigarette-style health warnings on some food products. It also called on the government to lead a cultural change to encourage more home cooking. As the Institute's policy officer, Jenny Morris, said:

'We need to tackle contradictory government policy and challenge the government to show real leadership to address key issues such as food advertising and the availability and affordability of healthier food. The time is past for yet more focus groups. We need positive and direct action.'

Positive and direct action? Other countries have taken quite prescriptive measures in their attempts to halt deteriorating eating habits, although none of them face an obesity epidemic of British dimensions. Sweden does not permit advertising aimed at children under 12, or allow programmes to be interrupted by advertising, and does not permit advertising before or after children's programmes. Norway is seeking a similar ban. The Canadian province of Quebec prohibits all adverts aimed directly at children under the age of 13. In the Netherlands, public broadcasters are not allowed to interrupt programmes aimed at the under-12s with adverts. The Flemish region of Belgium does not permit advertising five minutes before or after children's programmes. In Denmark,

Finland and the Netherlands, characters and presenters from children's programmes cannot appear in adverts. In the Republic of Ireland, regulators are drafting a code that would require fast-food advertisers to warn children that their products should only be eaten in moderation and would force adverts for cakes, biscuits, sweets and chocolates to show a toothbrush symbol. The code would also ban adverts for food and drink from portraying or referring to celebrities or sports stars. The state Senate in the US state of Connecticut has banned the selling of leading brands of soft drinks, crisps and potato snacks, and sweets in all schools. The French have removed junk food and drink vending machines from every collège and lycée in the country.

So what is happening in Britain? It sounded promising back in 2000, when the Labour government set up the Food Standards Agency as an independent government department 'to protect the public's health and consumer interests in relation to food'. Yet after only two years, the Agency was criticized by food campaigners as being too supportive towards the food industry and not truly independent: the two most obvious manifestations of this being its support for genetically modified food and the rubbishing of organic food. Five years on, an official review of the Agency concluded that it had 'deviated from its normal stance of making statements based solely on scientific evidence' when 'speaking against organic food and for GM food'.

The Food Standards Agency did ruffle industry feathers

in 2004, when it ploughed ahead with government efforts to get the industry to reduce the amounts of salt that go into the nation's food. The Agency launched a 'Sid the Slug' campaign to tell consumers that salt kills slugs, thereby inferring that salt is not that great for humans either. Britain's salt manufacturers promptly complained about the campaign to the Advertising Standards Authority, a complaint subsequently rejected. The food industry isn't used to having a hard time from regulators in Britain – in fact, quite the opposite. When it does, you can almost hear it squealing, 'Why are you having a go at us all of a sudden? We thought we were mates', followed closely by, 'If you keep it up, we'll turn nasty!' As evidence of this, back in 1994, when the government started drawing up plans to reduce salt intake in the UK, prominent food processing companies withdrew their funding from the Conservative Party.

Traditionally, politicians and regulators like to talk tough about taking action to get the country's food improved, although usually only when shamed into such a stance by health campaigners. They float schemes and threaten legislation, but then they back down when it comes to inconveniencing the food industry in any serious way, retreating under a protective suit of 'guidelines' and 'voluntary codes' dumped on cash-strapped councils or public bodies. Alternatively, they grab some easy headlines for radical-sounding initiatives that are subsequently shown to be ineffectual.

In 2001, for example, the government introduced its

'Better Hospital Food Programme'. It was announced with a great fanfare that £40 million would be spent on overhauling hospital food. Lloyd Grossman, television gastronome and pasta sauce figurehead, was appointed hospital food tsar and he drafted in a working party of leading chefs to devise ways of making Britain's notoriously bad hospital food more edible. They came up with fashionable dishes such as: navarin of lamb with couscous; steak and kidney pie with olive oil mash; spinach, tuna, egg and mung bean salad; and desserts such as 'posh' pear and chocolate crumble, and sticky toffee pudding – some of these (such as the latter) made less sense on paper than others.

All acute hospitals were meant to have the Grossman makeover by January 2002, but by that point, only 35 per cent had adopted the menus and there were reports that some of those that had, considered them to be a dismal failure. Nurses at one healthcare trust in Lancashire denounced the menus as even worse than before and described the food at Blackburn as 'slop'. As Lib-Dem MP Paul Burstow commented: 'Take-up of this initiative shows it is nothing more than a government gimmick at the expense of ward workload.' The failure of the government to get to grips with the problem was underlined in 2005 when it emerged that a startling 40 per cent of Britons of all ages admitted to hospital were suffering from malnutrition, a figure that increased for those leaving hospital. One contributor to *The Times* letter page hazarded a guess why this might be:

'Last January I was admitted to a three-star foundation hospital with a chest infection. Day 1, lunch was meat pie with soggy pastry, powdered potato and bullet peas. Pudding was pink mousse in a plastic pot with fake cream. On Day 2 it was dried-up Chinese, followed by pink plastic pudding. On Day 3 we had fish, but it was hard and dry as cardboard. Pink pudding again . . . Most of the food on my ward was untouched and returned to the trolley to be thrown away. I lost 4 kg in seven days and others on the ward looked equally frail by the time they escaped.'

An investigation by *ITN News* revealed that the average amount of money hospitals had to spend on patients' food was just £2.38 a day, although in some hospitals it was as low as £1.65. Footage was shown of relatives bringing in snack-bar sandwiches and fast-food meals to patients because they considered them to be better than the hospital food on offer. Such findings, although shocking, were scarcely surprising. Britain has never seen food or nutrition as part of the healing process – the standing joke being that if your illness doesn't kill you, then the hospital food will.

Facing deep-rooted, near intractable problems such as our national disgrace of hospital food, many governments might feel that more forceful measures were required. But British politicians of both left and right fear being branded as 'Nanny Staters'. In 1998, the Conservative Ann Widdecombe denounced the then Education Secretary

David Blunkett's proposed weak nutritional guidelines for school meals. 'It smacks of the Nanny State,' she said. In Britain, eating bad food routinely is considered quite normal, and any intervention from the state is likely to be interpreted as meddling with the British citizen's unassailable right to eat himself into an early grave. Once more the doctrine of personal responsibility is invoked, a sentiment expressed by one correspondent in a letter to the *Daily Telegraph*:

> 'Not every aspect of our lives is the responsibility of government and it is high time parents took more time in raising their children, and particularly providing healthy food . . . The solution to childhood obesity and other youth issues is not an overbearing government imposing ridiculous restrictions. Ultimately, we are all responsible for our own children.'

Such sentiments chime in nicely with the current government's strategy of 'personalization', making people more responsible for their own health. Back in 2003, there were rumours that the government seemed to be considering a ban on television advertising to children when Tessa Jowell, Secretary of State for Culture, Media and Sport, asked the telecommunications regulator Ofcom to look at the issue. But any enthusiasm cooled rapidly. Ms Jowell stated that she was 'sceptical' about whether such a ban would combat obesity and, in 2004, Ofcom ruled out such a ban, saying that other measures, such as encouraging exercise, would be a better way to tackle the problem. Does this sound familiar?

In that same year, there were press rumours, based on a leaked paper from the Prime Minister's Strategy Unit, that the government was considering imposing a 'fat tax' on products such as burgers, crisps, fizzy drinks, butter, cheese and whole milk. This was a clumsy idea because it blurred the crucial distinction between highly processed junk foods of dubious nutritional profile and whole, natural foods which though high in fat, offer other nutritional benefits. It was evident that a crude fiscal measure of this sort was no solution to Britain's obesity crisis. The government was forced to deny that it planned to impose such a levy. As Tim Yeo, the shadow Health and Education Secretary, observed, the government's approach to tackling the problems of obesity was 'haphazard and lacked coherence' – a criticism that he might also have aptly levelled at past Conservative administrations. The food industry, meanwhile, was cock-a-hoop at seeing off the 'fat tax'. As Martin Paterson, deputy Director General of the Food and Drink Federation, put it: 'The idea that any particular food is bad for you is out of date and simplistic. A balanced diet can include snacks and treats. Moderation is the key.'

Whenever a British government tries to make the food industry act more responsibly, it has a battle on its hands. Another major government initiative – conceived of from its inception as one that would be purely voluntary and not binding on food manufacturers and retailers – was to develop easy-to-understand labels that could be placed on the front of packs of processed foods such as ready meals, breakfast cereals, sandwiches, burgers and pies, to help consumers make healthier choices. After trialling various models with consumers, in 2005 the Food Standards Agency came up with a multiple traffic lights system showing a separate high, medium or low rating, and corresponding red, amber or green colour coding, for four criteria; fat, saturated fat, salt and sugar. This recommendation was not to the taste of the food industry, which continued to hold out for labels based on Guideline Daily Amounts (GDAs), an altogether more opaque label that has the convenient effect of drowning in undigested detail all but the most nutritionally-savvy consumers. Looking at 2006, *The Grocer* predicted that food industry bosses were 'on a collision course' with the Food Standards Agency. The Food and Drink Federation dismissed the traffic lights scheme out of hand: 'No traffic light system will work. They represent the same subjective views of good, bad and indifferent.' It was back once more, to the old 'no bad food, only bad diets' dictum.

Britain spends a phenomenal amount of time and energy in circular, endlessly repeating arguments about what has gone wrong with the nation's diet and what might be done about it. Like a car stuck in mud, the wheels go round endlessly, splashing an opaque liquid on everything around, but it doesn't move. It is just another example of how complicated the British find food, another example of the country's inability to see through food industry spin and grasp the essentials. Well-intentioned lobbyists and regulators become locked into futile discussions about what constitutes 'junk', and whether a 'fat-reduced' ice cream sundae or prawn sandwich is more or less insidious than a salty, high-fibre cereal or a tikka masala ready meal.

All this is beside the point. British politicians simply need to get their heads and tongues around one very clear, unequivocal public health message: Eat as little processed food as possible and base your diet on home-cooked meals, made from scratch from raw ingredients. But no government has the stomach for serving up this truth. It has become an alien message that the British no longer want to hear.

REFERENCES

BAD FOOD BRITAIN IN NUMBERS

page xv   'One in every four British households no longer has a table that everyone can eat around': *The Times*, 4 June 2005

page xv   Percentages of British men and women who have little interest in food: Institute of Grocery Distribution press release, 25 October 2005

page xv   'One out of every three Britons say they do not eat vegetables . . .': Institute of Grocery Distribution press release, 14 January 2005

page xv   The percentage of Britons who say that they enjoy eating: *Future Vision*, Institute of Grocery Distribution, October 2005

page xv   The year by which Britain ate more ready meals than the rest of Europe put together: **www.advfn.com/stocks/stanelco-plc-the-latest-information_8010773.html**

page xv   The percentage of patients entering and leaving British hospitals in 2004 with malnutrition: *Guardian*, 9 October 2005

page xv   The number of artisan British products with protected status in the EU in 2005: Country

Land and Business Association press release, 20 July 2005

page xv   'The percentage of food bought in Britain, but never eaten': *Observer Food Monthly*, August 2005

page xv   'The average amount in pence spent on food ingredients for a primary school meal . . .': Soil Association 'Food For Life' report, 2003; and speech by Sir John Krebs: **www.food.gov.uk/ multimedia/webpage/johnkrebs/ krebsspeech200504**

page xvi   'The percentage of Britons who say that they are fed up being told what to eat': Mintel report, *Daily Mail*, 27 April 2005

page xvi   The percentage of viewers who say that TV food programmes encourage them to cook: *Future Vision*, Institute of Grocery Distribution, October 2005

page xvi   Only four out of ten Britons enjoy eating meals with their children: *ibid*

page xvi   'The percentage of Britons who are still confused about which foods are healthy': Mintel report, *Manchester Evening News*, 27 April 2005

page xvi   'One out of every two meals eaten in Britain is now eaten alone': *BBC News*, 30 January 2005

page xvi   'The percentage of the food eaten by Britons in 2004 that was home-produced . . .': DEFRA report, *Farming Today*, 4 November 2005

page xvi   'Only one in five Britons will go out of their

way to buy British food': Institute of Grocery Distribution press release, 6 October 2005

page xvi   The percentage of all British shoppers who say that they do not care where their food comes from: *ibid*

page xvi   'The year by which at least a third of all British adults . . .': Department of Health, 2002

page xvi   'Britain eats more than half of all the crisps and savoury snacks eaten in Europe': 'Snackaholic Brits break European records', **www.just-food.com**, 2 May 2003

CHAPTER 1

page 1   'Sales of food and drink books grew by 22 per cent . . .': Nielson BookScan report, *Guardian*, 19 November 2005

page 1   Britain's obsession with food: *Vogue*, October 2005

page 4   Simon Hopkinson, *Roast Chicken and Other Stories – Second Helpings*, Macmillan, 2001, quoted in the *Guardian*, 11 August 2005

page 4   Jeremy Paxman, *Waitrose Food Illustrated*, March 2000

page 5   David Sexton, *Evening Standard*, 3 October 2005

page 10   Gary Rhodes and Delia Smith: *BBC News*, 26 October 1998 page 10   Antony Worrall Thompson and Delia Smith: *BBC News*, 25 September 2000

page 10   Delia Smith, *Food and Drink* programme, 25 September 2003

page 11   Delia Smith's retirement: *BBC News*, 21 January 2003

page 12   Yasmin Alibhai-Brown, *Evening Standard*, 17 August 2005

page 13   Tamasin Day-Lewis, *Observer Food Monthly*, August 2005

page 13   Arabella Weir: **www.thisisthenortheast.co.uk**, 23 January 2003

CHAPTER 2

page 15   'At a high-level meeting in Russia to celebrate the 750th anniversary of the founding of Kaliningrad . . .': *BBC News*, 4 July 2005

page 15   'We can't trust people who have such bad food': Associated Press, 5 July 2005

page 15   'Don't talk crepe, Jacques!': Associated Press, 5 July 2005

page 16   'How would Mr Chirac feel . . .': *ibid*

page 16   Egon Ronay, *Sunday Herald*, 10 July 2005

page 16   Fay Maschler, *Evening Standard*, 6 July 2005

page 17   William Grimes, *New York Times*, 4 August 1999

page 17   'More than London broil', *New Yorker*, 8 June 2001 page 18   Jamie Oliver and Jay Leno: *Guardian Weekend*, 24 September 2005

page 18   Jan Moir, *Daily Telegraph*, 13 October 2005

page 19   HRH, Charles, Prince of Wales: Slow Food UK *Snail Mail* no. 10, Message from the Prince of Wales

page 19   'As one Chinese writer . . .': *Guardian*, 27 June 2005

page 19   'I've heard that British food is boring': **www.britishcouncil.org/ japan-educationuk-faqs.htm**

page 20   'Foreign students contemplating taking a course at the University of Oxford are likewise pre-warned . . .': **www.oxford-info.com/ Rest.htm**

page 21   *Malaysia Tatler*, July 2005

page 21   Polish attitudes survey, British Council Poland: **http://elt.britcoun.org.pl/elt/o_survey.htm**

page 22   'Speak to people of diverse foreign origins . . .': interviews conducted by author between June and December 1995 with people of Austrian, German, Dutch, French, Danish, French Cameroonian, Italian and Nigerian origins

page 23   'The traditional fish supper . . .': 'Fish the dish' fact sheet, Seafish Industry Authority, 2000

page 26   'Grenouilles au Royaume Uni': **http:// albion.viabloga.com/lists/links/2.shtml**

page 26   Terry Durack, *Independent on Sunday*, 27 February 2005

CHAPTER 3

page 28   Best of British: **www.bestofbritish.fr**

page 30   '. . . one company that sends them to customers'
           doorsteps . . .': **www.britishexpatsupplies.co.uk**

page 30   British expat supper parties: author's experience

page 30   Curry suppers: *Independent on Sunday*,
           16 October 2005

page 31   Sybil Kapoor, *Simply British*, Michael Joseph,
           1998, p 3

page 32   William Black, *The Land That Thyme Forgot*,
           Bantam, 2005, pp 2, 3, 342 and glossary

page 34   'British food at Anuga', *The Grocer*, 15 October
           2005

page 35   Robin Cook and chicken tikka masala: Speech
           to Social Market Foundation, 2001

page 35   Origins of chicken tikka masala:
           **www.bbc.co.uk/worldservice/specials/
           177-food/page5.shtml**

page 35   James Martin: Mitchell Beazley press release,
           June 2005

page 36   Queen Elizabeth II: *Guardian* magazine,
           12 November 2005

page 36   'Seven out of ten Britons say that they "like
           foreign food" . . .': *Daily Telegraph*,
           17 December 2004

page 37   'One survey of European eating habits . . .':
           Mintel report, 'Eating Habits 2002', Executive
           Summary

page 37   George Bush UK menus, 2003: *Guardian*,
           21 November 2003
page 37   Matthew Fort: *ibid*
page 38   'By 2004, only 63 per cent of the food eaten in
           Britain was home-produced': DEFRA report,
           Farming Today, 4 November 2005
page 38   Friends of the Earth: *Daily Telegraph*,
           11 November 2005
page 39   Richard Burge: Countryside Alliance press
           release, 11 October 2002
page 39   British Food Fortnight:
           www.britishfoodfortnight.com
page 40   IGD survey: press release, 6 October 2005
page 40   Alexia Robinson, *Farmer's Weekly*,
           2–8 September 2005
page 43   George Dunn, Tenant Farmers' Association and
           Tesco: *The Grocer*, 22 October 2005
page 43   Taste of Britain competition:
           **www.sainsbury.co.uk/food/foodandfeatures/
           sainsburysandfood/tasteofbritain/
           tasteofbritaincompetition.htm**
page 44   Farmers For Action protest: Green MSP media
           release, 2 November 2005
page 45   Tamasin Day-Lewis, *Observer* magazine,
           9 October 2005

CHAPTER 4

page 47   'London began to be hailed . . .': Jonathan Meades, *The Times*, 16 May 2002

page 47   *Restaurant* magazine: **http://www.restaurantmagazine.co.uk**

page 47   'The World's 50 Best Restaurants': telephone interview with Ella Johnston, 15 July 2005

page 48   Richard Corrigan, *Independent*, 17 April 2005

page 48   Rod Liddle, *Sunday Times*, 24 April 2005

page 48   Fay Maschler, *Evening Standard*, 6 July 2005

page 49   *Harden's London Restaurants 2006*, pp 23, 25

page 49   Rules: **www.rules.co.uk**

page 49   *Field*, May 2004

page 50   Fergus Henderson, *Independent on Sunday*, 3 October 2005

page 50   Tom Aikens, *ibid*

page 51   *Good Food Guide 2006*; and 'Food Britannia', *The Times*, 20 October 2005

page 52   *Harden's London Restaurants 2006*, pp 23, 25

page 52   Rod Liddle, *Sunday Times*, 24 April 2005

page 54   Timothy Mo, *Sour Sweet*, (André Deutsch, 1982), Paddleless Press, 2003, p 111

page 55   Jonathan Meades, *The Times*, 2 February 2003

page 59   Bill Knott, *Caterer and Hotelkeeper*, 29 September 2005

page 60   Jay Rayner, *Observer* magazine, 16 June 2002 and 7 July 2002

page 61   *Ramsay's Kitchen Nightmares*:

**www.channel4.com/life/microsites/R/realdeal/
ramsay/nightmares-dplace.html**

page 63   Derek Cooper, *The Bad Food Guide*, Routledge
and Kegan Paul, 1967, p xv

page 66   Parents Jury: *Food* magazine, July/September
2003, p 17

page 66   'A subsequent survey of 141 children's
meals . . .': survey by Caroline Walker Trust,
reported in *The Times*, 17 September 2005

page 66   'Derek Cooper summed up his
conclusions . . .': *The Bad Food Guide*,
Routledge and Kegan Paul, 1967, p xvi

CHAPTER 5

page 69   'In 2001, the average British household cooked
from scratch . . . just 3.36 times a week':
'Eating and Today's Lifestyle Survey', *Nestlé
Family Monitor*, December 2001, p 11

page 69   'By 2002, 45 per cent of Britons agreed . . .':
Henley Centre, 2002, quoted in Edward
Garner's 'Consumer Behaviour and Future
Trends in Eating', Taylor Nelson Sofres, 2004

page 69   'While in 1980, the average meal took one
hour to prepare . . .': *Sainsbury's Magazine*, May
2003

page 69   '. . . now on average it takes 13 minutes':
www.geest.co.uk/ourmarkets

page 69   'On current trends . . .': *State of the Art in Food:*

The Changing Face of the Food Industry, Cap Gemini Ernst and Young, 2002

page 69 'As the convenience food manufacturer Geest observed . . .': **www.geest.co.uk/gst/ourmarkets**

page 70 '. . . four out of every five Spanish adults . . .': 'Eating Habits: Scratch versus Convenience', Mintel report, June 2005, Executive Summary

page 70 Mireille Guiliano, *French Women Don't Get Fat*, Chatto and Windus, 2005, p 51

page 70 'One survey of European food habits . . .': 'Eating Habits – Pan European Overview', Mintel report, December 2002, Executive Summary

page 70 '. . . seven out of every ten German women . . .': *ibid*

page 71 *Housekeeping Monthly*, 'Good Wife's Guide', 13 May 1955

page 72 Pat Mainardi, *The Politics of Housework*, Redstockings, 1970

page 72 'Another feminist collective denounced cooking . . .': 'Why Women's Liberation?', *Black Maria*, 1971

page 73 Derek Cooper, *The Bad Food Guide*, Routledge and Kegan Paul, 1967, pp 16–17

page 74 'Four miracle British products': from their packaging

page 76 'A 2002 report . . .': 'Eating Habits – Pan European Overview', Mintel report, December 2002, Executive Summary page 77 'Official data released in 2004 . . .': Keynote report on the food industry, 2004

page 78 Gordon Ramsay, *Daily Telegraph*, 24 October 2005

page 79 Deirdre Hutton on ready meals, *Observer*, 9 October 2005

page 80 'Once it was all sex and shopping. But now we're at it in the kitchen': Decca Aitkenhead, *Guardian*, 29 January 1999

page 81 Lynn Barber, *Observer Food Monthly*, November 2005

page 81 'The UK has the third highest rate of female employment . . .': **www.hrmguide.co.uk/hrm/ chap3/ch3-links6.htm**

page 81 'One survey found that in 61 per cent of British households . . .': 'Eating and Today's Lifestyle Survey', *Nestlé Family Monitor*, December 2001, p 9

page 82 '43 per cent of British mothers . . .': *Guardian*, 16 August 2005

CHAPTER 6

page 85 Oxo adverts: *BBC News*, 31 August 1999

page 86 'A 1997 poll found that two-thirds of British families . . .': *ibid*

page 86 *Observer* survey, 8 February 1998

page 86 Jonathan Meades, *The Times*, 22 February 2003

page 86   Raisingkids: press release, 14 July 2004;
           www.backtothetable.co.uk

page 86   Bisto adverts: *The Grocer*, 29 October 2005

page 87   '89 per cent of parents say . . .': *ibid*

page 87   '. . . one in every four homes no longer has a
           table . . .': *The Times*, 4 June 2005

page 87   '. . . people no longer even buy dining
           tables . . .': *BBC News*, 30 January 2004

page 87   Mimi Spencer, *Observer Food Monthly*,
           7 November 2004

page 88   'A substantial body of research suggests . . .':
           'Why are family mealtimes important?',
           www.backtothetable.co.uk

page 88   Cancer Research UK: 'Parents need to set
           example', press release, 7 March 2004

page 89   Julie Burchill, *Guardian Weekend*, 7 September
           2002

page 92   Raymond Blanc, *Guardian*, 4 January 2005

page 93   'Research in 2005 found that stress levels
           rose . . .': Institute of Grocery Distribution,
           press release, 25 October 2005

page 93   Christopher Gilmour, *Daily Telegraph*, 18 April
           1998

page 93   Gérard Depardieu, *My Cookbook*, Conran
           Octopus, quoted in the *Observer* magazine,
           11 September 2005

page 95   'Nearly half the meals eaten in the UK are now
           eaten alone . . .': *BBC News*, 30 January 2005

CHAPTER 7

page 96   Polish microwave ownership: 'Poland's EU
Membership Presents Packaging
Opportunities', 2 February 2005,
www.foodnavigator.com

page 96   Italian microwave ownership: 'Cosmopolitan
Tastes Marks UK Tastebuds', 21 February 2003,
www.foodnavigator.com

page 96   British microwave ownership: Economic and
Social Research Council, 'Consumerism in the
UK', 2004 fact sheet

page 97   French ready meals: visit by author to French
supermarkets in July 2005

page 98   'Demand for them grew by 70 per cent . . .':
The Grocer, 3 April 2004

page 98   'Britain already had the distinction of eating
49 per cent . . .': *BBC News*, 21 February 2003;
**www.advfn.com/stocks/stanelco-plc-the-
latest-information_8010773.html**

page 98   '. . . only a very slight variation in sales
"penetration" according to social class':
Keynote Ready Meals report, 2004

page 98   'Britons ate a staggering £900 million worth of
ready meals . . .': *Manchester Evening News*,
10 October 2005

page 98   '. . . the market for them is growing at 6 per
cent a year . . .': Institute of Grocery

Distribution research, 'Consumer trends drive convenience', 14 January 2005

page 98   Institute of Grocery Distribution: 'Meal Solutions' fact sheet, 29 January 2003

page 99   'The British food industry now classifies meal solutions into four types': *ibid*

page 100   Ikea's 'assemble and dine' food: *The Grocer*, 19 October 2005

page 101   'One day I saw a curry on telly . . .': 'Burger Boy and Sporty Girl' report, Barnardo's, 2004

page 101   *Daily Telegraph* survey of ready meals: 26 February 2005

page 102   David Gregory: *ibid*

page 102   Sainsbury's Taste the Difference Luxury Shepherd's Pie: *Guardian*, 8 June 2005

page 103   '. . . some 71 per cent of British shoppers said that they bought ready meals . . .': 'Attitudes Towards Processed Foods', Mintel report, May 2005

page 103   'As one market analyst put it . . .': Anne Bourgeois of Mintel, 'Cosmopolitan Tastes Marks UK Tastebuds', 21 February 2003, **www.foodnavigator.com**

page 106   'Pure & Pronto': **www.simplyorganic.co.uk**

page 106   Martha and Lawrence: *The Grocer*, 5 November 2005

page 106   Waitrose: **www.waitrose.com**

page 109   Cook!: **www2.marksandspencer.com/ foodmagazine/services/cook/index.shtml**

page 110   Waitrose Easy range: from packaging
page 110   Lynda Brown: letter to author, 24 October
            2005
page 111   'A sweet story of subterfuge and the
            disappearing soufflé packet': advert in
            Guardian Weekend, 12 November 2005; Tesco
            advert in *Observer Food Monthly*, November
            2005

CHAPTER 8

page 116   Gordon Brown's food preferences: *Guardian
            G2*, 26 April 2005
page 116   'Mr Whippy': *Guardian*, 3 May 2005
page 116   Tony Blair and broccoli: *Daily Telegraph*,
            20 April 2005
page 116   'On average the British consume . . .': British
            Heart Foundation statistics website:
            www.heartstats.org/datapage.asp?id=924
page 117   '. . . less than half that eaten by Mediterranean
            populations . . .': *BBC News*, 11 December
            1998
page 117   'Charles Kennedy conducted a key newspaper
            interview': *Guardian*, 30 April 2005
page 117   Boris Johnson and McDonald's: *Independent*,
            29 April 2005
page 117   'As one political commentator observed . . .':
            Michael White, *Guardian G2*, 26 April 2005
page 117   'Just under 3 out of every 10 Britons say . . .':

'Eating and Today's Lifestyle' survey, *Nestlé Family Monitor*, December 2001

page 120   Margarette Driscoll, *Sunday Times*, 21 November 2004

page 120   Barnardo's: 'Burger Boy and Sporty Girl' report, 2004

page 123   Boris Johnson, *Observer Food Monthly*, November 2005

page 123   *Posh Nosh*: **www.bbc.co.uk/comedy/posh**

page 125   Zoe Williams, *Guardian*, 26 April 2005

page 126   Chez Bruce: *Guardian*, 9 December 2005

page 126   Matthew Fort on school lunches: *Guardian* magazine, 6 November 2004

page 127   Julie Burchill, *Guardian* magazine, 28 October 2000

page 129   Letter to *The Grocer* from Andrew Jolliffe, 12 November 2005

page 129   '. . . a survey of markets carried out by the Mayor of London's London Food Board . . .': *Trading Places Report*, London Food Board, reported in the *Independent*, 7 November 2005

CHAPTER 9

page 131   'In 2001, the Food Standards Agency asked British consumers . . .': Food Standards Agency Survey press release, 28 September 2001

page 132   Scottish Executive survey: 'Public Perceptions

of Food and Farming in Scotland', reported in the *Sunday Herald*, 12 January 2003

page 133 Raymond Blanc, *Observer Food Monthly*, November 2005

page 133 '. . . anything from 8 to 23 per cent of the population . . .': Food Standards Agency Survey press release, 28 September 2001

page 134 '. . . but sales of chicken actually rose by 19.6 per cent . . .': *The Grocer*, 'Baffling rise in chicken sales', 3 September 2005

page 134 Deborah Orr, *Independent*, 22 February 2005

page 134 John Webster, *Guardian* Society, 7 September 2005

page 134 Richard D North, 'The Countryside: help the market build it', 2002; **www.richarddnorth.com/public-realm/ farming.htm**

page 134 'A 2003 government report suggested . . .': *ibid*

page 135 Carlo Petrini, *Daily Telegraph*, 26 February 2005

page 136 Hugh Fearnley-Whittingstall, *The Times*, 3 September 2005

page 137 'National statistics show . . .': National Statistics, Expenditure and Food Survey 2003–4, press releases 30 March 2005 and 8 June 2005

page 137 'The most recent government survey shows . . .': 2005 survey, *Guardian*, 30 November 2005

page 137   'Some £59 of the average British household's
           weekly budget . . .', *ibid*

page 137   Martin Samuel, *The Times*, 15 November 2005

page 138   Justin King, *Management Today*, May 2005

page 139   'In the words of one industry
           spokesperson . . .': Richard Ali, then food
           policy director of the British Retail
           Consortium, *The Grocer*, 1 February 2003

page 139   John Ruskin: **www.quotationspage.com/
           search.php3?homesearch=John+Ruskin**

page 141   'Britain's Organic Food Scam Exposed':
           Observer, 21 August 2005

page 141   'As one outspoken organic critic put it . . .':
           Richard D North, 'The Countryside: help the
           market build it', 2002;
           **www.richarddnorth.com/public-realm/
           farming.htm**

CHAPTER 10

page 145   Tessa Kiros, *Twelve – A Tuscan Cookbook*, press
           notice, Murdoch Books

page 147   '. . . less than 1 per cent of all retail food spend
           is being channelled through them . . .': *The
           Grocer*, 29 October 2005

page 147   Howard de Walden Estates:
           www.marylebonevillage.com

page 148   Jonathan Meades, *The Times*, 16 May 2002

page 148   '. . . the biggest share of food sales in 57 per cent of Britain': Study by retail analysts CACI, reported in *Daily Mail*, 3 November 2005

page 148   'Tescotowns': *The Grocer*, 22 October 2005

page 150   Antonio Carluccio, *Observer Food Monthly*, November 2005

page 151   'New food industry research': *Future Vision*, Institute of Grocery Distribution, October 2005

page 152   'Banbury, Gioia Tauro and Pont Audemer': letter to the author from Captain Nicholas Cooper, July 2005

page 154   Joanne Denney-Finch: Institute of Grocery Distribution, press release, 25 October 2005

page 155   David Potts, *Future Vision*, Institute of Grocery Distribution, October 2005

page 155   Andy Bond, *The Grocer*, 22 October 2005

page 155   'Bland, amorphous sameness': *The Grocer*, 5 November 2005

page 156   The Women's Institute and supermarkets: *The Times*, 20 October 2005; *Daily Telegraph*, 23 October 2005

page 156   Kate Hoey, *Observer*, 30 October 2005

page 157   Nigel Slater, *The Kitchen Diaries*, 4th Estate, 2005, p viii

CHAPTER 11

page 159   Mimi Spencer, *Observer Food Monthly*, August 2005

page 160   Kate Muir, *The Times* magazine, 19 November 2005

page 162   '77 per cent of British women say that they
            worry about their weight . . .': *Heat*,
            12–18 November 2005

page 162   Deborah Orr, *Independent*, 5 November 2005

page 163   'My girlfriend has become . . .', *Stella*,
            8 November 2005

page 163   'Orthorexia' definitions: Macmillan and
            Penguin dictionaries

page 164   Dr Steve Bratman: **www.orthorexia.com**

page 166   Tamasin Day-Lewis, *Observer* magazine,
            9 October 2005

page 167   *You Are What You Eat* magazine: May 2005

page 167   *You Are What You Eat*: **www.channel4.com/
            entertainment/tv/microsites/Y/yawye**

page 167   'An unrepentant nutritionist . . .': Gillian
            McKeith, *You Are What You Eat*, Michael
            Joseph, 2003

page 168   Rachel Cooke, *Observer Food Monthly*, June
            2005

page 169   'Super Consumers': James McCoy, senior
            market analyst at Mintel, quoted in the
            Manchester Evening News, 27 April 2005

page 169   Julian Hunt, *The Grocer*, 25 June 2005

page 170   'In 1998, research carried out by the food
            industry suggested that consumers seemed to
            have become "slightly desensitized" to food
            scares': Institute of Grocery Distribution
            research, 'Consumer attitudes to British meat
            and fresh produce', 1998

page 171   'By 2005, a survey by Mintel found that the British were in active revolt over nutrition and healthy-eating advice': *Manchester Evening News*, 27 April 2005

page 171   Lucy Mangan, *Guardian*, 18 November 2005

page 172   'No wonder only 50 per cent of Britons say that they really like eating': *Future Vision*, Institute of Grocery Distribution, October 2005

CHAPTER 12

page 173   Gérard Depardieu, *My Cookbook*, Conran Octopus, quoted in the *Observer* magazine, 4 September 2005

page 175   Gordon Ramsay and lobsters: *BBC News*, 23 August 2004

page 175   '. . . Britain, in the words of one *Times* commentator . . .': Martin Samuel, *The Times*, 15 November 2005

page 178   Numbers of vegetarians in European countries: Vegetarian Society press office

page 179   Benjamin Zephaniah: **www.benjaminzephaniah.com/rhymin**

page 181   Institute of Grocery Distribution research: 'Consumer attitudes to British meat and fresh produce', 1998

page 181   Advertising Standards Agency complaints: ASA adjudication on Burger King, 21 December 2005

CHAPTER 13

page 191   Saffron Walden Community Hospital: *BBC News* and *Daily Telegraph*, 29 July 2004

page 191   '. . . some 17 million hospital meals were being thrown away untouched': Philippa Davenport, *Financial Times*, 6 August 2005

page 191   'We have to adhere to strict hygiene criteria . . .': *BBC News*, 29 July 2004

page 192   'Norfolk Women's Institute markets close': *Guardian*, 15 November 2005

page 193   'An eminent professor commented . . .': Professor Brian Austin of Heriot-Watt University, quoted in the *Daily Mail*, 21 June 2005

page 193   Egg box ban: *BBC News*, 21 June 2005

page 196   Food Hygiene Mission Control: **http://archive.food.gov.uk/hea/index2.html**

page 196   Ros Coward, *Guardian*, 14 March 2000

page 198   '. . . over half of British chickens on supermarket shelves are contaminated with multi-drug-resistant strains of the potentially deadly *E. coli* bug . . .': *BBC News*, 16 August 2005

page 200   Cornish pilchards: interview with Nick Howell, 30 September 2005

page 203   James Aldridge: Select Committee on Agriculture, Minutes of evidence, 16 November 1999

page 203   'Chopping boards': *Science News*, 6 February
           1993
page 204   'PDO and PGI products in Britain': Country
           Land and Business Association, press release,
           20 July 2005
page 204   Richard Burge: Countryside Alliance, press
           release, 11 October 2002

CHAPTER 14

page 208   Ali Farrell: 'Food in the National Curriculum –
           Balanced diet or seriously malnourished?',
           www.foodforum.org.uk
page 209   'Britain's food illiterate pupils spend most of
           their timetabled hours . . .': *ibid*
page 209   Key words: Collins Total Revision, *GCSE Food
           Technology*, pp 135, 171,185 and 202
page 209   Saucy Chicken Animals: *ibid*, p 67
page 210   Coleslaw: *ibid*, p 47
page 210   Exam questions: *ibid*, pp 209, 171, 202 and 127
page 211   Home Economics syllabus: **www.aqa.org.uk/
           qual/gceasa/hom_assess.html**
page 212   'A government survey in 2003 . . .': 'Public
           Perceptions of Food and Farming in Scotland',
           the Scottish Executive, reported in the *Sunday
           Herald*, 12 January 2003
page 212   '. . . one out of every two young
           "housewives" . . .': 'Consumer Behaviour and
           Future Trends in Eating', article by Edward

Garner, Taylor Nelson Sofres, 2004;
www.readymealsinfo.com/index.cfm

page 213   Anita Cormac: interview with author, 17 July
2005; *Cook School* magazine, February 2005

page 213   The National Farmers' Union published a
disturbing survey . . .': NFU, 15 June 1999

page 214   Jamie Oliver: **www.channel4.com/life/
microsites/J/jamies_school_dinners**

page 214   British Heart Foundation survey: *Daily
Telegraph*, 7 November 2005

page 214   Peter Hollins: *ibid*

page 214   '60 per cent of schoolchildren thought that
potatoes grew on trees':
www.britishpotatoes.co.uk/press.asp?id=13

page 215   'The average Home Economics teacher . . .':
Anita Cormac: interview with author, 17 July
2005

page 216   MORI survey into the UK's eating habits,
'Eating and Today's Lifestyle': *Nestlé Family
Monitor*, December 2001

CHAPTER 15

page 217   Menus in Vigevano, City of Vigevano: schools
menus 2004–5

page 217   Menus in Genoa, Commune of Genoa:
elementary school menus, summer 2005

page 218   Menus in Limours, Mairie of Limours: primary
school menus, February 2005

page 218   Menus in the 13th Arrondissement, Caisse des
            Ecoles: primary school menus, May 2005

page 218   Menus in Helsinki: *Daily Telegraph*, 9 March
            2005

page 219   Jamie Oliver in Johannesburg: *The Times*, 26
            July 2005

page 220   '. . . the average amount spent on food
            ingredients . . .': Soil Association, 'Food For
            Life' report, 2003; and speech by Sir John
            Krebs

page 220   '£1.40–£1.70 for a meal': Soil Association,
            'Food For Life' report, 2003

page 223   '. . . researchers from the University of
            Edinburgh . . .': School of Clinical Sciences and
            Community Health/*Sunday Herald*, 10 July 2005

page 225   Kevin Morgan, *The Times*, 16 November 2005

page 225   Barnardo's: 'Burger Boy and Sporty Girl'
            report, 2004

page 226   'In 2003, when the Soil Association carried out
            a major survey into British school meals . . .':
            Soil Association, 'Food For Life' report, 2003

page 227   'As one 14-year old put it': Barnardo's: 'Burger
            Boy and Sporty Girl' report, 2004

page 227   'The Soil Association subsequently carried out
            a thorough nutritional analysis . . .': Soil
            Association press release, 28 October 2004

page 227   Food Standards Agency school lunchbox
            survey: **www.food.gov.uk/news/pressreleases/
            2004/sep/lunchboxtwopress**

page 227   '... the right to food is a binding right under international law ...': 'Getting Personal' report, Food Ethics Council, December 2005

page 228   Letter about Turkey Twizzlers: *The Times*, 19 April 2005

page 228   '... anything between 60 and 90 pence ...': *Daily Telegraph*, 9 March 2005; and *Jamie's Italy* – Puglia

page 228   '... a quarter of new schools being built in England ...': *Daily Telegraph*, 13 September 2005

page 229   '... these proposals would be subject to a consultation period ...': Department for Education and Skills press release, 3 October 2005

page 229   'Teachers' leaders ...': John Dunford, *Guardian*, 28 September 2005

page 229   'One major private catering contractor ...': Stephen Thorns of Sodexho, *ibid*

page 229   'Some British schools are signed up to catering contracts ...': *Daily Telegraph*, 13 September 2005

page 230   Local Authority Caterers Association: Neil Porter, Press Association, 1 June 2005

page 230   Barnardo's: 'Burger Boy and Sporty Girl' report, 2004

page 231   *Which?* magazine: March 2003

CHAPTER 16

page 233   David Cameron: *BBC News*, 4 January 2006

page 233   'The market for these chilled, microwavable delights . . .': *The Grocer*/Taylor Nelson Superpanel, 20 August 2005

page 233   'cup-holder cuisine': *Independent*, 3 July 2003

page 235   NHS Snack Box: **http:// patientexperience.nhsestates.gov.uk**

page 235   'When researchers from Barnardo's logged . . .': 'Burger boy and Sporty girl' report, Barnardo's 2004

page 236   'The British are Europe's most ardent consumers of snack foods . . .': Keynote report, 'Snack Foods', 2005

page 236   'The average Briton eats 7.2 kg of snacks per year . . .': *ibid*

page 236   '. . . by 2002, the United Kingdom was gobbling up 51 per cent of the European 'savoury snacks': 'Snackaholic Brits break European records', **www.just-food.com**, 2 May 2003

page 236   'Whereas 86 per cent of Britons eat such snacks, less than half of Italians do so . . .': *ibid*

page 237   Savoury Snacks Information Bureau: *The Grocer*, 'Guide to Snacking', September 2005

page 237   'Take your pick from prawn cocktail potato heads . . .': *ibid*/author purchases

page 237   Mini Pringles: 'Guide to Snacking', *The Grocer*, September 2005

page 237   Limited Edition Walkers crisps; and Gordon
            Ramsay: **http://walkers.corpex.com/cr15p5/
            news.asp?newsitemid=97&seq=5**

page 238   'The British eat their way through a £6.1
            billion mountain of confectionery': *The Grocer/*
            Nestlé Rowntree Confectionery Factfile,
            November 2005

page 238   'British children now consume . . .': *Which?*,
            March 2003

page 238   'It is essential to make it really easy for
            shoppers . . .': *ibid*

page 239   'Mini bites for maxi profits': 'Guide to
            Snacking', *The Grocer*, September 2005

page 239   'A survey by the National Consumer
            Council . . .': *BBC News*, 25 November 2005

page 239   'Food For Now': *ibid*

page 239   'Tesco Grab and Go': Tesco Annual Review, 2005

page 241   'Britons are now officially Europe's worst
            breakfasters': 'Focus on Breakfast', *The Grocer*,
            20 August 2005

page 241   'In the words of one market analyst . . .': Daniel
            Bone, Datamonitor, *ibid*

page 241   'deskfasts': *ibid*

page 242   'All-Day Lemon Croissant': *The Grocer*,
            19 November 2005

page 242   'Food To Go Breakfast Bar': 'Focus on
            Breakfast', *The Grocer*, 20 August 2005

page 242   '. . . sales of these grew almost sevenfold':
            Keynote report on the food industry, 2004

page 242   '. . . pre-cooked bacon bap': *ibid*

page 242   '. . . ready-made porridge': *The Grocer*,
           29 October 2005

page 242   'Three personal assistants . . .': *The Times*,
           7 January 2004

page 243   'As the managing director of one leading
           catering company put it . . .': Robyn Jones, *ibid*

page 243   Cardiff University's coffee shop:
           **www.cardiff.ac.uk/schoolsanddivisions/
           divisions/resid/cater/p1775.html**

page 245   Professor Mike Kelly: *Daily Telegraph*,
           8 October 2003

page 245   'Much of the rise in diet-related disease . . . is
           now attributed . . .': Food and Agriculture
           Organization and World Health Organization
           of the United Nations (1992) World
           declaration and plan of action for nutrition

page 246   'Baked cod versus fish finger': Soil Association,
           'Food For Life' report, 2003

page 246   'Around two-thirds of adult males . . .': 'Seeking
           bold solutions for Britain's obesity epidemic',
           International Obesity Taskforce, 2004

page 246   'Obesity has grown by 300 per cent over the
           last 20 years': *ibid*

page 246   'More than a fifth of Britain's adult population
           is obese': *Guardian*, 11 November 2005

page 246   'Nearly one-third of British children aged 2–15
           are overweight or obese': *Which?*, December
           2005

page 246   'Nowadays, nearly 16 per cent of children . . .':
            Melanie Johnson, *Hansard*, 4 July 2003

page 246   'In 2002, cases of maturity-onset diabetes in
            obese British children were reported for the first
            time . . .': Royal College of Physicians, 2004

page 246   'Fatty deposits . . . have also been identified in
            the arteries of teenagers . . .': Philip James and
            Karen McColl, 1997; Numbers of obese French
            children: *Sunday Herald*, 30 October 2005

page 247   'Currently, a third of the total number of obese
            children in Europe are British': *Guardian*,
            23 June 2005

page 247   National Audit Office's forecast: National Audit
            Office, 'Tackling Obesity in England', 2001

page 247   International Obesity Taskforce predictions:
            'Seeking bold solutions for Britain's obesity
            epidemic', 2004

page 247   UK dress sizes: *Heat*, 12–18 November 2005

page 247   'The average British woman's waistline has
            expanded by 6 inches since the 1950s': 'Size
            UK', *Independent*, 21 November 2005

CHAPTER 17

page 248   Institute of Food Science and Technology:
            www.ofst.org/ifstfaq.htm

page 248   Vincent Marks: *BBC News*, 3 October 2005

page 250   'A homemade spaghetti Bolognese . . .': *Which?*,
            December 2005

page 251   '. . . about half a billion pounds is spent on food advertising in Britain each year . . .': Tim Lang and Michael Heasman, *Food Wars*, Earthscan, 2004

page 251   '. . . 100 times more than the government spends on healthy eating campaigns . . .': Department of Health, 'Choosing Health: Making healthier choices easier', 16 November 2004

page 251   Malachy Reynolds, *The Grocer*, 26 November 2005

page 251   'Nestlé and wellness': *The Economist*, 13 December 2003

page 252   'In the US, there have already been two (unsuccessful) law suits against food companies . . .': 'Getting Personal' report, Food Ethics Council, 2005

page 252   'McDonald's nutrition labelling': *Independent*, 27 October 2005

page 254   'Britain's number one food brand': TNS Superpanel, 19 June 2005

page 254   'Walkers cheese and onion crisps alone are worth £81 million a year': *ibid*

page 254   Gary Lineker: **http://walkers.corpex.com/cr15p5/nutrition/keeping-active.html**

page 254   . . . the 'golden rule of food and lifestyle is balance': **http://walkers.corpex.com/cr15p5/nutrition/index.html**

page 254   McDonald's and free pedometers: **http://**

66.249.93.104/search?q=cache:
CyF-EoRzpi0J:www.fhf.org.uk/meetings/
2004–10-19_minutes.pdf+mcdonalds+free+
pedometers&hl=en

page 254   Miles to walk off fast-food calories: *Which?*,
December 2005

page 255   Gerard Hastings: *ibid*

page 255   Cadbury's Get Active!: *BBC News*, 29 April
2003; and Food Commission press release,
29 April 2003

page 256   Tessa Jowell and Get Active!: *Guardian*, 29 May
2004

page 258   Mike Lean: Scottish Free School Meals,
Campaign Report, 2004

page 258   Confed: *Independent*, 1 April 2005

page 258   British Medical Association: *Evening Standard*,
22 June 2005

page 259   Sam Everington, *Guardian*, 23 June 2005

page 259   Children's Food Bill: **www.sustainweb.org/
child_sup.asp**

page 259   'Top chefs and cooks . . .':
www.sustainweb.org/news-

page 259   The Chartered Institute of Environmental
Health: *Guardian*, 7 September 2005

page 260   Jenny Morris: *ibid*

page 260   'Interventionist measures . . .'(Sweden, Canada,
Norway, Belgium, Netherlands, Ireland,
Denmark, Finland): Keynote report on the
food industry, 2004

page 261   'Interventionist measures . . .' (Connecticut):
27 May 2005

page 261   'Interventionist measures . . .' (France):
Guardian, 7 September 2005

page 261   '. . . an official review of the Agency
concluded . . .': **www.food.gov.uk/multimedia/
pdfs/deanreviewfinalreport.pdf**

page 262   Sid the Slug: **www.food.gov.uk/news/
pressreleases/2004/sep/saltcampaignpress**

page 262   '. . . prominent food processing companies
withdrew their funding . . .': *Salt, Diet and
Health*, GA MacGregor and HE Wardener,
Cambridge University Press, 1998

page 263   Better Hospital Food Programme: **http://
patientexperience.nhsestates.gov.uk**

page 263   'Nurses at one healthcare trust in
Lancashire . . .': Liberal Democrat press release,
12 February 2002

page 263   Paul Burstow: *ibid*

page 263   '. . . a startling 40 per cent of Britons . . .':
Guardian, 9 October 2005

page 264   *ITN News* investigation into hospital food:
7 December 2005

page 264   Ann Widdecombe and David Blunkett:
Times Educational Supplement, 23 October
1998

page 265   **http://archive.food.gov.uk/hea/index2.html**;
letter from April-Tui Buckley to *Daily
Telegraph*, 7 October 2005

page 265   Personalization: 'Getting Personal' report, Food
            Ethics Council, 2005
page 265   Tessa Jowell and Ofcom: *BBC News*, 22 July
            2004
page 266   'Fat tax': *The Times/BBC News*, 19 February
            2004
page 266   Tim Yeo: *ibid*
page 266   Martin Paterson: *ibid*
page 267   'Multiple traffic lights': *BBC News*,
            16 November 2005
page 267   Food and Drink Federation and the 'traffic
            lights scheme': *The Grocer*, 19 November 2005

INDEX